POVERTY
CLOSE TO HOME

POVERTY CLOSE TO HOME

A Christian Understanding

Hilary Russell

MOWBRAY

Mowbray
A Cassell imprint
Wellington House, 125 Strand, London WC2R 0BB

215 Park Avenue South, New York, NY 10003

First published 1995

British Library Cataloguing-in-Publication Data

A catalogue record for this book is available from the British Library.

ISBN 0-264-67322-0

Typeset by York House Typographic Ltd
Printed and bound in Great Britain by Biddles Ltd, Guildford and King's Lynn

Contents

Acknowledgements   vi
Preface   vii
List of Abbreviations   viii
Introduction   x

Part I: The Wider Context – Attitudes and Assumptions   1
  1. Still News Today   3
  2. Always with Us?   23

Part II: Thinking about Poverty – Explanations
and Excuses   39
  3. An Exercise in Demarcation – Defining and Measuring
     Poverty   41
  4. Blaming the Victim – Individualist Explanations of
     Poverty   65
  5. Organized and Imposed – Structural Explanations of
     Poverty   85

Part III: The Experience of Poverty – Exclusion
and Expectations   107
  6. Jerusalem or Scar City?   109
  7. Poverty Earned and Unearned   133
  8. Public Issues, Private Troubles   157

Part IV: Responding to Poverty – Policies and Prophecy,
Pastoral Care and Protest   183
  9. The Arteries of the State   185
  10. The Building Blocks of the Good Society   206
  11. A House Built on Rock or Sand?   231
  12. Relationships of Justice   254

Index   272

Acknowledgements

The author and publisher wish to thank the following for permission to reprint copyright material. Although every effort has been made to contact the owners of the copyright material reproduced in this book, it has not been possible to trace all of them. If such owners contact the publisher, the appropriate acknowledgements will appear in any future editions.

T. S. Eliot, choruses from 'The Rock', from *Collected Poems 1909–1962*, published by Faber and Faber Limited. Reprinted by permission of the publisher.

Joel Lane, 'Saving Face', from *Private Cities*, published by Stride, 1993. Reprinted by permission of the author.

Billie Holliday and Arthur Herzog, 'God Bless This Child'. Reprinted by permission of Carlin Music Corporation.

Edward Shillito, 'Jesus of the Scars', published by Association Press, New York, 1952, in Thomas Curtis Clark (ed.), *Christ in Poetry*.

Preface

In this book, I have tried to adopt a descriptive and analytical approach to poverty issues. But I also make clear my basic beliefs, say where I am coming from, and indicate where both my beliefs and my analysis lead me in terms of political (though not party political) partisanship. So, in one sense it is a personal book. It is only in a more limited sense an individual one. It spans different facets of my life – my membership of Church Action on Poverty (CAP), my work in urban policy research and various sorts of involvement in church life on Merseyside. What is contained here, therefore, is very much a product of many influences and encounters, shared ideas and experience.

It would be impossible to name all those who have contributed directly or indirectly to my development and hence to the book. However, a number of people have helped me by discussing the issues and/or reading and commenting on specific sections of the book: Arthur Adlen and colleagues at the Merseyside Trade Union, Community and Unemployed Resource Centre, Tony Attwood, Pat Belvisi, Niall Cooper, Richard Evans, Nic Francis, Paul Goggins, David Horn, David Mathieson, Michael Parkinson, Alex Scott-Samuel, Derek Seber, Barbara Vellacott. In particular, I have especially appreciated Austin Smith's active support throughout, John Atherton's encouragement and constructive criticism, and the enthusiasm and patience of my publishing editor, Judith Longman. Their sustained interest in the project was invaluable.

I have said that the book is rooted in my working and private life. I am grateful to those who share these with me – my colleagues at work and my friends in CAP for their encouragement, and my husband George, our daughters Jean and Kate, and our son Duncan, for their love and forbearance while it was being written.

List of Abbreviations

ACORA	Archbishops' Commission on Rural Areas
ACRE	Action with Communities in Rural England
AHC	after housing costs
BHC	before housing costs
BSR	Board for Social Responsibility
CAB	Citizens Advice Bureau
CAP	Church Action on Poverty
CAWTU	Church Action with the Unemployed
CBI	Confederation of British Industries
CNHC	Churches National Housing Coalition
CPAG	Child Poverty Action Group
CRESR	Centre for Regional Economic and Social Research
CUF	Church Urban Fund
DoE	Department of the Environment
DSS	Department of Social Security
DTI	Department of Trade and Industry
EU	European Union
GNP	Gross National Product
GP	general practitioner
HIP	Housing Investment Programme
ICRC	Inner Cities Religious Council
ILO	International Labour Office
IMSY	Industrial Mission in South Yorkshire
IPPR	Institute for Public Policy Research
IS	Income Support
ISEW	Index of Sustainable Economic Welfare
IT	information technology
LEC	Local Enterprise Company
MIRAS	Mortgage Interest Relief at Source
NACAB	National Association of Citizens Advice Bureaux

NCH	National Children's Home
NHS	National Health Service
NIC	National Insurance Contribution
Nimby	'Not in my back yard'
Note	'Not over there either'
NVQ	National Vocational Qualification
OECD	Organisation for Economic Co-operation and Development
OFSTED	Office for Standards in Education
OPCS	Office of Population Censuses and Surveys
PSBR	Public Sector Borrowing Rate
RPI	Retail Price Index
SERPS	State Earnings-related Pension Scheme
SRB	Single Regeneration Budget
TEC	Training and Enterprise Council
TSB	Trustee Savings Bank
TUC	Trade Union Congress
UDC	Urban Development Corporation
UPA	Urban Priority Area
VAT	Value Added Tax
VET	vocational education and training
WHO	World Health Organization
YTS	Youth Training Scheme

Introduction

In this book, I try to bring together some of the material which is the context of the theological task of responding to poverty today. It draws on social and economic analysis and the day-to-day experience of individuals, families and communities to provide a picture of the place of poverty in Britain and discuss this in the context of Christian social thought.

There is surely no need to justify such an exercise. Ten years after the publication of *Faith in the City*,[1] there is still 'a grave and fundamental injustice' in the urban priority areas (UPAs). It remains the case that 'many residents of UPAs are deprived of what the rest of society regard as the essential minimum for a decent life'.[2] Five years after *Faith in the Countryside*,[3] over 25 per cent of households in rural areas still live in or on the margins of poverty. Poverty 'affects a substantial minority who find themselves living amongst a better-off majority'.[4] Polarization has been aggravated because

> Hand in hand with the encouragement of personal wealth has come a clear and unequivocal winding down of the public sector . . . the idea of a safety net for those poorer members of society, which for much of the twentieth century, and especially for the post-war period, has been seen as coming from state provision, has been seriously questioned and, many would argue, critically jeopardised.[5]

Disturbing contrasts in lifestyles and opportunities, though nothing new, have over the past few years become more open sores in our society, and people are beginning to wonder what infections they are spreading as, inexorably it seems, the features of social breakdown also appear. Just after Christmas 1993, the words of one commentator hit home:

> It has been a very 1990s Christmas. More people than ever spent Christmas abroad; more people than ever have found traditional Christmas excess beyond their means. The divisions opening up in our society are never starker than at this time of year; bleak beggars in the London subway while in Harrods £1,000 hampers are selling out. This inequality is no accident.[6]

All of the following strands interweave:

- the existence of poverty;
- the divided society within which it flourishes;
- the fact that it is not accidental.

It is these – set against the immediacy of the gospel imperative to 'remember the poor'[7] – which give the subject matter of this book its enduring importance and relevance. It is in these – not in any recitation of statistics which may soon be out of date – that the book's message is really to be found.

The book is in four parts. The first sets out some of the context of the later discussion. It looks at the historical ambivalence within both Church and society towards 'the poor' and seeks the roots of this ambivalence in Christian teaching and in human nature. The second part examines the conceptual tools that are brought to the study of poverty – the way that it is explained, defined and measured, all of which are critically interrelated with our perceptions, judgements and hence our responses. The third part looks at people's experience of poverty, at the circumstances in which it thrives today and the consequences for individuals and neighbourhoods. The last part examines public policy responses to poverty and cites examples of church reactions and initiatives. It identifies future questions for church and society.

I try throughout the book to interweave the secular and the religious, using material of different sorts for both aspects. In the secular discussion of poverty, the book contains a broad thematic discussion and an analysis of poverty, policy responses and descriptive examples. In parallel, it includes Christian reflection, reference to various theological approaches, examples of pastoral responses to poverty and ways in which local churches have shaped their ministry to local needs, and instances of church agencies seeking a more prophetic role.

NOTES

1. *Faith in the City: A Call for Action by Church and Nation*, Report of the Archbishop of Canterbury's Commission on Urban Priority Areas (London: Church House Publishing, 1985).
2. *Ibid.*, p. xv.
3. *Faith in the Countryside*, Report of the Archbishops' Commission on Rural Areas (Churchman Publishing, 1990).
4. *Ibid.*, pp. 92–3.
5. *Ibid.*, p. 93.
6. Will Hutton, 'Snow White ideology and the thirty million dwarfs', *The Guardian*, 28 December 1993.
7. Galatians 2.10. See also Chris Rowland, 'That we should remember the poor', Lattery Lecture No. 2 (1993), Von Hugel Institute.

PART I

The Wider Context – Attitudes and Assumptions

Christian hope is never naive wishful thinking, it always takes the mess seriously. (Thomas Cullinan, 'Eucharist and politics', in *The Passion of Political Love*, Sheed and Ward, 1987, p. 87)

The Church, for its part, must make politicians realise that its concern over things like poverty, unemployment, homelessness and racism is not just trendy secular fashion but is rooted in Christian concepts like creation, incarnation, redemption and grace. (Gerald Priestland, 'The church of the future', in *My Pilgrim Way*, Mowbray, 1993, p. 21)

THIS OPENING SECTION introduces the main theme of the book – that poverty is a personal and a social issue. It is also inescapably political and inescapably theological. The poor have a special place in God's kingdom. As Christians, we must work for a social order which strives to embody and express the alternative values and realities of that kingdom.

The first chapter looks at the interrelationship of theology and prevailing social and economic thought and the way theology can function either to reinforce or challenge the *status quo*. The second explores attitudes towards poverty in this country as they have veered between compassion and condemnation and looks at the personal defences we use to protect ourselves from understanding the reality and implications of poverty around us.

CHAPTER 1

Still News Today

Them that's got shall have,
Them that's not shall lose;
So the Bible said
And it still is news.
Billie Holliday and Arthur Herzog , *God Bless the Child*

IT CANNOT BE RIGHT ...

This declaration springs from the urgent concern of Christians across all the Churches. We have heard with our own ears the cry of the poor. We have seen with our own eyes our society being driven in a direction that contradicts the Gospel. Wounding effects are witnessed and experienced daily. They challenge us to seek a new social order founded upon that vision and possibility of human wholeness which is contained in the Christian message and which speaks to all human experience.

As we survey our society, our inescapable conclusion is that many are being hurt in Britain today, damaged and discounted by public policy. This is the story that emerges from the pastoral experience of teachers, social workers, community workers, doctors, clergy and others in urban and rural areas. Over recent years, social divisions have widened and community life has been gravely eroded. These trends and the suffering they cause diminish everyone. They must cease.

As we enter the 1990s, our lives are being reshaped radically by a changing technology. The economies of whole continents are increasingly interlocked and we grow more conscious of our global reliance on natural resources that are neither infinite nor indestructible. Choices have to be made about the way we want to live together and our vision of a future society.

How poor people are treated is a touchstone for the values that inform all our thought, policies and action. It is central to our Christian faith. It is central to our political challenge.[1]

Church Action on Poverty (CAP) published this declaration, *Hearing the Cry of the Poor*, in 1989. It issued out of bewilderment, sadness and anger that divisive tendencies in Britain were going unchecked – in fact, were being reinforced by the direction of public policy. It asked, 'What has happened to our common life?'

The statement had been over a year in the making following widespread consultation with national agencies, local church and community groups and individual Christians. Although it was an expression of '*urgent* concern', this thorough if lengthy process was felt to be essential to produce an authentic expression of concern. The declaration was formally adopted at the CAP annual conference held in Liverpool in September 1989. A group of nine delegates from Meadowell, a housing estate in North Shields, later wrote about that conference:

> We came away feeling that in some way Meadowell had left a mark in Liverpool – that we had been given an opportunity to make an impression. 'It was the first Conference I've come away from where I've felt folk had committed themselves in writing – had meant it all.' Folk had been listening through the year, and the declaration was the fruit. The cry of the poor is being heard.[2]

My reason for attempting this book is to try to say why Church Action on Poverty – or at least one member of it – sees poverty in Britain as a central challenge to Christians.

The book is largely about material poverty in Britain today. It will look at ways in which poverty is defined, measured and explained. It will also examine poverty's various manifestations and responses to it on a personal level, within Christian churches and in public policy. It will seek to show that poverty is about more than low income; more even than being unemployed or inadequately housed. Powerlessness, exclusion, lack of choice, are all dimensions of poverty.

All of these touch upon social relationships and what it means to be a member of our society. They get to the heart of how we value people and the way we express that value not only through our personal dealings, but through the policies and programmes that are enacted in our name and on our behalf. As such, they are also issues at the heart of our faith. And they show that the material and the spiritual are inextricable. The Christian faith is profoundly a matter of interpersonal relations and our interpersonal relationships are both material and 'material-transcending'.[3]

TOO CLOSE FOR COMFORT

The book is not about poverty in general or as an abstract concept. It is about poverty in Britain. One of the panel members at the Church Action on

Poverty declaration launch was Father Michael Campbell-Johnston, then the Provincial Superior for the Jesuits in Great Britain. Reflecting beforehand on what statement he might make, he wrote:

> When I was working in El Salvador, the people would often say to me: 'When you go back to your own country tell them that we here are poor and need help for food, clothes, educational equipment, etc. But more important, we would like the Christians in your country to know and understand why we are fighting for peace and justice. *Most important of all, we would like to know that they themselves are committed to peace and justice in their own country. Then we would be truly brothers and sisters in Christ.*' This seems to me to be a clear invitation to become committed to justice issues in our own society here in the UK as an essential dimension of our service of the faith.[4]

An authentic concern for people in poverty hundreds of miles away, they were saying, must be linked with commitment to justice on our doorstep. But this is not easy. This poverty is uncomfortably close to home. We are more obviously entangled in this situation. How far are we responsible for it, colluding in its causation and perpetuation? It is more painful to confront the contrasts which exist around us, more challenging to face up to the implications for ourselves and our society than to be concerned about poverty in far-distant places. Yet this is what our faith demands of us. It is demanded not merely as an ethical duty, an aspect of responsible citizenship, but as integral to our faith in God.

AN UNSHAKEABLE CONVICTION

In an address to the first conference of Church Action on Poverty in 1982,[5] David Jenkins talked about Christianity being 'the most this-worldly of other-worldly religions'.[6] The attributes of this-worldliness and other-worldliness have both to be taken into account in relation to poverty. In all biblical narratives, God who is other-worldly has a central and necessary part, as a transcendent resource and fact for the world and as 'offering a fulfilment to men and women who are in the world which comes from beyond the world and goes beyond the world'.[7]

Yet in parallel, for Christians, there is also a this-worldly story about God and people embodied in Jesus so that, 'as God is in himself, so he is in the flesh and blood of Jesus'.[8] And it does not end there. God's work – Jesus' work – is continued through the Holy Spirit. So the doctrine of the Trinity integrates the transcendent – the other-worldly – with the substance and particularities of the world – the this-worldly – in a unique, dynamic and utterly challenging way.

We believe ...

We believe that God, in whom we live and move and have our being, has chosen to reveal the meaning of our human story. God so loved this world as to send us his Son Jesus Christ and in him the true story – the Kingdom that he preached – is both revealed and made possible. It was in proclaiming this Kingdom, to which we are all invited and in which the poor have a special place that Jesus was rejected. But through his death and resurrection – the story's climax – the Kingdom is made present and we are invited to celebrate and live this new reality.

We believe that when we pray 'Thy Kingdom come, thy will be done on earth', we commit ourselves to be part of this story-in-the-making and we bind ourselves to work for a social order which mirrors, realises and incarnates the realities of the Kingdom.

Our human tragedy is to set our hearts on mirages or look-alikes of the real Kingdom. We turn God's gifts into idols which promise life but cannot deliver it. When we enthrone money, power, privilege and pleasure, God's gifts become God-substitutes.

We believe that God's Spirit speaks through the cries of the poor and the vulnerable to expose our illusions and break their power over us; calling us to our proper task of working for the emerging Kingdom, restoring us to the human story's authentic theme.[9]

The Old Testament understanding of God, which is particularly evident in the Prophets and the Psalms, is both fulfilled and transformed, says Jenkins, in the New Testament message. What is unfolded 'is the steadily deepening and unshakeable conviction that somehow or other there is a moral power and a moral possibility buried deep in, and at work in, the often savage randomness of human affairs'.[10] It is this conviction which gives the vision of what society might be and generates a longing for peace and justice. It is this conviction, too, which evokes the depth of anger at the way society actually is, which is 'an offence to the holiness, righteousness, love and peace of God'.[11] The issue of poverty is no mere secular concern. The anger and the outrage, as well as the vision and the longing, are integral to the recognition and worship of God.

A TASK FOR US ALL

I have brought this concern about the nature of God immediately upfront because what goes on in our world is profoundly about what we think about God. So the centrality of poverty to our faith is one belief driving this book. Another is that theology is not only relevant to the way we think about and react to poverty, but is a discipline in which all of us as Christians should be involved. 'Theology is one of a number of important subjects which are *too* important to be left to the experts. It is an enterprise which requires the critical attention of both experts in other fields and the ordinary public.'[12]

Theology is moving from being primarily a classic formulation of Christian doctrines. One of the activities of the Church from earliest times has been the development of a canon for the content of faith which could be used both to interpret and preserve the original Christian message as it was taken into new cultures. Christianity is a historical religion in two senses. It is based upon an historical person to whom Christians must remain faithful, and it exists as an historical entity which must adapt to its milieu in order to retain its meaning and vitality. It is an incarnational faith rooted in the human situation, and throughout its history it has necessarily drawn on prevailing categories of thought. The problem of theology in any age is to keep the right tension between the biblical message and current categories of thought; between the universal and the particular; the essential and that which should be properly subject to change; the transcendent and the historical. This clearly stretches theological skill beyond the rational articulation of the faith to being a critical discipline which additionally needs to 'read the style' of a culture or to 'trace God's hand in the events of our time'.[13] In our own country today, there is a clear need to provide a theological critique of a society which tolerates poverty in the midst of affluence.

Coming to terms with modern consciousness involves an awareness of other disciplines, including the social sciences. This is necessary not only for the insights they have achieved, but also because many of their tenets have become internalized as part of the twentieth-century person's cultural baggage. Individuals do not have to be Marxists to have been influenced by Marx's thought, or Freudians to have absorbed some of his ideas. Many of the categories of social scientific thought have passed into the currency of everyday life. They provide part of the language in which people speak of life around them and through which they formulate their self-awareness. They cannot be ignored as part of the context of contemporary theology. Although tending to oscillate 'between those very poles of withdrawal from the secular world and involvement in it which can be found also in Christian forms of organisation and activity',[14] theologians necessarily have ongoing 'conversations' with the world.[15] For these conversations to be relevant, they need to understand what the other party is thinking, feeling and experiencing.

It is this which should involve us all in 'doing theology'. Other disciplines, as well as the reality of all our lives, supply some of theology's raw material. They can enlighten and be enlightened by the Scriptures and the traditions we have inherited. This does not minimize the role of the theologian. As David Jenkins says, 'As a theologian it is my job and my duty to point to what seem to me to be relevant factors or features in the tradition.'[16] But this role has to be set beside the other sorts of expertise and an analytical and experiential critique of poverty. Our identity as Christians lays on us all the responsibility of engaging in the common task of working out an appropriate response to poverty.

WHOSE THEOLOGY?

> The insights of Christianity have become the almost exclusive possession of the more comfortable and privileged classes. These have sentimentalised them to such a degree, that the disinherited, who ought to avail themselves of their resources, have become so conscious of the moral confusions which are associated with them, that the insights are not immediately available for the social struggle in the Western world.[17]

Opening up the theological task to a wider constituency, of course, risks – or indeed ensures – that its ground will be shifted, that it will serve new purposes, meet new needs. *The Kairos Document*, published in 1985, analysed the different theologies co-existing in South Africa in relation to the political crisis in that country.[18] But the typology it gives could equally be applied elsewhere.

First, it identified 'state theology' which 'is simply the theological justification of the *status quo* with its racism, capitalism and totalitarianism'. It blesses injustice, canonizes the will of the powerful and reduces the poor to passivity, obedience and apathy.[19] Second, 'church theology', that is what is seen as the official views of the churches, is critical of apartheid but only 'in a limited, guarded and cautious way'.

> Its criticism, however, is superficial and counter-productive because instead of engaging in an in-depth analysis of the signs of our times, it relies upon a few stock ideas derived from Christian tradition and then uncritically and repeatedly applies them to our situation.[20]

It was inevitable that 'church theology' would be inadequate because it failed to address the realities of the South African situation. It contained no social analysis of what was really happening and why. Trying to apply principles of reconciliation, non-violence and justice must fail where the structures, mechanisms and effects of oppression and injustice are insufficiently understood.

Similarly it is impossible to develop a telling theological critique while skirting around politics and political strategy. Christian solutions to the world's problems are not alternative ones in the sense that they are lifted out of normal human institutions. They are alternative ways of working *within* and *through* these institutions with a new vision, motivation and driving spirit. But they will never be found if the Church persists in treating spirituality as divorced from worldly affairs. Regarding spirituality as wholly private and individualistic precludes people from being co-workers with God in building his kingdom.

> The Bible does not separate the human person from the world in which he or she lives; it does not separate the individuals from the social or one's private from one's public life. God redeems the whole person as part of his whole creation (Rom 8.18–24). A truly biblical spirituality would penetrate every aspect of human existence and would exclude nothing from God's redemptive will. Biblical faith is prophetically relevant to everything that happens in the world.[21]

Third, in contrast with state and church theologies, prophetic theology focuses on the heart of the message of hope at the heart of the gospel. *The Kairos Document* asks why this powerful message has not been central to the pronouncements of church leaders. 'Is it because they have been addressing themselves to the oppressor rather than the oppressed? Is it because they do not want to encourage the oppressed to be too hopeful for too much?'[22]

One of the hardest challenges of *The Kairos Document* for those of us in the UK is to unmask the extent to which our theology also ignores the reality of suffering in our society, also bypasses the need for political change, and is also implicated in systems of exploitation and injustice. It recalls what David Jenkins calls the 'contradiction of Christianity'.[23] 'Our behaviour as Christians and the performance of the institutions of Christianity have been such as to deprive us of the right to be Christians or to expect credibility for what Christianity stands for.'[24]

Ed de la Torre, the Filipino theologian, also talks about Christianity as

> a sign of contradiction that should force us to take sides, to make decisions … We believe that all of us have been hard of hearing or pretending not to hear. For if there is any portion of God's word that Filipinos ask for, it is that word which answers their questions. Why am I poor? Why am I jobless? Why am I treated unjustly? Our class thinks that the Christian social teachings have been kept secret too long … to be really relevant, Christianity must follow the pattern set by Christ. He became man. In the same way, Christianity must become Filipino.[25]

And, we must add, Christianity must become the Christianity of the homeless teenager, the unemployed miner, the lone mother and her children in a bed-and-breakfast hostel, the low-paid farm worker and all those others who are in some way sidelined in our society. What are the contradictions at the heart of our own beliefs and practices which must be faced and transformed if Christianity is to be meaningful to the marginalized?

DELUDING OURSELVES

And as he was setting out on his journey, a man ran up and knelt before him, and asked him, 'Good Teacher, what must I do to inherit eternal life?' And Jesus said to him, 'Why do you call me good? No one is good but God alone. You know the commandments: "Do not kill, Do not commit adultery, Do not steal, Do not bear false witness, Do not defraud, Honour your father and mother."' And he said to him, 'Teacher, all these I have observed from my youth.' And Jesus looking on him loved him, and said to him, 'You lack one thing; go, sell what you have, and give to the poor, and you will have treasure in heaven; and come, follow me.' At that saying his countenance fell, and he went away sorrowful; for he had great possessions. (Mark 10.17–22)

In his book *The Culture of Contentment*[26] the economist J. K. Galbraith looks at contemporary American society and sees that those who are gaining most from it have not only lost sight of those who are gaining least; they have lost any sense of interdependence.

[It] has been conveniently neglected [that] the comfort and economic wellbeing of the contented majority ... is ... supported and enhanced by the presence in the modern economy of a large, highly useful, even essential class that does not share in the agreeable existence of the favoured community.[27]

The most general characteristic of the contented majority, he says, is the assumption that its members are receiving their just deserts. What they have got, they have got through their own efforts, virtue and intelligence.

This way of thinking has particularly characterized the last decade. Whereas in the past, on either side of the political divide, many might have had a sense of unease at seeing those who did not share in the well-being of the fortunate, Ronald Reagan betrayed no such squeamishness. The 'presidentially ordained script', says Galbraith, was that 'Americans were being rewarded as they so richly deserved. If some did not participate, it was because of their inability or by their choice.'[28] As with Reagan, so it was with Thatcherism. And sadly, though the mood has changed a little, perhaps becoming less bullish, that attitude has taken considerable hold – again across the political divide – at least to the extent that we tend to have lost a sense of interconnectedness.

What Galbraith identified as a political culture underpinning and justifying a divided society can also be interpreted as 'profoundly godless and is a very corrosive acid on the bonds of our common life'.[29] In biblical terminology, it is an expression of idolatry. It reveals how far as a society and as individuals we have departed from acknowledging our total dependence upon God. All we are and all we have is given to us by God. Claiming credit for our lives and achievements is a denial of this. Our equal standing before God is not only in his love for each one of us but in our essential poverty and powerlessness.

In the story quoted above, Jesus tells about a man who apparently led an ethically exemplary life. He was thoughtful, responsible and keen to do good. But, when it came to answering Jesus' call, he just could not let go of his possessions and the life that he treasured. Early in the conversation, Jesus had gone to the nub of the issue by asking him 'Why do you call me good?' In other words, how did he assess goodness? What did he understand by it? In what was it grounded? Only by understanding the true nature of goodness could he know how to respond to Jesus' challenge. But this man, variously called a rich young man or a ruler, could only conceive of eternal life – the blessing he was seeking – as a reward, a good conduct certificate, rather than life in God's company. He could not bring himself to transfer his trust from his own wealth and his ethical as well as material achievements to place it in God. So he could not answer a call to go beyond the moral limits of an ethical life to one of obedience and faith. Yet the Scriptures are precisely about going beyond these moral limits. The Bible is not a rule book; Christianity is not a code of conduct. 'What the Scriptures are *about*, first of all, is the gift and goal of human existence as it has been called into being by the one God who reveals himself in the world and in the history of his creatures.'[30] And our attitude towards, and use of, possessions should be rooted in this premise that our very existence is the gift of God.

OWNERSHIP OR STEWARDSHIP

The things that we own and use daily are closely bound up in our identity and sense of self – individually and collectively. It is hard to be dispassionate about them or objective in looking at our relationship with them. We talk about certain things having sentimental value. Their value or significance comes from those who gave them to us, the circumstances in which we received them or the memories they hold for us. Similarly, when people are burgled, have their homes entered and ransacked, they often have a sense of outrage and violation – of having been intruded upon – which affects them far more deeply than the monetary value of what they have lost. Our belongings and surroundings are an extension of ourselves.

'Ownership' is a slippery concept and one which is closely related to the exercise of power. The multiplicity of property laws indicates that so-called private ownership is rooted in a social context, showing for example the wide range of possibilities for disputed ownership. Social ties altogether are set within an intricate framework of definitions of what is yours, mine, ours, theirs, and the relationships which flow from these, whether they are established in law or by custom and practice or survive by mutual understanding and trust.

Questions of the ownership and efficient use of land, capital and labour are fundamental to economics. The distinction between public and private ownership remains basic to political debate. This was illustrated most colourfully in recent years by Harold Macmillan's description of the disposal of hitherto public resources as 'selling off the family silver'. But it is also central to issues about the welfare state, taxation and the extent to which provision for personal needs should be made publicly or privately. When the Conservative Party calls itself the party of freedom, much of this self-image has to do with minimizing the redistribution of income and contribution towards social provision through taxation – which is often depicted as, if not theft, at least confiscation of personal income – and increasing the individual's free disposal of his or her income. This emphasis on individual rights underplays any sense of goods held in common or communal obligations. It detracts from the notion of stewardship – the socially responsible use of our resources. The deregulation of private enterprise also risks the neglect, pollution or squandering of resources, with serious consequences not only for today but also for future generations. When allied to a dominant goal of economic growth leading to increasing consumerism, it adds up to a possessive individualism which is particularly destructive of a sense of community.

However, the idea of ownership and possessions extends beyond material things to ourselves and other people. People can be physically taken over by others in slavery, but we also talk about minds being 'possessed' by others, for example, through forms of political or religious indoctrination. Women and children at different times and in different societies have been regarded in various degrees as men's chattels. 'You think you own me' can be the frustrated reaction to a jealous lover or an over-protective parent. Phrases such as 'a woman's right to choose' and 'I can do what I like with my own body' suggest a realm of private power in relation to an individual's ownership of his or her body. But we can also be possessive about 'our' time, 'our' ideas or 'our' status or dignity.

Much of the importance attached to possessions – of whatever type – is symbolic. Their meaning arises out of their cultural, social or economic context. What is highly prized here and now may mystify someone on the other side of the world or from the past or future. Changing fashions can be bewildering even to those in the same society. But the importance to many adolescents of having trainers or jeans with the 'right' label illustrates the power of commodities to impart or withhold a feeling of belonging. For another generation, 'keeping up with the Joneses' expressed this same link between identity and occupying a desired place in society and possession of those things which are the badges of membership.

HAVING OR BEING

In the Bible, too, it is not the *fact* of possessions – or their quality or quantity – which is singled out as important, but their meaning to the person claiming or wanting possession. God is shown to us as the ultimate reality. If possessions of some sort have usurped God in our affections, what it means is that we have lost real meaning in our lives for the sake of illusion. We are building on shifting sands; seeking or relying on false security. Jesus tells the parable of the man who built bigger and bigger barns to store his riches only to find that such material wealth could guarantee him nothing (Luke 12.16–21). '. . . his death disclosed his essential poverty. The only possessions worthy of man's striving are those death cannot take away.'[31]

Later in Luke's Gospel, Jesus reminds the disciples about Lot's wife who, when fleeing from cataclysmic events, yet had to look back, because she found it so hard to relinquish the things she had left behind (Luke 17.32ff referring to Gen 19.26). 'Whoever seeks to gain (possess) his life will lose it, but whoever loses his life will preserve it' (17.33). The mistake that the rich fool made and that Lot's wife made was to confuse *having* with *being*. Their measurement of themselves and the value of their lives was in what they owned rather than what they were. And, ultimately, they were treating life itself as something they owned, which they could control and hold in their own grasp. In contrast, Jesus asks 'Which of you by being anxious can add a cubit to his span of life?' (Luke 12.25). The question is, of course, a rhetorical one. No one can exercise that power, so the reality of human powerlessness and, consequently, the ultimate folly of preoccupation with material provision is revealed.

Yet our society is based upon the value of having rather than being – estimating people by their possessions, their status or their power rather than by their human qualities.

GOD AND MAMMON

Mammon led them on,
Mammon, the least erected Spirit that fell
From heav'n, for ev'n in heav'n his looks and thoughts
Were always downward bent, admiring more
The riches of heav'n's pavement, trodden gold,
Than aught divine or holy else enjoyed
In vision beatific.

Milton, *Paradise Lost*, Book I, 678–84

If an ancestor were brought back to life in the late twentieth century he would surely assume that the world was under the sway of a powerful new religion. He would see the glittering buildings reaching up to the sky, dwarfing the old churches or shrines alongside them. He would see the same architectural styles, as alike as Gothic cathedrals, proclaiming the same beliefs. Inside the cathedrals he would come into high atria, with the same hushed, self-contained atmosphere, the same kind of foliage, like flowers on altars. And in the surrounding cloisters he would see hundreds of acolytes sitting silently in front of flickering screens, watching mystical patterns of digits taking shape, and pressing keys as if reciting ritual responses or telling beads.

He would see these new cathedrals across half the world, whether in New York, Tokyo, London, Hong Kong or Singapore all apparently interchangeable across the continents ... and everywhere the same screens display the same magic numbers, subjugating a hundred different cultures and traditions to the same universal homage to its language, proclaiming with total faith the first commandment: that money makes the world go round.[32]

To understand our attitudes towards poverty it is also necessary to think about our attitude towards wealth, to gain a deeper understanding of people's attitudes towards possessions in general and money in particular. Anthony Sampson introduces his book on 'money, people and power from East to West' by describing money as the central tenet of a faith which has gathered around it the sorts of accretions of reverence and ritual fitting to the present-day universal religion.

Money is an essential mechanism for enabling societies to function. When it replaced bartering, symbolic tokens were introduced to substitute for commodities. Early currencies were otherwise useless objects which were only invested with special significance by becoming a means of exchange. It then became the standard means of payment and thus the foundation of systematizing all credit and debt transactions, necessarily underpinned by the state acting to guarantee its value. Money moved from being only a means of exchange to a commodity in itself. It became an end in itself as 'it acquired its own magic and awe as an instrument of worldly power'.[33] Thus money as an anti-religion became a recurring theme in literature. At the same time, gold came to be a symbol of wealth and ultimate value. As its power grew, most religious teachings, including the Old and New Testaments, warned about the potentially corrupting influence of money – the love of money is the root of all evil[34] – and about financial practices such as usury.

There is nothing new, then, about the association between money and God. It is the most abstract of all commodities and represents to us the relationship between all other commodities. If interpersonal relationships are seen as being built on an intricate network of transactions, then money defines a high proportion of those transactions. Even if there is no exchange of cash, there may be indirect payments such as taxes. As such, it shapes not only our most basic social institutions, such as the family, but also our personality structures. God is often referred to as the ground of all being: that within whom all other beings find relationship. In one sense, the same can be said of money. Money substitutes an impersonal standard for the intrinsic content of goods and services. It enables anything to be exchanged for anything. How can you put a price on a beautiful view or fresh air or a work of art or devoted care? Well, with money you can.

However, the indispensability and the mundane functionalism of money as the mechanism of trade ensured that it would win out over religious scruples. Now its role has enormously expanded and undergone qualitative change. It was integral to industrialization and the spread of commerce. 'Money was becoming so all-enveloping in industrial society that like a religion it gave its own meaning and purpose to life.'[35] The German philosopher, Georg Simmel said in 1907, 'Money is everywhere conceived as purpose, and countless things that are really ends in themselves are thereby degraded to mere means.'[36] It had become inextricable from the complex organizational and behavioural framework needed to support and advance capitalism.

It has been argued that there was a cross-fertilization between, in the words of Max Weber's famous title, *The Protestant Ethic and the Spirit of Capitalism.*[37]

> Weber wanted to show how certain types of Protestantism became a fountainhead of incentives that favoured the rational pursuit of economic gain ... to show how the secular ethical concepts of the Reformation were related to its theological doctrines, and hence to verify that the new worldly orientation was indeed related to the religious ideas of the period.[38]

Reformers such as Calvin were not setting out to promote the spirit of capitalism but, said Weber, their doctrines nevertheless contained implicit impulses in this direction. They tended towards asceticism.

> The usefulness of labour was judged by the fruits that signified its favour in the sight of God. Profit and wealth were ethically bad only insofar as they led to idleness and dissipation; they were commended insofar as they resulted in the performance of duty ... As long as it involved unremitting effort and an absence of self-indulgence, the successful pursuit of gain was therefore the duty of the businessman.[39]

David Landes more recently still saw Puritan virtues, in the widest sense of self-denial and discipline, as having a crucial role in the organization of industry and economic growth: 'They constituted in effect an imposition of the criterion of efficiency on every activity, whether or not directly connected with getting and spending.' If Puritan virtues so defined remain key, their connection with Protestantism is no longer supreme, as capitalism has advanced across the world. Whatever virtues were necessary have survived being transplanted into very different cultural and religious soil, judging from the economic success of Japan, Korea and Taiwan.

TIME IS MONEY

Money is all-powerful and omnipresent. Its influence is the more pervasive not just because it saturates everything, but because we take it for granted. Its ascendancy is all the greater because we cannot see it, we fail to recognize it; it is part of the givenness of things. The global spread of this 'religion' has had a number of consequences. The world is an instant market-place. Boundaries of time and space have been overcome. Financial markets have become the new means of imperialism and missionary inculturation. Financial power is as potent as military strength for gaining access to and controlling the world's scarce resources. And, at the same time, those countries rich in natural resources, such as those of Latin America, have become crippled with debt as their capital has drained away to richer countries. The language of money often uses the analogy of water – money streams, liquidity, flotation. As Sampson says, the scale and speed of flows around the world have suddenly increased, but rather than streams and rivers which 'refresh all parts', it is more like a single dynamic and mobile pool criss-crossing the world without necessarily watering the seeds of growth in its temporary resting places. The pursuit of new markets and the ease of transnational relocation are also driving down the value of labour as multinational companies shift their operations to areas of cheaper and less organized labour markets.

Sampson points out that

> the religion of money exacts its harshest tribute in its demands on time
> . . . . The old cathedral clocks which summoned monks to prayer and
> measured the time which belonged to God have long been superseded by
> the digital microseconds which measure the time which belongs to
> money.[40]

One consequence is that on a personal level, 'time misers' have replaced
'money misers'. Busyness, and how long in advance it is necessary to book an
appointment with someone, has become a new status symbol. The speed of
transactions which technology makes possible has imprisoned instead of
liberated. Everything has gathered a bewildering momentum. People become
locked into urgency. International travel timetables take over, dealing takes
place across international time zones, telephone calls cannot wait but have to
be made while in transit, replies have to be faxed. Time is parcelled out in
smaller and smaller portions and has to be organized in a Filofax or even
electronically. More and more people complain of overloaded and stressful
lives. At the other extreme, people who are unemployed have an excess of time
but lack the resources to use it. There is a danger that their time loses all
meaning, with no incentive to get up in the morning and no shape to the day
thereafter. No wonder that one of the main problems of adjusting to work
after long-term unemployment is (re)acquiring the discipline of being ruled
by the clock.

  In other ways, the poorer someone is, the more time takes on an immediacy
with regard to money. Money has moved beyond material coinage or paper
money. 'Today, "money proper" is independent of the means whereby it is
represented, taking the form of pure information lodged as figures in a
computer printout.'[41] Money was already a means of deferring payment,
providing a way of connecting credit and liability in circumstances where the
immediate exchange of products was impossible. The transition to plastic
money and computer information enlarges the possibilities of credit. But these
possibilities are only open to those deemed credit-worthy. A distinctive
feature of the lives of poor people in countries such as this is that they are
much more limited to cash transactions than other people. Their payments,
therefore, have to be immediate and visible – no bank loans or overdrafts, no
store accounts, no monthly or quarterly standing orders. It is cash over the
counter, feeding meters with coins or tokens and getting cut off when the
money runs out. Less money is also less control. The use of credit cards and
indirect and deferred methods of payment can mean that people become very
hazy about the cost of things and their real level of expenditure. There is no
such danger if you have to count out every pound and penny.

Another aspect of money and time is the effect that our financial systems have on the timescale of our collective thinking. Sampson quotes an interview with John Reed, Chairman of Citicorp, America's largest bank. 'The global markets and large pools of capital have had the effect of shortening our time horizons . . . we define out of existence certain types of problems that have a longer time-cycle.'[42] The accusation of being more interested in the hereafter than the here and now can certainly not be levelled at money! Michel Albert in his study of different types of capitalism sees the creeping advance of the neo-American model, also prominent in the UK, over the European and Japanese models. Its distinguishing feature, he says, is that it deliberately sacrifices the future for the present, even though quality and well-being are tied to investment in the future.

WHAT GETS COUNTED COUNTS

If short-termism is one problem, another is the false perspective that money brings when it becomes the measure of all things. Economic growth and prosperity have become the icons of the age. The emphasis on individuals as economic beings which has been a mark of the last fifteen years has effectively denied our social nature, cultural interests and spiritual concerns. It is only a short road to reducing human identity to self-interested consumerism. This has been expressed – and reinforced – by a number of developments.

First, the nature of trust has changed.[43] Trust is still indispensable to the operation of financial systems and the use of money. But that trust is no longer in people but in abstractions. With money, as with many other aspects of life, we rely upon expert systems. We do not live in daily fear of our house falling down because we have faith in the skills and expertise of the people who built it, even if we have not got the knowledge ourselves to verify that faith. We may think more highly of one builder than another, one plumber than another, but underpinning those judgements about their individual competence is a more fundamental trust in the authenticity of the expert knowledge they apply. So it is with money. We rely upon it retaining its value. We take for granted – and therefore trust – the whole panoply of structures and transactions in which we are involved, touching on governments, employers, retailers, banks, building societies, insurance companies, pension schemes – the list is endless. Trust in people is relevant to faith in the systems, but that is to do with whether they work properly, not whether they work at all.

The importance of this sort of trust underlines the significance of some proper apprehension of the way systems actually work. Even if we are not electricians, we need to know enough about electrical systems not to misuse them or have false expectations, for example, about how much we can load onto them. There have been some unpleasant surprises recently for people with misplaced confidence. Will Hutton in an article entitled 'Poverty's posh relations' has pointed out that the 1990s have brought a rude awakening.

> The 1980s offered the British middle class a delightful release from having to make hard economic choices. Gross incomes grew handsomely; after-tax incomes even more so. Inflation was high enough to swallow the debts run up by private schooling and foreign holidays without devaluing those solid earnings. The wonders of the property boom which made housing equity of a couple of hundred thousand pounds commonplace added a further feel-good glow.[44]

Everything seemed affordable and, as he said, 'even marriages seemed disposable: the two family father could flourish, knowing he had the means to maintain children by a first and a second wife'. For these people, the disinflationary 1990s, said Hutton, have brought 'an emerging crisis of expectations . . . Redundancy, job insecurity and the Child Support Agency have befallen them.'

Even without such a dramatic scenario, people with mortgages – as well as the Church Commissioners – were caught out by the fall in the property market. After a seemingly inexorable growth in house prices which gave people confidence to borrow hugely, millions of people were left with houses whose resale value was far outstripped by what they owed. A British legacy of the 1980s was the highest ratio of mortgage debt to disposable income in the industrialized world. Lloyd's 'names' have also found that they have tried to build financial security on shifting sand.

The elevation of material possessions as individual goals and as the measure of human happiness and achievement is one way in which money can erode human values. Another is when money is introduced as a measure instead of the common good. Charles Handy cites a range of distortions that can result. We take for granted measuring *per capita* income nowadays as a basis for international comparisons. Yet national income statistics fail to count so many things which probably actually contribute more to quality of life than simple income levels. Unpaid work, for example, home or voluntary (gift) work goes uncounted. Handy points out the irony that by this way of accounting, a society is richer if your parent lives in a home for the elderly than with you. 'More insidiously, if the cars and the highways are so bad that accidents proliferate, then hospital, car repair and insurance bills increase, and so does the supposed wealth of the country as these transactions find their way into the national accounts.'[45] By this measure leisure activities would be ranked in value according to the money spent on them, and so on. Yet as Handy says, 'Adding up all the financial transactions by all the companies and institutions in a country, converting it into dollars and dividing it by the number of people in a society does not tell you how comfortable they are.'[46] There are other forms of measure, such as those relating to health, employment and unemployment, and the environment, but these are not given a fraction of the prominence given to money figures.

THE COSTS OF CONSUMPTION

Attempts have been made in America and in the UK to develop an 'Index of Sustainable Economic Welfare' (ISEW)[47] which adjusts a consumer expenditure-based measure to account for a variety of social and environmental factors not generally included in measuring economic progress. The index covers factors such as the costs of commuting, road accidents, water, air and noise pollution, the loss of wetlands and farmlands, the depletion of non-renewable resources and the cost of long-term environmental damage between 1950 and 1990. Although it was an immensely fraught technical exercise, the authors, Tim Jackson and Nic Marks, adopted what they felt to be conservative assumptions throughout and therefore felt they could present their findings with some degree of confidence.

'The results suggest that welfare in the UK has not improved over the study period at anything like the rate that a conventional measure of GNP would have us believe. In particular, sustainable economic welfare appears to have declined in this country since the mid-1970s.'[48] Adjustment for the long-term costs of environmental damage was the largest negative contribution to the index. Modern prosperity has fuelled consumer aspirations and competitive instincts and led to a 'can't wait' culture. Its effects are seen in an erosion of community services and support networks, polarization and increasing personal stress.

Jackson and Marks also look at the – admittedly complex – relationship between equity and welfare.

> It is intuitively obvious that a society which looks after the interests of a few, at the expense of the welfare of the majority, is likely to incur real economic costs in terms of policing, security, and damages arising from civil unrest. It is also to be expected that a growth in *per capita* consumer expenditure is less likely to be a growth in *per capita* welfare, if it applies more to the rich than it does to the poor.[49]

Although there are difficulties in measuring the economic effects of distributional inequality, nevertheless it should not be excluded altogether from such an index. Rather the authors emphasized the need to examine it more closely.

VALUE FOR MONEY OR MONEY INSTEAD OF VALUE?

Money shapes our notions about what is important individually and collectively. In this way, it is affecting both our personal and our structural relationships. Britain is becoming more and more a society of competing individuals and interest groups. With the privatization of public services and public utilities such as water, gas and electricity, market operations are being introduced into spheres in which not so long ago the profit motive was deemed wholly inappropriate. The free-market philosophy which has been dominant over recent years measures policies by their efficiency. This presupposes a greater concern with costs than quality of service, a greater concern with the smooth running of the market than with the dignity and respect of those caught up in its machinations. It heightens competition for scarce resources and therefore allocates them according to competitive strength rather than need. Competition sets prices for essentials without necessary reference to what the poorest can afford. Competition searches out the most lucrative markets and focuses on meeting those demands rather than assessing the relative needs of different groups and areas.

This chapter has indicated some of the basic presuppositions that underpin this book and it has begun to identify some of the major questions that need to be addressed if poverty is to be confronted. It has come back full circle to the 'urgent concern' of the CAP Declaration about society being driven in a direction that contradicts the gospel. The next chapter continues the process of scene setting by turning to look at attitudes towards people in poverty.

NOTES

1. Church Action on Poverty, *Hearing the Cry of the Poor* (1989).
2. 'A Really Good Weekend', an account of CAP National Conference 1989, in *Hearing the Cry of the Poor, Poverty Network 12* (Autumn 1989), p. 5.
3. J. Philip Wogaman, *A Christian Method of Moral Judgement* (London: SCM Press, 1976), p. 65.
4. Fr Michael Campbell-Johnston SJ, in a letter to Church Action on Poverty 1989 (my italics).
5. David Jenkins, 'Christian doctrine: the challenge to and from poverty' in *God, Politics and the Future* (London: SCM Press, 1988).
6. *Ibid.*, p. 46.
7. *Ibid.*, p. 48.
8. *Ibid.*, p. 49.
9. *Hearing the Cry of the Poor.*
10. Jenkins, *op. cit.*, p. 49.
11. *Ibid.*, p. 51.
12. Stephen Sykes, *Christian Theology Today* (London: Mowbray, 1983), p. 7.
13. V. A. Demant, *Religion and the Decline of Capitalism* (London: Faber and Faber, 1952), p. 177.
14. Alasdair MacIntyre, *Secularization and Moral Change* (Oxford: Oxford University Press, 1967), p. 67.
15. MacIntyre asserts that in these ongoing conversations with the world, theologians have tended to adopt characteristic conversational strategies. He makes a firm connection between the claims of Christian theology and the relation between church organization and different forms of social life. He sees in theology's adaptations the same 'two poles of sectarian apartness and denominational assimilation' (*ibid.*, p. 66). II. Richard Niebuhr also addressed the 'enduring problem' of the relation

between Christianity and civilization in *Christ and Culture* (London: Faber and Faber, 1952) in which he too saw 'a series of typical answers which together, for faith, represent phases of the strategy of the Church militant in the world' (p. 18).

16. Jenkins, *op. cit.*, p. 45.
17. Reinhold Niebuhr, *Moral Man and Immoral Society* (London: SCM Press, 1963), p. 255.
18. *Challenge to the Church: The Kairos Document*, published in the UK by Catholic Institute for International Relations (CIIR) and British Council of Churches (BCC), September 1985.
19. *Ibid.*, p. 6.
20. *Ibid.*, p. 11.
21. *Ibid.*, p. 17.
22. *Ibid.*, p. 23.
23. David Jenkins, *The Contradiction of Christianity* (London: SCM Press, 1976).
24. *Ibid.*, p. 9.
25. Ed de la Torre, *Touching Ground, Taking Root* (CIIR with BCC, 1986), p. 16.
26. J. K. Galbraith, *The Culture of Contentment* (London: Sinclair Stevenson, 1992).
27. *Ibid.*, p. 29.
28. *Ibid.*, p. 28.
29. John Austin, 'Nurturing the green leaf of faith', in *The Place of the Wound: Poverty Network 19*, February 1993, p. 8.
30. Luke T. Johnson, *Sharing Possessions* (London: SCM Press, 1981), p. 43.
31. G. B. Caird, *St Luke* (Harmondsworth: Penguin, 1963), p. 163.
32. Anthony Sampson, *The Midas Touch: Money People and Power from West to East* (Coronet edn, 1990), p. 17.
33. *Ibid.*, p. 21.
34. 1 Tim 6.9–10: 'But those who desire to be rich fall into temptation, into a snare, into many senseless and hurtful desires that plunge men into ruin and destruction. For the love of money is the root of all evil; it is through this craving that some have wandered away from the faith and pierced their hearts with many pangs.'
35. Sampson, *op. cit.*, p. 24.
36. Georg Simmel, *The Philosophy of Money* (English translation, London: Routledge and Kegan Paul, 1978), p. 431.
37. Max Weber, *The Protestant Ethic and the Spirit of Capitalism* (London: Allen and Unwin, 1930).
38. Reinhold Bendix, *Max Weber, An Intellectual Portrait* (London: Heinemann, 1960), p. 79.
39. *Ibid.*, pp. 83–4.
40. Sampson, *op. cit.*, p. 27.
41. Anthony Giddens, *The Consequences of Modernity* (Cambridge: Polity Press, 1990), p. 25.
42. Sampson, *op. cit.*, p. 33.
43. See Giddens, *op. cit.*, pp. 29ff.
44. Will Hutton, 'Poverty's posh relations', *The Guardian*, 21 April 1994.
45. Charles Handy, *The Empty Raincoat: Making Sense of the Future* (London: Hutchinson, 1994), p. 220.
46. *Ibid.*, p. 221.
47. Tim Jackson and Nic Marks, *Measuring Sustainable Economic Welfare – A Pilot Index: 1950–1990* (Stockhold Environment Institute in co-operation with the New Economics Foundation, 1994).
48. *Ibid.*, p. 36.
49. *Ibid.*, p. 34.

CHAPTER 2

Always with Us?

Christ does tell us that the poor will always be with us. He does tell us that we should help the poor, but I would put limiting factors on that. (Christian Aid, *The Gospel, the Poor and the Churches*)

What thoughtful rich people call the problem of poverty, thoughtful poor people call with equal justice a problem of riches. (R. H. Tawney, 'Poverty as an Industrial Problem')

WHAT'S THE POINT?

It was now two days before the Passover and the feast of Unleavened Bread. And the chief priests and the scribes were seeking how to arrest him by stealth, and kill him; for they said, 'Not during the feast, lest there be a tumult of the people.'

And while he was at Bethany in the house of Simon the leper, as he sat at table, a woman came with an alabaster jar of ointment of pure nard, very costly, and she broke the jar and poured it over his head. But there were some who said to themselves indignantly, 'Why was the ointment thus wasted? For this ointment might have been sold for more than three hundred denarii, and given to the poor.' And they reproached her. But Jesus said, 'Let her alone; why do you trouble her? She has done a beautiful thing to me. For you always have the poor with you, and whenever you will, you can do good to them; but you will not always have me. She has done what she could; she has anointed my body beforehand for burying. And truly, I say to you, wherever the gospel is preached in the whole world, what she has done will be told in memory of her.' (Mark 14.1–9)

The gospel story of the woman anointing Jesus is frequently quoted to justify inaction over poverty – not, it might be imagined, what Jesus had in mind when he said that the woman's action would always be remembered. Yet the story is sometimes used as if Jesus was telling it to provide a fatalistic interpretation of poverty, suggesting that attempts to prevent it are pointless.

The primary message is surely a different one. Jesus knew he was soon to die. He had been trying to prepare his followers for this, to convey to them the significance of the moment and the impending challenges they would face. Not surprisingly, they could not understand what he was really saying. But perhaps this woman intuitively recognized the importance of the occasion, had a feeling it was a moment to be grasped and cherished. And so she brought the expensive oil. The disciples' indignation may have been tinged with annoyance that they had not thought of something similar, pique that they were pushed out of the limelight, as well as mystification that such an extravagant act was so unexpectedly appreciated and justified by their Master who hitherto had seemed to turn worldly values on their head. For Jesus, the outpoured oil was the woman's love unstintingly given and expressed as she responded with her heart to his true message. His reply to his disciples swept aside the way they rationalized their grudging reaction. He was not saying, 'It's no use bothering to do anything about poverty because it's a never-ending problem that will never be resolved.' The point of his rebuke was not to give a long-term forecast about poverty at all. Rather, he was exposing the hypocrisy of their complaint. 'The opportunity is always there to help those who are poor.' That they raised the concern now distracted from the immediate issue. At worst, they were using it as a smokescreen. At best, they were asserting an ethical demand detached from Jesus' wider teaching about the nature of God.

THE TRUE TEST

> 'A decent provision for the poor is the true test of civilization . . . The condition of the lower orders, the poor especially, was the true test of national discrimination.'

Despite Samuel Johnson's true test of civilization, social attitudes towards poverty seem always to have veered between pity and blame and this has also been reflected in the wide range of explanations, responses and solutions offered. The political positions and ideological stances that are adopted today invariably pick up old themes adapted to current circumstances. That there is scope for diversity – and confusion – is not surprising since poverty relates to economic and social structures and individual behaviour. It straddles the realms of the social sciences and morals, the material and the spiritual. It is a public problem with personal consequences.

The historian Gertrude Himmelfarb points out that an ambivalent conception of poverty can be seen in the Middle Ages when it was

> at the same time a blessing to be devoutly sought and a misfortune to be piously endured. The 'holy poor' embraced poverty as a sacred vow, the

better to do God's will; the 'unholy poor' tolerated it (or railed against it) as an unhappy fact of life, a cross to be borne with Christian fortitude or resisted with unchristian defiance.[1]

The rich had a duty of charity – an obligation equally to sustain those who had voluntarily adopted the mantle of poverty and to relieve the sufferings of those who had no option. Poverty and charity were inextricably bound together and permeated with religious significance; '. . . the church inevitably became the instrument both of social amelioration and of spiritual salvation; indeed the one was a function of the other'.[2]

Gradually the idea of poverty became largely secularized and, for most purposes, synonymous with involuntary poverty. By the eighteenth century, even such an unsentimental high Tory as Samuel Johnson had no illusions about the ennobling quality of poverty:

> In the prospect of poverty there is nothing but gloom and melancholy; the mind and body suffer together; its miseries bring no alleviations; it is a state in which every virtue is obscured, and in which no conduct can avoid reproach; a state of which cheerfulness is insensibility, and dejection sullenness, of which the hardships are without honour and the labours without reward.[3]

Johnson's observation of the no-win situation of those in poverty still rings very true today.

Poverty was viewed as a natural condition, an inevitable consequence of the fall of man through which men were condemned to toil all their days and eat by the sweat of their brows.[4] Yet it was one which should be alleviated if at all possible, and society had a role to play in this alleviation. It was because the state had assumed some responsibility for those in poverty that Johnson and others judged England to have passed the test of a civilized society. No matter how unsatisfactory their effects or uneven the application of the laws was in practice, the principle of the Elizabethan Poor Laws was important. They had established in law the principle of a national system of relief: ' . . . compassion had become public policy.'[5] Even those who thought the laws themselves were counter-productive and rebounded in their effects on the very people they were meant to serve nevertheless implicitly accepted that the primary locus of moral responsibility had shifted. The public responsibility was taken for granted and, while there was room for debate about how that responsibility should best be discharged, to have retreated from this commitment would have been perceived as moral failure.

The Poor Laws introduced at the end of the sixteenth century, though much reformed and amended, remained on the statute books until finally replaced after World War II. Yet throughout this time private charity continued to gain strength.

> Indeed, it flourished most when public relief was most generous, thus belying the familiar prediction that the assumption of responsibility by the state would diminish the sense of private responsibility; clearly the same moral impulse that expressed itself in charity also expressed itself in parish relief.[6]

Over recent years, government ministers have tended to talk as though we must choose between private Good Samaritans and corporate state provision on the assumption that the latter inevitably erodes the good impulses of the former. Gertrude Himmelfarb's reading of history suggests that feelings of responsibility are not divisible in this way.

AMBIVALENCE AND AMBIGUITY

Looking at social policies going back to Elizabethan times, the story is not one of steady development in one direction, but rather of pendulum swings between progressive and retrograde steps, between punitive and repressive policies and more generous amelioratory ones. Distinctions were made between types of poverty and classes of poor people. Some policies were deemed to have backfired. Reforms inspired by benevolent intentions could have negative results. In other words, the story is also one of ambivalence and ambiguity.

It is a task for historians to trace the link between the social and economic circumstances of the day and moral judgements made about poverty, and examine the way the intellectual and moral climate affected both the condition of the poor and the inclinations of reformers. Ideas about poverty changed, redefinitions took place. At each stage, however, the way poverty was defined derived from a moral position. Even later when attempts were made to reach more 'objective' definitions based upon minimum income requirements, this could not be a value-free exercise. 'Hard facts' are only seen as such and accepted insofar as they are mediated through contemporary perceptions, concepts, attitudes, values and beliefs. Thus some of the 'facts' of history appear very different in succeeding decades or centuries.

The period of rapid social and economic change from the mid-eighteenth century to the mid-nineteenth when Britain became an industrial nation can be described in terms of the prevailing social conditions. A picture can be built up by assembling material on standards of housing, employment and social amenities, wage and income levels and differentials, mortality rates, patterns of family life, crime rates and other features which might convey a flavour of life at the time. Alternatively, its history can be written in terms of legislative reform – the policies and agencies developed to meet changing needs.

Putting these two together more often shows disjunctions than apt solutions to evident problems. This is not just because of the social lag – the fact that it takes time to come to terms with a problem so that its solution tends always to be belated – but also because other factors interpose between the perception of a problem and the formulation of a solution. In particular, different interests and ideologies can preclude what may with the benefit of hindsight be thought a more obvious and appropriate response.[7] Reading history in this way may not provide us with the answers to any of our current problems, but it should at least lead us to retain some ideological suspicion of both the diagnosis of 'problems' today and the accompanying prescriptions.

Notions of poverty – what it was and how the problem could be resolved – were one of the key mediating influences on perceptions and policies. It is here that social history strays into the realm of the history of ideas, raising questions about how and why conceptions changed.

Quite striking changes of social climate – changes of mood – can be seen in retrospect. Poverty provided the subtext for Adam Smith's *The Wealth of Nations*.[8] Published as the Industrial Revolution was getting underway, it identified the significance of the division of labour in boosting production and thus increasing the economic wealth of the nation. Other themes were the role of self-interest and the 'invisible hand' which made the individual's self-interest an instrument in achieving the common good. Although best known for its arguments against government regulation of the economy and for a *laissez faire* system, the book's political economy is embedded in a wider moral philosophy. In any case, for Smith, political economy was not an end in itself. It was a means towards attaining 'the wealth and well-being, moral and material, of "the people", of whom the "labouring poor" were the largest part. And the poor themselves had a moral status in that economy – not the special moral status they enjoyed in a fixed, hierarchic order but that which adhered to them as individuals in a free society sharing a common human, which is to say, moral nature.'[9] He attacked those private interests that were in conflict with the general interest and in conflict especially with the interests of the poor. 'It is the industry which is carried on for the benefit of the rich and powerful that is principally encouraged by our mercantile system. That which is carried on for the benefit of the poor and the indigent is, too often, either neglected or oppressed.'[10] Smith could see that the poor were the chief victims of the existing system which kept wages low and drove prices up, whereas he wanted them to be the chief beneficiaries. And to the extent that he associated the interests of the labouring poor with the general interest of society, he recognized that there was nothing 'natural' about their present plight.

A VICIOUS CIRCLE

The mood changes that have been discerned in the twentieth century as commentators mark out the differences in the 'feel' of decades, for example, between the 1960s, 1970s, 1980s and 1990s, were also evident in the eighteenth and nineteenth centuries. By contrast with Smith's optimism about the potential of general benefit from economic advance, Thomas Malthus was profoundly pessimistic. His *Essay on Population*, published at the end of the eighteenth century, brought about a profound ideological shift which undermined both the moral status of the poor and the promise of material improvement held out by Smith.[11] Whereas Smith had assumed that an expanding industrial economy would bring about a direct link between 'the wealth of nations' and the well-being of the poorer members of society, Malthus' 'principle of population' pointed to a completely contrary conclusion. For him, while the growth of industry would promote the country's overall economy, it would be at the expense of the poorest because it would lead to an increased population without any associated increase in food. The ones to suffer would be those already struggling to subsist. His theory also allowed reactionary politicians to argue against giving poor relief or raising wages because they too would lead to this vicious circle of larger families, more mouths to feed and consequently less food to go round. 'The spectre of Malthusianism, in its original, stark, unqualified, ineluctably tragic form, gripped the imagination of contemporaries for half a century, making even more fearful a period fraught with anxiety and insecurity.'[12]

This anxiety brought to a head the movement for the reform of the old Poor Law though it did not lead to its total abolition as Malthus advocated. Instead, a distinction was made between 'pauper' and 'poor' by extending relief to able-bodied paupers only in the workhouse and on the condition of 'less-eligibility'. The outcome was the reverse of what was intended. Rather than separating out the pauper from the poor, the entire body of poor people was stigmatized in the public mind, precisely reinforcing the ambiguity the reformers sought to remove. 'The new ambiguity, however, was different from the old in one important respect. Where the old had assimilated the pauper into the body of the poor, the new unwittingly assimilated the poor into the class of the pauper.'[13] According to Disraeli, the implicit message of the new law was that 'poverty is a crime'. Whether it was pauperism or poverty that was defined as the problem, and whether the problem was seen as a disease or a crime, for Disraeli as for other Tories, this solution was worse than the problem itself. The new law undermined the social order. It may have been an order embodied in paternalistic structures, but at least its legitimacy rested on an ethos binding rich and poor together.

Attacked from right and left – though for different reasons – the reaction against the New Poor Law became bound up with a variety of other moves to improve prevailing conditions and extend the rights of various groups. These ranged from legislation on factory safety and public sanitation through to female and child labour and universal suffrage. The speed of social change had brought with it a deep sense of both social and moral disarray and the question of how to respond to poverty focused some of this unease.

> However poverty was viewed – as an inexorable fact of physical and human nature, as an unfortunate by-product of a particular law or institution, or as a fatal flaw of the entire system – it was seen as primarily, fundamentally, a moral problem. It was a moral problem for the poor and for society – for the poor as responsible moral agents, and for society as a legitimate moral order.[14]

'A GREAT GULF BETWIXT US'

There was a rich man, who was clothed in purple and fine linen and who feasted sumptuously every day. And at his gate lay a poor man named Lazarus, full of sores, who desired to be fed with what fell from the rich man's table; moreover the dogs came and licked his sores. The poor man died and was carried by the angels to Abraham's bosom. The rich man also died and was buried; and in Hades, being in torment, he lifted up his eyes, and saw Abraham far off and Lazarus in his bosom. And he called out, 'Father Abraham, have mercy upon me, and send Lazarus to dip the end of his finger and cool my tongue; for I am in anguish in this flame.' But Abraham said, 'Son, remember that you in your lifetime received your good things, and Lazarus in like manner evil things; but now he is comforted here, and you are in anguish. And besides all this, between us and you a great chasm has been fixed, in order that those who would pass from here to you may not be able, and none may pass from there to us.' (Luke 16.19–26)

One of those incensed by the New Poor Law was Charles Dickens. *Oliver Twist* – as much a morality play as a social novel – was a swingeing indictment of the law and workhouses. In it, he said that the New Poor Law gave the poor the alternative 'of being starved by a gradual process in the house, or a quick one out of it'.[15] A number of Victorian novels were influential in bringing alive to their readers the situation portrayed in a more arid way in parliamentary and other reports, 'namely, that the gulf between Dives and Lazarus was there, systematised at the very foundation of Victorian prosperity'.[16] It was Disraeli who made 'two nations' a household term, but the theme it summed up was developed by a number of commentators and novelists as the nineteenth century wore on. Thomas Carlyle in 1843 had divided the country into 'two sects', the 'dandies' and the 'drudges'.[17] If this fabulously wealthy Britain was to become a real civilization, he asserted, then the wealthy and the poor had to have a genuine relationship.

Disraeli used his novel *Sybil* (published in 1845) as a vehicle for putting across his views on the state of the nation – or, in the more contemporary phrase, 'the condition of the people' – because he felt this might be a more effective way of influencing public opinion than the political platform. As he had already told his constituents, he was convinced that there was something rotten at the core of the British social system. Individuals were amassing fortunes and Britain was becoming the most prosperous nation in the world, while at the same time the working classes, the real wealth creators, lived in abject poverty.

> 'Say what you like, our Queen reigns over the greatest nation that ever existed.'
>
> 'Which nation?' asked the younger stranger, 'for she reigns over two ... Two nations; between whom there is no intercourse and no sympathy; who are as ignorant of each other's habits, thoughts and feelings, as if they were dwellers in different zones, or inhabitants of different planets; who are formed by different breeding, are fed by different food, are ordered by different manners, and are not governed by the same laws.'
>
> 'You speak of ... ' said Egremont hesitatingly.
>
> 'THE RICH AND THE POOR.'

Disraeli's analysis in this passage, which, according to one modern commentator, 'can still send a *frisson* of emotion through any thoughtful Conservative',[18] strangely echoed that of someone with very different political views. Friedrich Engels wrote at around the same time that the bourgeoisie and the working class were 'two radically dissimilar nations, as unlike as difference of race could make them'.[19]

Elizabeth Gaskell also depicts the schism between the two nations in a novel about mid-nineteenth-century Manchester. When it was published, *Fraser's Magazine* said: 'People on Turkey carpets, with their three meals a day, are wondering, forsooth, why working men turn Chartists and Communists ... Do they want to know why? Then let them read *Mary Barton*.' The dangers of such lack of knowledge and communication between the social classes are graphically drawn in the incidents of the book, but Elizabeth Gaskell also speaks through the words of the Chartist, John Barton:

> 'Don't think to come over me with the old tale, that the rich know nothing of the trials of the poor. I say, if they don't know, they ought to

know. We are their slaves as long as we can work; we pile up their fortunes by the sweat of our brows; and yet we are to live as separate as if we were in two worlds; ay, as separate as Dives and Lazarus, with a great gulf betwixt us: but I know who was best off then,' and he wound up his speech with a low chuckle that had no mirth in it.[20]

In the original story, too, Dives could not plead ignorance. When in the after-life their situations were reversed, he recognized Lazarus and knew his name.

'A ONE-MAN ROYAL COMMISSION'[21]

This type of social novel was a distinctively Victorian phenomenon, though a similar service of translating reports and statistics into a more accessible and immediate medium may now be performed by television documentaries, such as *Breadline Britain*, and drama, such as *Cathy Come Home*. Henry Mayhew, who also worked around the middle of the nineteenth century, was a yet more prolific chronicler of his time. He was a journalist, playwright and novelist, and a series of his newspaper articles published in 1849 – written with all his dramatic panache – did more to alert people to poverty in London than any other single work. He continued to produce pamphlets over the next ten years until his four-volume *London Labour and the London Poor* was published in 1861–2.

What was specially notable about Mayhew's work was that he popularized a new image of poverty – a poverty defined in cultural rather than economic terms. What caught the public imagination was his description of the 'moral physiognomy' of London street folk whom he likened to the 'wandering tribes' world-wide in contrast to the majority of settled civilized peoples. They included a range of rural and urban 'paupers, beggars and outcasts' – vagrants, peddlers, thieves, pickpockets, prostitutes, street performers and street traders. Each group had its own distinctive features, he said, but all shared certain qualities such as 'lax ideas of property', 'a general improvi-dence', 'repugnance to continuous labour', 'pugnacity', 'an utter want of religion'.[22] Mayhew himself was not hostile to these people. In fact, he held society largely to blame because nothing had been done to avert the privation and insecurity which inevitably brought about this moral degradation. But this was not the impression that remained with most of his readers. Compas-sion, explanation and exculpation were overshadowed by his descriptions of the depths to which people had sunk. His language and metaphors – beasts, barbarians, pestilence, dungheap – passed judgements which spoke louder than his more measured analyses or pleas for understanding and help.

OURSELVES AND POVERTY

If I truly struggle to understand myself, I will discover my dependency, contingency and frailty. In a word, I am forced to acknowledge my ultimate poverty.[23]

Today, we are still readier to judge and categorize than to understand; to base our thinking on impressions, hearsay and 'horror stories' than an exploration of the causes and consequences of poverty. In 1993, Christian Aid commissioned a piece of research to investigate church people's attitudes to poverty, their perceptions about its nature and causes, their understanding of Christian teaching about poverty and their views about the church's role in relation to poverty.[24]

The research findings were illuminating. Although the study focused on poverty, many of its messages were more general ones about the interrelationship between faith and life. It revealed a wide array of theological approaches and positions, as well as showing that a multitude of meanings can be attached to the same set of words. In general, it confirmed that many of the divergences between Christians cut across denominational lines. It also pointed to a Church which is inward-looking and preoccupied with its internal 'domestic' concerns. Implicit in the findings was the Church's general fear of, and confusion about, politics. Consequently it operates with an inadequate concept of personhood and neglects our relationships in community. Artificial boundaries are drawn over what is political and what is not. The illusion reigns that it is possible to be non-political and confine oneself to moral or cultural questions.

A key feature of the report revolves around the similarities and differences between perceptions of poverty in the UK and in developing countries. The main findings correspond with, and reinforce, personal observation. First, people are more judgemental about poverty in the UK. Information and imagery about poverty are taken largely from the media – certainly more from secular sources than church ones. Their understanding tends to be narrow and extreme, associated more with the character of Third World poverty than that in the UK. Poverty in the UK has not necessarily been directly witnessed or experienced; it has remained hidden.

Second, people are inclined to see things as more clear-cut – not necessarily correctly – when they look outside their own society. They identify social evils to be condemned and fought against, whereas in relation to life around them, there is greater reliance on impressions and comparisons with times past, a greater focus on individuals' norms. Their views tend to be more complex and fragmented. Judgements are more hedged around with 'buts' and 'maybes' and this gets in the way of taking a positive stand.

Many of the responses in this survey about what can or should be done about poverty revolved around giving what it is assumed is ours to give. They implicitly denied the biblical view of the givenness of things – that nothing is merited, nothing is ours. Such responses left untouched the question of the basic distribution of both goods and power. They proceeded from a concept of charity rather than of justice. They also, therefore, failed to recognize any concept of common wealth or the common good – with the associated issues of taxation and so on – that such a concept would raise.

Poverty is an emotive topic. Rational consideration and empirical evidence are influenced by the premises people start with and are heavily overlaid with stereotypes and prejudices. But also people can be disturbed by their own reactions to it. 'The subject of poverty can arouse complex and disturbing emotions. People described compassion, sympathy, admiration, sadness, horror, desperation, frustration, guilt, a sense of being selfish or greedy, a desire to help or a constant nagging pressure to "do something about it".'[25] The study describes a number of 'coping mechanisms', which can be active or passive. The active ones involve people dealing with their feelings in a constructive way, attempting to identify with poor people and to 'enter into their experience'.[26] Passive coping stances, on the other hand, included trying to avoid the issue, disbelieving reports about poverty in this country, leaving the problem in God's hands, emphasizing 'the differences between themselves and poor people who were seen to have "given up" whereas others had successfully "made the best of their situation" '.[27]

It would be easy to be critical of passive 'copers'. But there is surely a passive coper lurking in all of us. Once the report was delivered, Christian Aid drew together a reference group to explore the research findings and identify their implications. It was a disparate group – men and women, black and white, from different social, economic, geographical and church backgrounds, theologians and sociologists, clergy and lay, community activists and academics, people with and without Third World experience. What united us was a concern about the response of Christians to poverty in Britain and overseas.

The experience of the group in discussing the report was telling. It was not an exercise that could be conducted with intellectual detachment. Once people started to probe the underlying significance of the range of reactions evoked by poverty which emerged from it, the process inevitably led to the need to acknowledge our own personal feelings and reactions and the reasons for them. It is no easy task to be open and honest even to ourselves. We tend not to question whether our inner feelings or gut reactions actually conform to our publicly expressed views; whether what we say *ought* to be the case actually *is* the case. It is even harder to be candid in a group in which it is assumed there is a strongly held shared ethic.

We give a dollar when we pass and hope our eyes don't meet.[28]

However, in talking about our feelings when seeing someone begging in the streets of London or Manchester, for example, it was clear that we all experienced the same ambivalence, the same mix of sympathy, guilt, anger and confusion. Variations on similar questions and thoughts tend to run through our minds. Am I being conned? I can't give to everyone, so how do I choose? Shouldn't I find out more before giving? But that would mean me getting more involved and I haven't time and I don't know where it might lead. Is this kind of giving really in their best interests? Surely it's better to stick to giving to charities that work with people like this. Why has he got a dog with him – isn't it just a ploy to get more sympathy? What about her child – surely there must be a better way?

Guilt and confusion are perhaps understandable, but why anger? Is my feeling of anger directed at the situation or the person or myself? Is it indignation that anyone in Britain in the 1990s should have to beg? Or is it because I feel repelled by the manner of the approach? Or think 'I'd never resort to that'? Do I want to help, but only on condition that it is an impersonal transaction? With money, I can decide how much I can afford and limit my giving accordingly but spending emotions is by definition more difficult to control. Is it an all-too-painful reminder of my own insecurity and weakness?

ENCOUNTERING THE STRANGER

Nicholas Lash's discussion of hermeneutic practice, that is, the interpretation of different cultures and contexts of meaning, in terms of our experience of interpersonal relations, is very relevant to the question of our self-identity when we have such disturbing encounters. He asks, how do we enter into the lives of people from other eras – such as Jesus and his contemporaries – and those from different cultures in our own time? How can we understand the stranger? We are all classified as human beings. To deny any possibility of understanding would be to make that classification meaningless. On the other hand, too easy an identification or sympathy can amount to colonizing the other. It starts from ourselves as the reference point. It assumes that our experience and understanding are normative, the appropriate frame within which all else fits.

A hundred years ago, still riding the crest of colonial and missionary expansion, the white man knew he was the centre of the universe of meaning. More specifically, the educated, middle-class or bourgeois white man knew what was good for the black man or the working man, for the 'lower orders' or for Kipling's 'lesser breeds without the law'.[29]

Once such superiority is overthrown and in so far as other individuals or groups are experienced as equals, 'they are also thereby experienced precisely *as* other . . . *as* a stranger'.

> And once you admit that you do not understand *him*, you are gradually forced to admit that you do not understand yourself.
>
> In the encounter with the stranger, he is experienced as a potential threat, and a potential partner. We are obliged to choose between treating him as an enemy or as a friend. If we decide to treat him as an enemy, as one who threatens our self-understanding and identity, then the only way in which we can 'understand' him, can comprehend him, is either by destroying him or by assimilating him. And assimilation is itself a form of destruction: it negates his particularity, his otherness . . . If, on the other hand, we decide to treat him as a friend, as a potential partner, then we are taking the risk of having *our* self-understanding radically transformed. And not only our self-understanding, but also those economic, social and political patterns and structures of which our beliefs and attitudes are the conscious expression.[30]

Thus understanding the stranger entails not only altering our attitudes of mind but also our lives. It calls for us to change social, cultural and economic structures as well as structures of feeling. It is an encounter which carries the threat or the promise of total transformation.

POOR IS A FOUR-LETTER WORD

> Two years ago Ronald Reagan was addressed by reporters on the ever-deteriorating situation of the poor in the United States. In his answer he avoided the word *poor* and spoke instead of the nonrich. This term shocked me, although I knew that the only foreign language that Reagan commands is the Orwellian. What does it mean, I asked myself, when someone no longer uses the word *poor*? Is it one of the dirty four-letter words that should not be used? The distortion of language signals a new political paradigm. Most importantly, it expresses a denial of reality: the poor are not even poor . . . Reality may not be seen and named. The most important media in the US follow this scenario: the nonrich are invisible and are nonpersons. Speaking about the 'nonrich' implies at the same time an attack on the dignity of the poor. What I call their spiritual reality has to be neutralised.[31]

Ralph Ellison, the black American writer who died in 1994, constructed his classic novel of the 1950s, *Invisible Man*, around a central metaphor of black America just not being noticed:

I am an invisible man. No I am not a spook like those who haunted Edgar Allan Poe; nor am I one of your Hollywood movie ectoplasms. I am a man of substance, of flesh and bone, fibre and liquids – and I might even be said to possess a mind. I am invisible, understand, simply because people refuse to see me.[32]

Denial is a way that we hide things that we do not like from ourselves. We are not rational beings. Whole education programmes have been based on the premise that if you give people 'the facts' then they will think the 'right' things, will revise their attitudes to meet reality. Such programmes fail – unless they also allow people the opportunity to accommodate their new learning in their old selves without being too threatened, unless there is scope for them to dismantle their resistances. Denial, too, is a way of coping with our own weakness and vulnerability. It is perhaps this that we are chiefly running away from when we shut our eyes to other people's suffering. Is it also our own weakness or badness that we are projecting on to others when we adopt very punitive attitudes towards them? Admitting our own frailty and dependence – our own essential poverty and powerlessness – becomes the first step towards journeying with the poor.

THE QUESTIONS DON'T CHANGE

The purpose of this chapter has been twofold. The brief glance back over attitudes towards poverty aimed to show that questions which are raised later in the book have surfaced and resurfaced in the past. Recognizing these as recurring themes may help to put current concerns into a wider perspective:

- *Diagnosing the problem.* Personal and policy responses to poverty are influenced by perceptions of its nature and causes. The pendulum still swings back and forth between compassion and condemnation. The invisibility of much poverty in Britain – and the extent to which we can close our eyes to it – is still a problem today. So too is the tendency to stereotype and scapegoat.
- *A disjunction between problems and solutions.* A second issue that is still relevant is the dubious ability of governments to respond appropriately and quickly to the changing landscape of poverty. The advent of widespread and long-term unemployment and the changed position of women are just two examples of the radical shifts that have taken place since the Beveridge Report of 1942. Even within their own value systems, political parties of all shades are currently struggling to formulate policy responses to these changes.

• *The test of a civilized society.* What is the extent of corporate responsibility? The issue of how much Britain can afford to spend on social security and public services is an ongoing question. But so also is the question of whether we can afford *not* to take steps towards closing the gaps in society. The costs – financially and socially – of ignoring the divisive effects of market forces and allowing the seeds of social disintegration to take root may be far greater.

THE INTEGRATION OF THE POLITICAL AND THE PERSONAL

The other aim of this chapter was to underline the fact that while poverty *is* an inescapably political question, it is not *only* a political question. In some ways, it would be easier to cope with if it was. But it also affects us emotionally. Our relationships with others – and their justice or injustice – are tied up with our own identity and integrity. And, as a political and a personal issue, it is at the centre of our faith.

Christian teaching is traditionally ambivalent towards poverty just as it is towards riches and, indeed, to materiality altogether. Discipleship means a total reorientation. We have to face our own poverty – in all its dimensions – and align it with that of others. The gospels set us new standards. They tell us not to seek riches and to renounce worldly indicators of success and the good life. This is what 'poor' means in the Beatitudes. It is less a matter of not having any material resources and more one of not being encumbered by them, not being shackled by possessions or consumed by a wish for riches. Thus material poverty *per se* is not what is being put forward here, but rather a detachment from material goods. Preoccupation with acquiring possessions and maintaining a particular lifestyle enthrones Mammon as master instead of God. Those who are materially poor may be in a better position to recognize what is truly important and of lasting value. We are to be in but not of the world. It is this independence from the world, enabled by and founded upon a relationship of trust in and dependence on God, which is the basis of Christian integrity.[33] 'The offer of God's goodness is ultimately shown and revealed, when nothing gets in the way of receiving and acknowledging it – hence the privileged place for the powerless and the weak and all those who are prepared to be vulnerable to the presence of pain and suffering.'[34]

NOTES

1. Gertrude Himmelfarb, *The Idea of Poverty: England in the Early Industrial Age* (London and Boston: Faber and Faber, 1985), p. 3.
2. *Ibid.*, p. 4.

3. Samuel Johnson, *The Rambler*, 18 September 1750.
4. Genesis 3.17–19.
5. Himmelfarb, *op. cit.*, p. 4.
6. *Ibid.*, p. 5.
7. See Himmelfarb for further discussion and relevant references.
8. Adam Smith, *An Inquiry into the Nature and Causes of the Wealth of Nations* (1776).
9. Himmelfarb, *op. cit.*, p. 63.
10. Smith, *op. cit.*, p. 609.
11. Thomas Malthus, *Essay on Population* (1798).
12. Himmelfarb, *op. cit.*, p. 525.
13. *Ibid.*
14. *Ibid.*, p. 526.
15. Charles Dickens, *Oliver Twist* (1837/8), p. 29.
16. Stephen Gill in the Introduction to Elizabeth Gaskell's *Mary Barton: A Tale of Manchester Life* (First published 1848; Penguin edn, 1988), p. 10.
17. Thomas Carlyle, *Past and Present*, 1843.
18. David Willetts, *Modern Conservatism* (London: Penguin Books, 1992), p. 11.
19. Marx and Engels, *Collected Works*, Vol. IV (New York: International Publishers), pp. 419–20.
20. Elizabeth Gaskell, *op. cit.*, p. 45.
21. Himmelfarb, *op. cit.*, p. 312, describing Henry Mayhew.
22. Henry Mayhew, *London Labour and the London Poor*, quoted in Himmelfarb, *op. cit.*, p. 325.
23. Austin Smith, *Journeying with God: Paradigms of Power and Powerlessness* (London: Sheed and Ward, 1990), p. 100.
24. Liz Spencer and Dawn Snape, *The Gospel, the Poor and the Churches*, a research study conducted for Christian Aid by Social Community Planning Research (Christian Aid, 1994).
25. *Ibid.*, p. 63.
26. *Ibid.*, p. 65.
27. *Ibid.*, p. 66.
28. From 'Stones In The Road', a song by Mary-Chapin Carpenter.
29. Nicholas Lash, *Theology on Dover Beach* (London: Darton, Longman and Todd), 1979, p. 71.
30. *Ibid.*, pp. 71–2.
31. Dorothy Soelle, *On Earth as in Heaven: A Liberation Spirituality of Sharing* (Westminster/John Knox Press, 1993), p. 8.
32. Ralph Ellison, *Invisible Man* (Harmondsworth: Penguin) 1965.
33. See Frank Field, *The Politics of Paradise* (London: Fount Paperback, 1987), chapter 3.
34. Donald Reeves, *For God's Sake* (London: Fount Paperback, 1988), p. 26.

PART II

Thinking about Poverty – Explanations and Excuses

For it is written, 'I will destroy the wisdom of the wise, and the cleverness of the clever I will thwart.' Where is the wise man? Where is the scribe? Where is the debater of this age? Has not God made foolish the wisdom of the world? (1 Cor 1:19–20)

Poverty may be apprehended at any one of at least three levels: as a technical or scientific phenomenon to be measured and defined; as a moral issue involving moral imperatives or judgements; or as a personal question relating to individuals' identity or status. (Hartley Dean, 'Poverty discourse and the disempowerment of the poor', *Critical Social Policy*, Vol. 12 No. 2, 1992, p. 80)

POVERTY IS a multi-faceted and necessarily relative phenomenon. A precise quantitative definition is therefore impossible. Even establishing a measure for an adequate quality of life is difficult, given the different cultural norms influencing the conception of 'adequate' and the variety of factors affecting a person's cost of living. However, to say there is no exact definition of poverty is not the same as saying that poverty does not exist. Nor does the complexity of measuring poverty mean that the task should not be attempted. Chapter 3 looks at approaches to the definition and measurement of poverty and at some of the wider related issues.

Chapters 4 and 5 go on to review explanations of poverty. Attitudes towards people in poverty, and personal and social responses to them, are influenced and often justified by judgements about what has caused them to be poor. One raft of explanations focuses on causes which, in one way or another, are associated with the individuals concerned, their genes, their family or cultural background. Or they identify welfare policies deemed to have undermined individual self-reliance. Other explanations look rather to the way social and economic structures and processes play a large part in determining individual access to society's goods, such as employment, housing, education, health and social care.

These chapters look at the mix of social scientific analysis, empirical evidence and moral judgement which these different explanations comprise and at the extent to which they resonate with different theological approaches.

CHAPTER 3

An Exercise in Demarcation –
Defining and Measuring Poverty

They don't call it poverty in Cheshire. The strategy being developed by the county council to help the poorest and most vulnerable is called 'economic disadvantage'. (Pat Healy, 'Turning Tables on Poverty', *The Guardian*, 30 September 1992)

> . . . we may buy the poor for silver
> and the needy for a pair of sandals
> (Amos 8.6)

Poverty is not only about shortage of money. It is about rights and relationships; about how people are treated and how they regard themselves; about powerlessness and exclusion, and loss of dignity. Yet the lack of an adequate income is at its heart. (*Faith in the City*, p. 195)

> If living was a thing that money could buy,
> You know the rich would live but the poor would die.
> ('All My Trials', traditional song)

The lack of agreement about what constitutes poverty cannot be used to write off its existence any more than the lack of consensus on the definition of wealth can be used to argue that there are no wealthy persons in Britain or the US or other affluent countries. (Vic George and Irving Howards, *Poverty Amidst Affluence: Britain and the United States*, Edward Elgar, 1991, p. 22)

WHAT IS POVERTY?

Over recent decades, the developed world has faced the challenge of living with affluence. It is a challenge which so far seems to have defeated us in Britain. Despite rising standards of living, we have failed to make this an inclusive society. A sizeable minority remain in poverty and the gap between rich and poor is increasing. In a society which is not only increasingly prosperous, but also seems to set more and more store by that prosperity, a significant number of people are excluded from effective participation. Yet now, as throughout history, people try to ignore or question the existence of poverty. Or they minimize its extent and its consequences.

Some people would say – and have said – 'there is no *real* poverty in Britain'. This flies in the face of evidence. Just as there is no consensus over what constitutes wealth, so there is no agreement on a definition of poverty. But this is not the same as saying poverty does not exist. Rather it means that charting its extent will be influenced by the definition used.

Defining and measuring poverty are not just technical issues. Any definition must be influenced by the values of the person concerned. It will depend upon his or her assumptions about what are basic needs, what are the 'necessities' or 'normal' essentials required to meet these needs and what should be the quality and quantity of provision.

Four levels of definition have emerged over the years, which range over varying depths of want:

- starvation
- subsistence
- social coping
- social participation

Starvation – as it suggests – makes food the only requirement. For *subsistence*, more – though still minimal – requirements are identified. Fuel, clothing, household expenses would all be counted in. This was the definition used by Rowntree in his three studies from 1899 to 1950. He wanted to explore the question of how much poverty was 'due to insufficiency of income and how much to improvidence'. In order that there could be no quibbling about his findings, he constructed a primary poverty line, a standard which erred on the side of 'stringency rather than extravagance'. He excluded almost every item of expenditure not positively required to maintain a family in physical health, with no allowance for contingencies. This standard was used to demonstrate that poor people needed more money than they were actually getting. It was not intended, as has sometimes been thought, to prescribe a minimum income on which anyone could live an adequately social life.

In our sort of society, this may be seen as defining absolute poverty – the minimum needed to sustain life. To be below subsistence level is to experience absolute poverty. However, as Pete Alcock says:

> On the face of it this is a contradiction in terms – how do those without enough to live on, live? The answer, according to absolute poverty theorists, is that they do not for long; if they are not provided with enough for subsistence they will starve, or perhaps more likely in a developed country like Britain, in the winter they will freeze. Indeed every winter significant numbers of elderly people in Britain do die of hypothermia because they cannot afford to heat their accommodation.[1]

Thus, although the post-1945 welfare reforms were widely assumed to have put an end to subsistence poverty, it lives on. Other contradictions to this comfortable assumption will be cited later in the book.

The *social coping* definition introduces, albeit modestly, a reference to lifestyle. It takes account of prevailing standards and expectations. It is summed up in the words of J. K. Galbraith in *The Affluent Society*:

> People are poverty-stricken when their income, even if adequate for survival, falls markedly behind that of the community. Then they cannot have what the larger community regards as the minimum necessary for decency ... They are degraded for, in the literal sense, they live outside the grades or categories which the community regards as acceptable.[2]

The *social participation* definition also adopts this line but interprets it more generously. Its frame of reference is the whole of society, not just the working class. Additionally, it is concerned not merely with providing a standard of living just above subsistence but with reducing inequality. It focuses the level of income which will give an individual or household access to a tolerable lifestyle and addresses the implications of the existence of wide disparities of income for the quality of social relationships.

Translating these definitions into what people need to stay out of poverty becomes more difficult the more sophisticated the definition used. What advocates of the social coping and participation models tend to do, therefore, is identify some percentage of national average income – 40, 50 or 60 per cent – as the poverty line. This clearly moves away from the idea of the level of income which is essential for subsistence, though it could be one of these percentages. It makes the connection instead with what others in the same society have to live on. It is a relative measure.

Relative to what?

> People's needs, even for food, are conditioned by the society in which they live and to which they belong.[3]

The distinction between absolute and relative poverty is frequently made. It can be a source of confusion because the word 'relative' is used in different ways. It may mean relative in historical terms – 'you don't see the poverty today that you saw in the 1930s'. It might be used to compare countries – 'there's no comparison between poverty here and in India'. The third use of relative is in relation to other groups in a given country at a given time. Conditions and norms in the immediate environment are taken into account and, as they change, so the specification of poverty must change.

All definitions are relative in the first two senses. Even views about what constitutes starvation or subsistence will have changed slightly over time and will to some extent be shaped by the prevailing conditions in different countries. However, it is its use in the third and fourth senses that is controversial. Taking the existing living standards and changing expectations as the standard of comparison rather than subsistence is more appropriate to more affluent societies in which it is assumed (rightly or wrongly) that the most basic survival needs are met. Nonetheless, the social policy debate since 1979 has been marked by repeated attempts to deny the validity of any but the most absolute definition. The tone was set by Keith Joseph in 1979: 'An absolute standard means one defined by reference to the actual needs of the poor and not by reference to the expenditure of those who are not poor. A family is poor if it cannot afford to eat.'[4] Ten years later, the then Secretary of State for Social Security, John Moore, was still calling relative concepts of poverty 'bizarre'.[5]

To say that poverty is relative in the sense of needing to refer to prevailing living standards is not to say that it is wholly subjective. Peter Townsend is very explicit:

> Individuals, families and groups in the population can be said to be in poverty when they lack the resources to obtain the type of diet, participate in the activities and have the living conditions and amenities which are customary, or at least widely encouraged and approved, in the societies to which they belong. Their resources are so seriously below those commanded by the average individual or family that they are, in effect, excluded from ordinary living patterns, customs and activities.[6]

Townsend and others drew this conclusion from observing trends which had occurred in the 1950s and 1960s despite the achievements of the welfare state. Although a safety net was in place to prevent most people falling below subsistence level, nevertheless most poor people were no better off relative to average living standards than they had been in the 1940s. So they were unable to participate fully in their own society. There was nothing novel about thinking that a society's custom and practice and rising standards should figure alongside absolute necessities as the basis of comparison for defining poverty. For Adam Smith, this was a natural extension of the moral status of the poor. 'By necessaries, I understand not only the commodities which are indispensable necessary for the support of life but whatever the custom of the country renders it indecent for creditable people, even of the lowest order, to be without.'[7]

Faith in the City certainly accepted the concept of relative poverty in this participatory sense saying, in words reminiscent of Galbraith's:

Of course this is not poverty as it is experienced in parts of the Third World; people in Britain are not actually starving. But many residents of UPAs are deprived of what the rest of society regard as the essential minimum for a decent life; they live next door to, but have little chance to participate in a relatively affluent society; by any standards theirs is a wretched condition which none of us would wish to tolerate for ourselves or to see inflicted on others.[8]

It could have gone on to say that the consumer goods which exemplify the lifestyle we are all supposed to hanker after shout at us daily from magazine stalls and television screens. To lack them is to be without your badge of belonging.

They advertise on TV all the time for a couple of months up to Christmas and the toys are so expensive and the children ask and naturally they expect but it is not always possible to provide.

I think they just naturally expect. They don't understand. When the children are young they don't understand poverty .... They watch television and they see other children and what they have and they can't understand why they can't have that.

You have to explain. They just don't understand. It's very depressing.[9]

BASES OF MEASURING POVERTY

Measuring poverty is an exercise in demarcation. Lines have to be drawn where none may be visible and they have to be made bold.[10]

If poverty is difficult to define, it is just as hard to identify a measure which gains widespread acceptance and can be readily applied. At first sight, the starvation or subsistence definitions of absolute poverty may seem easier to pin down. But, if they are about the means to support life then, as Alcock says, they still beg the question of what is life. In practice, what we require depends upon time and place. What constitutes adequate shelter will depend upon climate; fuel-needs similarly vary according to weather, time of year, the condition of a person's dwelling and the state of their health. A reasonable diet hinges upon the availability of particular types of food, cooking facilities, the energy needs of the individuals and their age and health. All these variables demonstrate the virtual impossibility of disembedding the concept of poverty from the context in which it is occurring and treating it as definable or measurable by some single yardstick without reference to prevailing lifestyles or social and economic conditions.

However, while absolute notions are unreal and impractical, relative ones are also fraught with difficulty. It can be argued that any dividing line between the poor and others is arbitrary and involves a subjective judgement about what is an acceptable minimum standard given the time and circumstances. It is all the more difficult to find that dividing line because, of course, life does not stand still. Economies grow and shrink. General living standards change. Many people may be worse off during a recession, but how does this affect the relative position of the poor? Conversely, what is their situation during a period of economic growth? And is it poverty that is being measured or inequality? As Alcock says,

> ... absolute definitions of poverty necessarily involve relative judgements to apply them to any particular society; and relative definitions require some absolute core in order to distinguish them from broader inequalities. Both it seems have major disadvantages, and in pure terms neither is acceptable or workable as a definition of poverty. If we wish to retain poverty as a basis for analysis, measurement and ultimately political action, therefore, we need to avoid the disadvantages, or rather capitalise on the advantages, of both.[11]

Looking at necessities and circumstances

Defining poverty is not the same as measuring it. But the types of measures used tend to reflect stances on definitions. In practice, however, they do generally incorporate in differing degrees features of both absolute and relative concepts of poverty. First there is the 'budgeting' approach based upon that of Rowntree. A list of necessities is compiled and costed and used to draw a poverty line. It has been criticized on at least two counts, that it is elitist and prescriptive. It is said that the line is drawn by so-called experts without reference to actual spending patterns and without allowing people choice over how they use their resources. However, the criticisms tend to assume that such budget standards have a prescriptive purpose, which is not necessarily the case. Just as Rowntree was seeking to demonstrate the inadequacy of certain income levels so others more recently have used this way of making a point to policy makers. In 1979 the Child Poverty Action Group (CPAG) published *The Cost of a Child* by David Piachaud which sought to introduce a greater realism in setting the level of what was then Family Allowance.

Then there is the 'deprivation index' approach of Peter Townsend. He devised a questionnaire with sixty questions covering a wide range of factors impinging on people's lives: diet, clothing, household conditions and amenities, conditions at work, health, educational and environmental conditions. He was trying to measure styles of living. Having used this questionnaire in a survey of just over 2,000 households, he analysed the answers to discover which gave the strongest correlation with income levels. A 'yes' answer was most likely to be associated with a poor household. From this, the index was constructed by adding up the 'yes' answers to the 12 questions which showed the most marked correlation. Looking at these indices in relation to the households' net income, taking into account their size and composition, he came to the conclusion that deprivation begins to increase significantly below 150 per cent of the supplementary benefit level.

Apart from the statistical complexity of this method of arriving at a poverty threshold, it can be criticized as being unable to distinguish between choices which are constrained by income and those which express personal taste. For example, is the lack of a cooked breakfast a sign of deprivation or of individual likes and dislikes? Not only do yes/no answers fail to elicit reasons, but the questions selected may be more a reflection of the investigator's tastes than a real measure of deprivation.

A consensual approach

This raises the issue of who should say what is poverty – where to draw the line. It is seldom poor people themselves. Professional experts can help, but for a poverty threshold to have any political relevance, ultimately it must be accepted by public opinion. So when London Weekend Television commissioned MORI to conduct a poverty survey in 1983 as the background to the documentary series *Breadline Britain*, it was precisely to see whether there was a consensus about what was a minimum standard. As the authors said, they were seeking an acceptable measurement of a minimum standard of living which everyone should be able to enjoy. Whether or not people falling below this standard would be accepted by critics as being 'in poverty' would not alter the fact that they were 'falling below a society-approved minimum'.[12]

> The definition of what it is to be poor is something which comes out of the relations between people. If you take a country like ours which is a democratic country, what in effect you are doing in this kind of approach is to say let's all vote together on what we think constitutes poverty. If you get some kind of social consensus about that definition, then that actually fits the reality of what people experience.[13]

Thirty-five items were listed in the MORI survey and people were asked which of those were things all adults/families should be able to afford and not have to go without. ' ... the "necessities" of life are identified by public opinion and not, on the one hand, the views of experts or, on the other hand, the norms of behaviour *per se*.'[14] A majority of respondents agreed that 26 items were necessities; over two-thirds agreed that 17 were necessities. To

BREADLINE BRITAIN

Necessities for adults only	*Necessities for families with children*
heating	heating
indoor toilet	indoor toilet
damp-free home	damp-free home
bath	bath
enough beds	enough beds
refrigerator	refrigerator
carpets	carpets
celebrations on special occasions	celebrations on special occasions
a roast joint once a week	a roast joint once a week
a washing machine	a washing machine
new clothes	new clothes
meat or fish every other day	meat or fish every other day
present for family or friends once a year	presents for family or friends once a year
a holiday away from home for one week a year	a holiday away from home for one week a year
two hot meals a day	three meals a day
a warm waterproof coat	enough bedrooms for every child over 10 of different sex to have his or her own
two pairs of all-weather shoes	
a hobby or leisure activity	leisure equipment/toys

examine how many people were falling below minimum standards, two lists of 18 items were drawn up, one to examine deprivation amongst adults only, the other deprivation amongst families with children.

In asking respondents whether or not they had these items, it was further asked whether they went without them through choice or because they could not afford them. To some extent this got around the possible confusion between taste and financial constraints. The concept of 'an enforced lack of necessities' was central to the study. It was found that although those with higher incomes might forego one or even two necessities, they did 'not choose the lifestyles associated with the lack of necessities'. On the other hand, those in the lower income groups fared very badly, not just compared with others, but by reference to the standards set by the majority of people as minimal. In fact in the bottom half of the income range, the income differences were not very great. But, of the bottom 10 per cent, over one-half could not afford at least two necessities; over one-third could not afford four or more; over one-fifth could not afford six or more. In each income bracket, families with children fared worse than others and, additionally, more families were concentrated in the lower income ranges.

> The personal consequences are a life that is often depressing and nearly always full of worry.[15]

The main importance of *Breadline Britain* was to shed light on the character of relative deprivation in the mid-1980s. However, the authors also tried to draw their findings together to establish a measure of the extent of poverty in Britain. They could do this either by looking directly at those whose needs went unsatisfied or by counting those living on an income below the level at which it was possible to meet these needs.

These researchers chose the former, on the basis of which they estimated:

- 12 million lived in or on the margins of poverty (unable to afford more than two necessities).
- 7.5 million (5 million adults and 2.5 million children) were living in poverty (unable to afford more than three necessities).
- 2.6 million (including 1 million children) were in intense poverty – about 1 in 20 people (lacking more than seven necessities).

Some calculations were made about those in poverty that took into account various ways in which the figures might be adjusted according to particular variables. Making deductions to allow for spending patterns which suggested that the lack was not necessarily enforced brought the figure down to 6.75 million. On the other hand, some people, especially pensioners, had such low expectations that they did not recognize that they were forced to do without. Allowing for such low aspirations increased the number to 9.7 million. Again adjustments could be made for the marginality or intensity of deprivation according to how seriously people's lives were affected by the type of necessities lacked. This gave a range from 6.7–11.7 million. Taking all the adjustments together the estimated number in poverty was 8.5 million.

Although Joanna Mack and Stewart Lansley used this direct measure of poverty, they were also able to reach some conclusions about the likelihood of poverty at different income levels. Tests were applied to their data to see if there was evidence of a poverty threshold. Was the relationship between deprivation and income rises or falls a steady continuum? Or was there an income level at which a fall in income suddenly meant a much sharper increase in deprivation? Was there 'an income level below which people are forced to withdraw from a whole range of activities and are unable to afford a whole range of goods'? This sort of break had been found with Peter Townsend's data in 1981 and his findings were reinforced by *Breadline Britain* data. In both cases the cut-off point was around 150 per cent of the supplementary benefit level amount. This was the threshold of deprivation. Households on incomes below this were *much* more likely to be deprived and, therefore, the risk of poverty was greatly increased.

Measuring the extent of poverty

The fact that something is difficult to do is no reason for not attempting it. This is the case as far as measuring poverty is concerned, especially as there is a danger that the conceptual and technical difficulties can be used as a smokescreen to duck the issue altogether. It is politically convenient to avoid bringing the extent of the problem under the spotlight. Despite the inherent difficulties much can be learnt.

Two sorts of measures can be used – quantitative or qualitative. The former, statistical method has the advantage that it can be employed on a large scale and is anonymous. Its limitations stem from these virtues. Statistics speak more to the head than the heart. They fail to convey the experiential meaning of poverty in the way a qualitative measure can. A.B. Atkinson tells the story of Ernest Bevin at an enquiry in dockworkers' pay in 1922.[16] A researcher had given evidence on need – subsistence – in the form of a minimum basket of goods. Bevin went out and bought the recommended items of the meagre diet of bacon and fish scraps and bread and presented them to the enquiry. Were they sufficient, he asked, for a man having to hump heavy bags of grain all day? This had greater persuasive power than volumes of statistics.

The main source of quantitative data is government statistics, produced by government departments or the Central Statistical Office. A regular Family Expenditure Survey is produced based on spending patterns of a relatively large sample – 1 in 2,500 – of the population. This and other official sources provide the material for the annual *Social Trends* and *Economic Trends* statistical reports. The Department of Social Security (DSS) also produces *Households Below Average Income* reports, though a more comprehensive series of reports on incomes produced by the then Royal Commission on the Distribution of Income and Wealth was discontinued by the Government in 1980.

Even official statistics have to be handled with care. When they are based on households rather than individuals, they automatically omit the homeless and those based in institutions. Surveys always have problems with non-response rates and, for this reason too, they may under-represent poverty and low income. However, as CPAG has shown through its regular analyses, using the government's own figures to demonstrate the failure of its policies can be extremely effective – in winning the argument, if not in prompting the necessary policy changes.

Independent researchers, such as Rowntree, Townsend, Mack and Lansley, have also collected their own data. This enables them to decide on the breadth of their study and the level of detail required. Compatibility of data sets is a problem with official and non-official studies alike when it comes to trying to track change over time or compare one area with another. There can be different approaches over what information is collected, how it is collected, and how it is analysed and presented. Over the last few years, there has been increasing interest in overcoming these problems in the European Commission in order to be able to make comparisons between member states, for example in relation to the European Poverty Programmes. Eurostat, the Commission's statistical survey, is attempting to assemble cross-national computer databases. The advances in information technology increase the possibility of retrieving, transferring, adapting and re-analysing data, always of course remembering that its use depends upon the quality of the information which has gone in. Rubbish in still means rubbish out no matter how sophisticated the techniques in between!

Very often statistical surveys are accompanied by case studies which describe the individual experience of poverty and which are designed to breathe life into arid arithmetic. Organizations such as The Children's Society and National Children's Home (NCH) are well placed to produce this kind of direct evidence. Child Poverty Action Group's *Hardship Britain* contains interviews with people in poverty which amply illustrate the struggle they have to cope.[17] It follows in the long tradition of commentators using descriptive material, from Mayhew and others in the nineteenth century, through to George Orwell's *The Road to Wigan Pier*, and more recently, Paul Harrison's *Inside the Inner City*, Jeremy Seabrook's *Landscapes of Poverty* and Robert Wilson and Donovan Wylie's *The Dispossessed*. Such works have the power to convict people and capture their imaginative sympathy, but they still probably rely upon the reader's predisposition to believe. Their strength is also their weakness. They can be dismissed as anecdotal, unscientific and lacking statistical rigour.

Readiness to reject findings about poverty, whether quantitative or qualitative ones, springs from its political sensitivity as a subject. It gets to the heart of politics. It raises questions not only about the distribution of income, but also our own place in the scheme of things. They are about the distribution of power and society's cohesion and integrity. The next two sections of this chapter will turn to these other dimensions of poverty: inequality and powerlessness.

POVERTY AND INEQUALITY

The concept of relative poverty is closely linked with that of inequality, though they are not the same thing. There can be inequalities even amongst society's highest earners but this is not to say that those in the lower part of that top band are poor. The inequalities which evoke more concern, however, are those where the range of incomes is unacceptable because some fall below the level deemed necessary for a decent existence. Poverty is 'that part of inequality which is unnecessary, and consequently, unfair'.[18]

Putting poverty in terms of inequality at once connects it with the distribution of income and the allocation of society's goods. It underlines that poverty cannot be removed without cost. It makes clear the personal and political challenge. As we have seen over the past few decades, a general rise in the standard of living does not necessarily eliminate poverty. If improvement is evenly spread, it raises expectations without doing anything to reduce inequality. What has happened over the last fifteen years is even more striking. The rising tide has not lifted all ships. Instead, the gap between rich and poor has widened. Many policies have had a specially harsh impact on the most vulnerable groups and, in many ways, the poorer members of our society have had to bear a disproportionate burden in times of both boom and recession.

The likely effects of such policies are not, of course, specified when they are introduced, even though they are foreseeable. Although policy moves are sometimes justified in general terms as tactics necessary for the success of a longer term strategy – 'if it isn't hurting, it isn't working' – it is less often, if ever, made clear precisely who will be hurt and who the eventual beneficiaries will be. The injustice would be more glaring if it was admitted from the outset that today's victims may remain losers even in the long term.

Words such as 'unfair' and 'unacceptable' show that any definition of poverty must be based upon value judgements. How we respond to poverty also depends upon our values – values that are derived from our beliefs, our experience and our circumstances. Later in the book, some consideration will be given not only to the sorts of values expressed, but *whose* values chiefly affect the political process and hence determine the level of poverty and inequality that is tolerated in our society.

Equality

> There is neither Jew nor Greek, there is neither slave nor free, there is neither male nor female; for you are all one in Christ Jesus. (Gal 3.28)

Equality, like poverty, is a concept open to various interpretations. Tawney accepted that the word has different meanings. Broadly it may either purport to state a fact or it may refer to an ethical judgement. On the one hand, it may affirm that people are very similar in their natural endowments of character and intelligence. On the other, it may assert that, while individuals differ profoundly in capacity and personality, as human beings they are equally entitled to consideration and respect. The statement of fact is clearly untenable. It is the ethical position that Tawney upholds. People are not all equally endowed with intelligence, aptitudes, beauty and personality attributes. Yet Christians as well as people of many other faiths and philosophies would assert that in a deeper sense all are equal. Christianity teaches that all are created in God's image. Yet we all have 'fallen natures', that is, we have all been subject to, and implicated in, that distortion and diminishment of what God intended for us as a result of what we call sin. Christ died to restore all to a right relationship with God and one another, to enable all to develop according to God's purposes for humankind.

> We are the Body of Christ,
> In the one Spirit we were all baptised into one body,
> Let us then pursue all that makes for peace
> and builds up our common life.
> (The Alternative Service Book 1980,
> Order for Holy Communion Rite A)

How then does this reading of basic human equality translate into principles that can be applied to public life? In this country, the ideals of equality before the law and within the political sphere are taken for granted. Yet are they really possible in the absence of social equality? Can they co-exist with a high degree of material inequality? The American philosopher, John Rawls, states firmly that they cannot.

> Historically one of the main defects of constitutional government has been the failure to insure the fair value of political liberty. The necessary corrective steps have not been taken, indeed, they never seem to have been entertained. Disparities in the distribution of property and wealth that far exceed what is compatible with political equality have generally been tolerated . . . [19]

However, the desirability of social equality is disputed. Raymond Plant has pointed out that the authors of *Faith in the City* seemed to assume that people across the political spectrum still upheld the aim of a fair society, whereas in reality it had been jettisoned by the New Right and was no longer a guiding principle for political policy. There had been a quite deliberate move away from redistributive welfare and fiscal policies towards trying to raise overall standards using economic growth promoted by free market policies. Insofar as free market mechanisms notoriously produce winners and losers, it was a 'strategy of inequality'.[20] This meant that when the Archbishop's Commission expressed their view 'that the nation is confronted by a *grave and fundamental injustice* in the UPAs'[21] they were using a yardstick of justice which was not necessarily shared by the policy makers they hoped to influence.

Only a few years before, Hayek had written a book called *The Mirage of Social Justice* in which he argued that attempts to secure social justice misconceive the nature of economic relations between individuals. First, there is no adequate or generally accepted standard by which to judge the justice or injustice of the shares that different groups have of society's goods. Second, to adopt a particular conception and pursue it would necessarily entail considerable state intervention and thus be incompatible with personal freedom. Hayek believes this rules out government measures to create a more just society. Such actions, he says, would have no moral legitimacy and, insofar as they would be chasing an illusory goal, they would also breed resentment amongst those who felt unfairly treated.

Instead, governments should leave it to the market to govern distribution and let its outcomes lie as they fall. Suffering may result but it will have come about as an unintended result of an aggregate of individual decisions taken for a whole array of reasons. And, as market transactions are not deliberate in the sense of intending to cause harm, they cannot be said to be either coercive or unjust. The poor may be poorer in the end but their freedom will not have been diminished.

Tawney held a rather different view of freedom.

> A society is free insofar, and only insofar, as within the limits set by nature, knowledge and resources, its institutions and policies are such as to enable all its members to grow to their full stature, to do their duty as they see it and – since liberty should not be too austere – to have their fling when they feel like it.[22]

The relationship between liberty and justice is put even more directly in a World Council of Churches document.[23]

> ... freedom depends on structures which ensure fair opportunities for all. Liberty and justice are not opposed to each other and they do not exclude each other, at least when they relate to human beings. But when freedom is no longer the liberty of human beings, but of commodities, of enterprises, of private property, of the market, then it follows that the

aspiration of human beings for liberation is suppressed, and injustice is perpetuated.

John Rawls wrote about the two principles of justice. First, each person should have an equal right to the most extensive basic liberty compatible with a similar liberty for others. Second, social and economic inequalities should be both (a) reasonably expected to be to everyone's advantage, and (b) attached to positions and offices open to all. By this account, justice hinges upon freedom and vice versa. When the connection between the two is severed, then either justice suffers or freedom is reduced.

The New Right also assert, however, that there is a necessary trade-off between equality and efficiency. But if this is deliberate policy, then the moral innocence of 'leave it to the market' policies is open to question. It implies that, instead of spreading the cost of increased efficiency, the burden is deliberately being put on to particular groups to bear for the rest of us. Yet, the New Right argued, if this inequality comes about as a result of a multitude of market transactions, then no one holds the moral responsibility for the outcome. However, if the results can be foreseen – which they can be in broad terms if not in detail – then there is an agent responsible for their impact on the weakest members of society. 'If their deprivation is an infringement of their freedom, the state, which even for the vast majority of conservative capitalists is the ultimate guarantor of individual liberty, has a responsibility for it.'[24]

Further, as Plant argues, moral responsibility is not confined to *how* a given thing occurred. It also lies in the response which is made to it. To allow painful and divisive consequences to go on happening repeatedly without intervention is a failure of justice and responsibility. 'Even if the result of the market is impersonal, failure to organise collectively to meet the needs of people disadvantaged by the operation of the market would be an injustice.'[25]

'Equalities do not need special justification, whereas inequalities do.'[26]

The arguments against the New Right are an echo of Richard Tawney's views in the early years of this century. Tawney's starting point for his classic book on equality was the inequality he saw around him. He had already tackled this to some extent ten years earlier. In the post-World War I period there was much talk of increasing productivity. Tawney had wanted to show that social institutions were basic to any consideration of productivity or poverty because they set the framework for what would be the end result. Social institutions, he said, express moral values – or the absence of them – and the *laissez-faire* assumptions of what he saw as an acquisitive society sidelined human moral principles. He attacked the concentration on a purely personal morality and the abandonment of any corporate Christian social tradition.

In *Equality*, he looked at the inequalities stemming from the Industrial Revolution and its aftermath. He began by recalling that Matthew Arnold at the end of the nineteenth century had observed that in England 'inequality is almost a religion'. This, Arnold said, was incompatible with a spirit of humanity and a sense of the dignity of man as man, which are the marks of a civilized society. 'On the one side, in fact, inequality harms by pampering; on the other by vulgarising and depressing. A system founded on it is against nature and, in the long run, breaks down.' Tawney, looking later at 'the heightened tension between political democracy and a social system marked by sharp disparities of circumstance and education, and of the opportunities which circumstance and education confer' felt that there was a strong element of prophetic truth in what Arnold had said.

He returned to Arnold's feeling that inequality is unhealthy when referring to the frequent challenge to those seeking to mitigate the consequences of inequality. This is the accusation that what they want is not to make the poor richer, but the rich poorer. Usually, the defence was to disclaim any such intention. To Tawney, this was mistaken. Rather it should be acknowledged that both are desirable, because the extremes of riches and poverty are degrading and anti-social. After becoming Prime Minister, John Major talked about looking towards a classless society. Roger Scruton responded that 'a classless society is neither possible nor desirable'. He went on to make the familiar barb about levelling down: 'socialism prefers equality of failure to unequal success'.

Tawney, like Arnold, saw the acceptance of inequality as a peculiarly British phenomenon. 'An indifference to inequality ... is less a mark of particular classes than a national characteristic.' Even the working-class movement, 'standing for the ideal of social justice and solidarity as a corrective to the exaggerated emphasis on individual advancement through the acquisition of wealth' he saw as being liable to forget its mission – too easily bought off, too willing to accept the moral premise of their masters, too ready to believe in the minority that has always exercised authority.

> They denounce, and rightly, the injustices of capitalism; but they do not always realise that capitalism is maintained, not only by capitalists, but by those who, like some of themselves, would be capitalists if they could, and that the injustices survive, not merely because the rich exploit the poor, but because, in their hearts, too many of the poor admire the rich.[27]

Equal but not identical

Tawney was looking for equality of circumstances, institutions and manner of life. Social institutions, such as property rights, economic organization, health and education, should be planned as far as possible to emphasize and strengthen the common humanity which unites people rather than the class differences that divide them. Today we might add race, gender and disability to class as examples of divisive categories. He recognized, of course, that people varied in intellect, skills, aptitudes and other qualities, 'but to recognise a specific difference is one thing; to pass a general judgement of superiority or inferiority, still more to favour the first and neglect the second, is quite another.' Apart from anything else, we are notoriously bad at such judgements. As he said, 'the failures and fools – the Socrates and St Francis – of one age are the sages and saints of another.'

Tawney also accepted that people have different needs and that, therefore, different forms of provision are needed to meet them. Equal provision does not mean identical provision. Different needs should be treated not in the same way but by devoting equal care to ensuring that they are met in ways most appropriate to them. Thus, 'the more anxiously . . . a society endeavours to secure equality of consideration for all its members, the greater will be the differentiation of treatment which, once their common human needs are met, it accords to the special needs of different groups and individuals among them.'

Reference was made earlier to the potential confusion between equality as a fact and equality as a value. Tawney pointed out that the justification of inequalities in circumstance or opportunity is often based upon a similar misunderstanding. Such inequalities are often 'explained' by reference to differences of personal quality. But for the argument to be valid, it must be shown that the differences in question are relevant to the inequalities. Usually this is not the case. Instead, people try to validate an ethical opinion by appealing – as they think – to a matter of fact. Examples can be drawn from the experience of black people, women or disabled people where some attributed characteristic is deemed appropriate to justify some limitation of opportunity or treatment. Movement towards equal opportunities for these groups still has a long way to go. Nevertheless, progress so far demonstrates that cultural and ethical resistance has been a far greater barrier to change than any supposed matters of fact.

Room for improvement

Equality may seem like a utopian dream – though perhaps a few more such dreams would impel us more forcefully to necessary change. Nevertheless, striving for a *fairer* society is well within our sights. There is ample scope to reverse some of the trends of recent decades.

- There has been a rise in inequality in post-tax income distribution. The independent organization, the Institute for Fiscal Studies, in an analysis of the distributional effects of actual and prospective changes in personal taxes and benefits for the period 1985–95, show they will leave the poorest 10 per cent of households £156 a year worse off, while the top 10 per cent are £1,627.60 a year better off.[28]
- There has been a rise in inequality in pre-tax income distribution. The measure called the Gini coefficient symbolizes the way income is spread: the higher the figure, the more distribution is skewed to a smaller number of high-income earners. Zero indicates a completely equal distribution, 1 means that one person has everything. Between 1977 and 1989, the figure rose from 0.35 to 0.42.[29]
- In 1986, the top 10 per cent of male, full-time manual workers earned 1.4 times the average. Now they earn 1.6 times. Over the same period, the wages of the lowest paid 10 per cent fell from 0.69 to 0.64 of the average.
- The value of income support for a married couple as a proportion of average full-time male earning has fallen over the last fifteen years from 26 per cent to 19 per cent.
- Male employment fell by 2 million between 1977 and 1991, but only half of this change showed up as a rise in unemployment. Some 1.8 million jobless men were counted as out of the labour force and thus excluded from the unemployment count.[30]
- The harsh clawback of benefits means there is an increasing divide between two-earner families and no-earner families. In 1992, nearly 60 per cent of women with an employed husband were in work compared with only 24 per cent with a non-employed husband.
- Women in full-time work still on average only earn 75 per cent of the wages of full-time men. Women in part-time jobs earn lower hourly rates than men. The gap between full- and part-time rates has grown. Women also tend to work in lower-paid occupations.
- Unemployment rates for black ethnic minorities are twice those of the white population.
- Only 31 per cent of disabled adults below pension age were in paid employment compared with 69 per cent of the general population. This low rate was not the inevitable outcome of disability itself, but the product of a combination of barriers in the labour market, not least discrimination. Nearly one-third of those actively looking for work had been doing so for three years or more.[31]
- In 1989, almost three times as many employed people with disabilities had gross weekly earnings of less than £150. One quarter surveyed said they earned less than others doing the same job.

POVERTY AND POWERLESSNESS

Poverty is at the root of *powerlessness*. Poor people in UPAs are at the mercy of fragmented and apparently unresponsive public authorities. They are trapped in housing and in environments over which they have little control. They lack the means and opportunities – which so many of us take for granted – of making choices in their lives.[32]

Structures of power

To be in possession of power means being able to determine the behaviour of others in accordance with your own ends. It lies also in 'the freedom to act otherwise'.[33] Power can be positional or personal. Structural power rests on an individual's status or office in the economic and social system. It may be defined legally or take its authority from the custom and practice of the society concerned. On the other hand, power is also exercised in informal, personal relationships by force of personality and this may or may not reflect the standing of the people concerned. The domineering wife and bossy secretary are frequent motifs in literature and jokes. Power, therefore, can derive both from a person's position – his or her status and office – and from the way that he or she performs the role.

Two questions arise in relation to structural power. The first is: how does someone come to occupy a given position, and how open was it to other people? 'From log cabin to White House' was the 'anyone can do it' myth which nourished the American dream, feeding America's perception of itself as an open and egalitarian society. Reality is a little different, as the sociologist Kingsley Davis writing forty years ago pointed out:

> But the Constitution forbids anyone to compete for this office who is not a native born citizen, not thirty-five years of age or over, and not at least fourteen years a resident within the country. Furthermore, we know that there are certain customary limitations that are as effective as if they were written into the Constitution. No woman, no Negro, no Oriental, no Catholic, no Jew has ever been president. It is conceivable that one of these might someday get the office, but it will be only by overcoming a great handicap. Thus approximately 120 million out of a total of 140 million people in the United States are effectively excluded from becoming president of the United States.[34]

Some things have changed, of course, in the intervening period. But the story illustrates that there is no level playing field for the acquisition of power. It is not solely a matter of achievement. *Ascribed* status also goes a long way towards affecting an individual's chances of occupying particular positions. The most common bases of ascribed status are sex, kinship and race. As in America, we probably delude ourselves in Britain about the extent to which this is a meritocratic society and these things no longer matter. The examples of inequalities already quoted demonstrate the significance of race and gender. A child's prospects are also clearly influenced by his or her family background. Apart from the extremes of inherited titles or wealth, there is the more fluid ascription of status which gives some people a competitive edge because they have attended the 'right' school or university, or have the 'right' accent, or know the 'right' people.

In *Friends in High Places*, Jeremy Paxman tries to dissect the British Establishment in the 1990s. Even while John Major was asserting his personal rise from Brixton to Downing Street as a symbol of the new Britain, his 'protestations about being "Mr Ordinary" depended for their force upon a belief that the British class structure was somehow still alive and well: why else should he make such a fuss about wanting to see it overcome?'[35] In his study, Paxman found that there is still a ruling class of considerable homogeneity in this country. He was not primarily concerned with the actions of government. 'This book is about the network of powerful individuals, institutions and professions linked together through the spider's web from which madly buzzing flies like Margaret Thatcher, Tony Benn and the rest, rarely escape unscathed. It is the spiders who really run Britain.'[36]

Spiders can make webs work for them, use them to protect themselves, to ensnare the unsuspecting and feed off what has been caught. If even senior politicians can be counted as flies in this context, how much more do these, and other webs woven by smaller spiders, trap the poor? And, of course, there are flies and flies. Some encounter far more predators than others.

> In the context of persistent poverty, the degree of respect accorded to the family will depend upon the judgement of social services, the local authorities and the courts. These bodies have to make difficult decisions. The poorer the family is, the more crucial are the decisions to ensure the family's survival in a state of dignity. At the same time, the poorer a family is, the weaker are its means of defence. In considering this subject we must always keep in mind the perseverance with which men, women and children try to keep together as families. Minimum levels of security are essential to enable them freely to make family choices and plans.[37]

Differences of access to status and office, and to the goods that go with them, mean differences in the power to determine one's own and other people's lives. The most obvious form of power in Western economies is the possession of money. Money gives security, protection against misfortune, the ability to exercise some control over circumstances. As has already been discussed, money is also a measure of a person's standing so that people tend to behave differently towards someone seen to have money. Money opens doors. It commands respect. It often also increases self-assurance. In these days of plastic money, it gives people control over time. They can accumulate by deferring payment. One of the ironies of credit systems is that they are more open to the more affluent and cheaper for them to use. For low income households, use of credit is a matter of necessity and not choice, and this is reflected in the terms of credit they can obtain. Free choice does not operate in this arena. Access is closely determined by factors such as income, occupation, housing tenure, sex, age and home address. Creditors, understandably, want to minimize their risks. High income and high status occupations are taken to signify low risk. A house may be accepted as security. Ordinary types of commercial credit, such as bank loans, credit cards, store cards, are often closed to people on low incomes. They have to resort instead to unregulated money lenders who exact extortionate amounts of interest. Loan sharks are able to prey on the most disadvantaged precisely because their borrowing is driven by extreme need. Similarly, it is the poorest sections of the community living in the most deprived neighbourhoods who, assuming they can get insurance cover at all, will be charged the highest rates.

So for those who do not have money, the problem is greater than not having purchasing power. It is also more expensive to be poor. Horizons are reduced to meeting immediate needs. Timescales are reduced to getting through until the next Giro or meagre pay packet comes, or until the next payment is due. It extends to knowing how to play the system, having the right information, having the standing and confidence that will ensure that people take notice when you complain.

Once I went to the Council office to complain because under my floor boards in the kitchen I could smell something was wrong – it smelled like bad eggs. A friend of mine took all the floor boards up and said that all the pipes underneath had burst. That was going to be not healthy, diseases and things like that, and more rats would live. It got very bad.

I kept going to the council, ringing up, writing. In the end, I went to the council early in the morning as soon as the office opened and I said to them, 'I am staying here, I am not leaving' and I stayed all day and they were going to close the office and this woman said to me, 'Would you please leave?' and I said, 'No! You are going to have to throw me out! I am not moving. I will move when you give me some proof that you are going to change the situation.' She said that she would get the police, I said 'I don't care. You get the police, I am not going back to that house

because it is going to go next door to my neighbours. They don't want
to have overflowing drains in their garden.' All the houses are the
same.[38]

Keeping the system in place

> ... there is no virtue or liberating potential in powerlessness simply as
> such.[39]

The second question about structural power is: what keeps it in place? Put
another way, if some people are disadvantaged by the system and have clearly
little likelihood of radically changing their position, why do they put up with
it? Power is not the same as oppression or domination. Nevertheless, the
extent to which power systems work – if they are not to be upheld by force –
depends upon their legitimacy in people's minds. The majority of the
population have to see the system as fair, or the 'natural order' of things, or
defensible on some other grounds such as national security or economic
necessity. They also need to feel there is something in it for them. This may
be the belief that it is possible for them to 'get on', to get a better job or house
or ensure their children climb the social ladder.

This takes us back to the importance of myths and symbols. Social
structures and social divisions are held in place by a multitude of codes,
symbols, assumptions and role definitions which people learn from birth.
These operate as an internal policing system to instil conformity just as
powerfully as an external force would do – perhaps even more powerfully
because they are less likely to be recognized or questioned, and therefore less
likely to be resisted: ' ... as long as the delusional assumptions remain
unconscious, they are seldom effectively transcended.'[40] This is why liberation
theology puts such stress on conscientization. This is why it was suggested at
a Church Action on Poverty Conference that perhaps we should shift our
sights, it was more important to persuade poor people that they *have* rights
than to convince the middle classes that the poor should have rights.

Where there is domination, it can attach to either positional or personal
power. But domination is more than a power relation. 'It is a *spiritual state of
being*. The dominator exerts power by extracting being from the dominated
... Thus domination always entails more than injustice. It wounds – and it
intends to wound – the very soul itself.'[41] It depersonalizes, treats people as
objects or as less than human, denies their particularity.

Powerlessness, therefore, can be both an objective and a subjective state.
The two sides reinforce each other. Poor people have fewer resources, fewer
choices, less control. But they can also have a sense of powerlessness. They can
have internalized and accepted the view that it is their fault. Governments
frequently brush aside poverty issues by 'blaming the victims'. Perhaps the

most insidious effect of this is when these same victims accept the blame. Once this happens, resistance evaporates, low self-esteem takes over, hopelessness sets in, expectations are diminished, the possibility of change is reduced. The next chapter looks at some of the ways in which explanations of poverty have in one way or another blamed the victim and dodged the issue of its roots in social and economic structures.

NOTES

1. Pete Alcock, *Understanding Poverty* (London: Macmillan, 1993), p. 58.
2. J. K. Galbraith, *The Affluent Society* (Harmondsworth: Penguin, 1963), p. 261.
3. Peter Townsend, *Poverty in the UK* (Harmondsworth: Penguin, 1979), p. 59.
4. K. Joseph and J. Sumption, *Equality* (John Murray, 1979), p. 27.
5. John Moore, 'The End of the Line for Poverty.' Speech to the Greater London Conservative Party Conference, 11 May 1989.
6. Townsend, *op. cit.*, p. 31.
7. Adam Smith, *An Inquiry into the Nature and Causes of the Wealth of Nations* (London: Routledge, 1982), p. 691. (First published 1776)
8. *Faith in the City: A Call for Action by Church and Nation*, Report of the Archbishop of Canterbury's Commission on Urban Priority Areas (London: Church House Publishing, 1985), p. xv.
9. *Women in Poverty in Europe*, World Council of Churches (WCC) on Interchurch Aid, Refugee and World Service (CICARWS) and William Temple Foundation Consultation in Manchester, May 1990, p. 20.
10. Meghnad Desai, 'Drawing the line: on defining the poverty threshold', in Peter Golding (ed.), *Excluding the Poor* (London: CPAG, 1986), p. 1.
11. Alcock, *op. cit.*, p. 62.
12. Joanna Mack and Stewart Lansley, *Poor Britain* (London: Allen and Unwin, 1985).
13. A. H. Halsey quoted in Mack and Lansley, *op. cit.*, p. 47.
14. *Ibid.*, p. 45.
15. *Ibid.*, p. 277.
16. A. B. Atkinson, *Poverty and Social Security* (Harvester Wheatsheaf, 1989), p. 27.
17. R. Cohen, J. Coxall, G. Graig and A. Sadiq-Sangster, *Hardship Britain: Being Poor in the 1990s* (Child Poverty Action Group, 1992).
18. R. Berthoud, *The Disadvantages of Inequality* (MacDonald and Janes, 1976), p. 53.
19. John Rawls, *A Theory of Justice* (Oxford: Oxford University Press, 1972), p. 226.
20. A. Walker, 'The strategy of inequality. Poverty and income distribution in Britain 1979–89', in I. Taylor (ed.), *The Social Effects of Free Market Policies: an International Text* (Harvester Wheatsheaf, 1990).
21. *Faith in the City*, p. xv.
22. R. H. Tawney, *Equality* (1931).
23. Julio de Santa Ana, Konrad Raiser and Ulrich Duchrow, *The Political Economy of the Holy Spirit* (WCC Commission on the Churches' Participation in Development 1990), pp. 14–15.
24. *Faith in the City: Theological and Moral Challenges*, an occasional paper prepared by the Theology and Social Values group of the Diocese of Winchester's Working Party to consider the report of the Archbishop's Commission on Urban Priority Areas (Diocese of Winchester, n.d.), p. 21.
25. *Ibid.*, p. 23.
26. Ronald Preston, 'Equality', in John Macquarrie and James Childress (eds), *A New Dictionary of Christian Ethics* (London: SCM Press, 1986).
27. Tawney, *Equality*, p. 29.
28. Alissa Goodman and Steven Webb, *For Richer, for Poorer: The Changing Distribution of Income in the United Kingdom 1961–1991*, Institute for Fiscal Studies commentary No. 42 (1994).
29. P. Cregg and S. Machin, in Barrell (ed.), *The UK Labour Market* (Cambridge: Cambridge University Press, 1994).

30. Edward Balls and Paul Gregg, *Work and Welfare: Tackling the Jobs Deficit* (The Commission on Social Justice, Institute for Public Policy Research, 1994).
31. OPCS Report (London: Office of Population Censuses and Surveys, 1988).
32. *Faith in the City*, p. xv.
33. Anthony Giddens, *A Contemporary Critique of Historical Materialism*, Vol. 1: *Power, Property and the State* (London: Macmillan, 1981), p. 4.
34. Kingsley Davis, *Human Society* (London: Macmillan, 1959), p. 117.
35. Jeremy Paxman, *Friends in High Places: Who Runs Britain?* (London: Penguin, 1991), p. viii.
36. *Ibid.*, pp. xiii–xiv.
37. *The Wresinski Report* (ATD Fourth World, 1987), pp. 95–6.
38. *Women in Poverty in Europe*, WCC Churches' Commission on Interchurch Aid, Refugee and World Service (CICARWS) and William Temple Foundation Consultation in Manchester, May 1990, p. 6.
39. Nicholas Lash, *Theology on the Way to Emmaus* (London: SCM Press, 1986), p. 193.
40. Walter Wink, *Engaging the Powers: Discernment and Resistance in a World of Domination* (Philadelphia: Fortress Press, 1992), p. 96.
41. *Ibid.*, p. 101.

CHAPTER 4

Blaming the Victim –
Individualist Explanations of
Poverty

Increasingly the real division within the world of Christianity does not run along historic
denominational lines. It is a division between those who believe that the Kingdom of God
involves the transformation of the world and its structures of injustice and those who do not.
(Ken Leech, 'Turbulent priests', *Marxism Today*, February 1986, pp. 11–13)

In the Christian Aid research investigating church people's attitudes towards
world poverty, some clear differences emerged between their views about
poverty in the UK and poverty in developing countries.

> ... there was considerable variation in the extent to which people felt
> they understood the question of origins, and in the range of factors they
> cited as possible causes of poverty. For some, part of the process of
> thinking about origins involved making attributions of fault. What or
> who was 'at fault' and therefore responsible for poverty differed accord-
> ing to individual perspectives, but governments, unfair systems, and the
> poor themselves were all cited as contributors to the creation of
> poverty. Generally speaking, however, fault was more commonly attrib-
> uted to poor people themselves in this country whereas in the Third
> World, the poor were typically seen as 'victims of circumstance'.[1]

The extent to which poverty nearer home is more difficult for people to
cope with personally has already been discussed and the way that this can lead
to making personal judgements about those in poverty. This chapter is
concerned to look at the sort of thinking – the understanding of poverty's
causes and effects – on which some of these moral judgements may be based.
What are the explanations used to rationalize or justify particular attitudes? It
was notable in the Christian Aid research that Christians acquired their
information about poverty largely from the media and other secular sources.

Although this was not tested by the research, it seems likely that the range of views expressed by these church respondents was not dissimilar from that which could have been obtained from a group of non-church members of similar age and social background. What theories and views then have been prevalent in Britain which would have influenced people's thinking? This chapter will review some of the main sorts of explanations of poverty and deprivation which have affected post-war thinking and, therefore, have also been instrumental in shaping responses to poverty.

Broadly, explanations fall under a number of headings – individual, cultural, agencies of welfare, which are considered in this chapter, and social and economic, which will be covered in the next. Although they will be separated out here for the sake of analysis and although some explanations are clearly at odds with others, very often the views of any one person will be a more untidy mix than this presentation suggests, sieving together an amalgam of ingredients drawn from across two or three of these categories.

FOCUSING ON THE INDIVIDUAL

The tendency to adopt a punitive approach towards people in poverty has already been mentioned. To say that people are to blame for their plight or failure assumes that human beings are autonomous and self-determining, that they have full control over their lives and that they can, therefore, be wholly responsible for the way that it is conducted. To accept this means that people can be held personally responsible for their poverty. Of course, some exceptions to this have always been accepted – that particular misfortunes could befall people which were no fault of their own. However, with the introduction of the welfare state, it was then supposed that social insurance and other provision stood between the individual and social deprivation if only he or she cared to take advantage of it.

There are different types of explanations stressing the relationship between individuals and poverty. They do not necessarily attribute blame, but they all see poverty as in some way stemming from the limitations or deficiencies of individuals whether these are biological, psychological or economic.

It's all in the genes

The biological case rests largely on intelligence. If intelligence is required to get on in life – to acquire the qualifications which will lead to higher earnings and social standing – then intelligence, it is argued, is a key factor. The argument is strengthened by saying that the effects of different environments have been mitigated by such developments as the opening up of educational opportunities to all. The intelligent working-class person has been enabled to rise up the social scale.

There are a number of flaws in this case. First, genetic transmission of intelligence is not as simple as is suggested here. It is as likely to produce differences between generations as similarities. 'The influence of genetic factors on intelligence has been over-emphasized but even where they do operate, they do not separate out a biologically self-perpetuating class of paupers.'[2] Secondly, intelligence is not wholly inherited. Social circumstances such as bad housing, overcrowding and poor nutrition play a part in impairing development just as a stimulating environment and experiences will encourage it.

A third objection to this reliance on an association between poverty and low intelligence is that it takes an unduly optimistic view of existing conditions of educational opportunity in this country. It is still the case that children from particular social backgrounds – irrespective of their level of intelligence – are more or less favoured in terms of educational chances. Apart from the major difference between private and public schools, it is known that within the public sector, schools in certain areas are more likely to suffer from overcrowded conditions or rundown buildings, a lower level of resources and higher pupil–teacher ratios. A Government report has signalled that in some inner city and outer estate schools, pupils are underperforming in part because of the low expectations of teachers.[3] The effects of attempts to introduce market forces into schools will be discussed in a later chapter. Children of comparable intelligence but more advantageous backgrounds are more likely to move on to higher education. In particular, the clear class divide in Britain can still be detected by looking at the intake into Oxford and Cambridge and recruitment into particular occupations.

Over forty years after the legislation which opened secondary education to all, the public schools account for seven out of nine of the army's top generals, two-thirds of the external directors of the Bank of England, thirty-three of the thirty-nine top English judges, all the ambassadors in the fifteen most important overseas missions, seventy-eight of the Queen's eighty-four lord lieutenants and the majority of the bishops in the Church of England. Even the bold thrusting entrepreneurs who have become such folk heroes have failed to cast aside old money; of the two hundred richest people in Britain, thirty-five were educated at a single school, Eton. Reports of the death of the class system have been greatly exaggerated.[4]

Free to compete?

'Indigence was simply the punishment meted out to the improvident by their own lack of industry and efficiency. Far from being a blessed state, poverty was the obvious consequence of sloth and sinfulness.'[5] Here is a typically

Victorian voice ascribing poverty largely to individual laziness. The language may have changed but the outlook survives today. It has been articulated by New Right thinkers such as Friedman and Hayek,[6] but it permeates thinking on the right more pervasively and explicitly or implicitly underpins various aspects of employment and welfare policy.

As expressed by the New Right, this outlook is one plank of a wider philosophy based upon free-market economics. The development of the market economy in the late eighteenth and nineteenth centuries both accompanied and facilitated the rapid industrialization of the period. Large-scale private enterprise grew up alongside advanced specialization and division of labour and the development of larger markets. Price became the mechanism for regulating the supply and demand not only of goods, but also of land, labour and capital. (A later chapter will look at the extension of the market system beyond consumer goods to include welfare goods such as pensions and health care.) Competition was the stimulus to higher standards and greater adaptation in production and distribution in order to gain success through greater efficiency and responsiveness to the market. The 'laws' of supply and demand work because people will seek to sell their goods or labour to the highest bidder and buy goods or labour from the lowest.

In many ways, the free-market scenario can be seen as an ideal – in the sense that for it to fulfil all the promises held out by its supporters, there has to be a perfect balance between demand and supply. In fact, this never does – and never can – occur. Further, not only does the market system create winners and losers, the whole basis of competition depends upon winners and losers.

Free-market advocates link the operation of capitalism with certain freedoms. Firms are free to produce what they want and should be untrammelled by state interference if they are to be able to exercise this freedom fully. The consumer is king and can decide his or her own wants by exercising choice in what he or she purchases. Taxation is criticized because it reduces the individual's freedom to spend his or her income as he or she likes. Such economic freedom is seen as a condition for all other freedoms. Milton Friedman linked the early development of the free-market system with a philosophy of freedom:

> ... the intellectual movement that went under the name of liberalism emphasised freedom as the ultimate goal and the individual as the ultimate entity in society. It supported laissez-faire at home as a means of reducing the role of the state in economic affairs and thereby enlarging the role of the individual.[7]

It can be seen that such a philosophy centres upon people as economic beings to the extent that it puts forward a form of social organization designed mainly to advance this facet of their lives. Economic relationships are the pivotal ones. There are a number of corollaries. First, if people are given these economic freedoms then, as Friedman says, they can be considered individually responsible for their own lives and futures. It is open to them to reap the monetary rewards that the market gives to those who are talented and industrious. If they fail, then it is their own moral or physical limitations which are to blame.

A combination of these arguments appears to underlie the assertions of individuals who see themselves – or their fathers – as self-made and who are heavily critical of others who have not similarly managed to pull themselves up by their bootstraps. Margaret Thatcher, Norman Tebbit ('Get on your bike') and Rhodes Boyson are all MPs for whom this has been a recurrent theme.

Shifting the blame

These assumptions have also lingered in the policies – or absence of policies – on unemployment during the 1980s and 1990s. The implicit message throughout this period has been that if people really wanted to work and were 'employable', they could do so. This is a convenient way of distracting attention from the scale of the unemployment problem but, for those looking for jobs in areas where the ratio of applicants to vacancies is 30 to 1, it only compounds a sense of failure and alienation. The change of name from 'unemployment benefit' to a six months' 'jobseeker's allowance' symbolizes this deflection of responsibility on to the unemployed person. Anyone who is really trying, it says, will get another job within six months. Unemployment is only a matter of gear-changes in the economy, inevitable as adaptation takes place. This might ring true if the unemployment rate was 2 or 3 per cent but not when millions of people are out of work and in mid-1994 the male unemployment rate stands at 12.5 per cent for the country as a whole and rises to nearly 30 per cent in some areas. Even official figures show this, despite the twenty-nine changes in ways of calculating the number of unemployed made during the 1980s, all of which resulted in a lower figure.

Minimizing the lack of jobs is one side of the picture. Blaming people's alleged lack of 'employability' is another. People's ability to compete in the labour market will always be constrained by various factors, such as inheritance of wealth, their level of education and training, the suitability of their skills for the current market needs. This is a fact conveniently discounted in the free-market philosophy. Since Britain entered the European Common Market, we often hear industrialists asking to be allowed to compete 'on a level playing field'. It is an indication that competition does not take place in a vacuum. If this is true for industries, it is also true for individuals who are affected by wider social and economic trends which can put insuperable barriers in the way of even the most strenuous individual efforts. Some obstacles can be surmounted by the acquisition of new skills but however employable people become there remains a massive jobs deficit in this country.

Unrealistically high expectations have been shifted not only on to the unemployed themselves, but also on to educational and training institutions. They have then been criticized when they fail to measure up to this standard of effectiveness. In the 1980s, the 'solution' to youth unemployment was seen as vocational preparation. In addition to post-school youth training schemes, there were moves to adapt the school curriculum to provide an introduction to, and skills for, the world of work. Some elements of these changes were welcome. But it was a solution to a problem that had been misdefined: that young people were unemployed because of their lack of qualifications rather than because the job market had collapsed. Although training issues are vital as we move into an 'intelligence' economy, the training being offered was not necessarily appropriate. Rather, education was being used as an instrument to respond to a non-educational crisis. 'Many people believe, with good reason, that unemployment is here to stay. If this is merely an economic trough then it is so long that the youth of Knowsley and similar places have not seen and will not see the peaks within their youth.'[8] Unemployment was being used as a motivational stick to beat the students with or regarded as a personal problem to be 'treated', and some of the blame for it could also be laid at the teachers' door. Training and Enterprise Councils are caught in the same bind as their effectiveness is, in part, measured by the number of people they get into jobs irrespective of the current state of the labour market in their area.

There is a second corollary of seeing economic relationships as central to life. It means that the maximum effectiveness of such an economic system depends upon a view of human motivation which states that men and women act primarily out of economic self-interest. Yet people's motivation may not be so singular. They may be driven by a variety of non-economic motives. A higher paid job may be turned down in favour of a lower-paid one because the latter affords more job satisfaction or entails less stress or less overtime. (Wanting to 'spend more time with my family' can sometimes be taken at face value!)

If seeing self-interest as the prime driving force is, on the one hand, too pessimistic a view of human nature, in other ways it is too optimistic. Where does self-interest end and selfishness or greed begin? As John Atherton points out, Adam Smith knew from experience that shared values of truth, honesty, obligation and trust are needed to regulate market behaviour and to restrain uncurbed self-interest which could otherwise damage both the market operation itself and have devastating social consequences. 'The damage to individuals and communities through unemployment and deprivation is closely related to the functioning of an unregulated free market with uncontrolled self-interest at its heart.[9] Irresponsible dealings on the money market, insider share dealing and the misuse of pension funds are all examples over recent years of what can happen when either the legislative framework is relaxed or such values are eroded.

A class apart

Another continuing theme in accounts of poverty has been the identification of 'problem' individuals or families. In the 1950s and 1960s, the term 'problem families' was common currency. It is an ambiguous phrase. According to the context in which it is used, it can either mean people with problems or, as a more prevalent castigation, people who present a problem to society. But it was not a new phenomenon. Richard Titmuss put it in the context of a long but discontinuous concern with ' . . . a segment of families in the population, supposedly characterised by similar traits and thought to represent a closed pathological entity'.[10] Victorian philanthropists, it seems, were moved as much by the moral and social degradation that they saw in city slums as by the material deprivation. 'This they attempted to remedy by measures designed to restore individuals and families to self-respect and independence, hoping by a slow but sure process of personal reclamation to raise the standards of the people as a whole.'[11]

In the early part of this century, there was some reaction against this individualistic approach with reforms such as the introduction of minimum wage legislation, social insurance and preventive health services designed to raise the standards of the 'submerged tenth'. By 1939 there was a general feeling that the situation was much improved, although social and health workers 'were aware of the existence of families in the slum areas of the big towns, on the new housing estates, and even in the country villages, who remained sunk in squalor and apathy'.[12] Penelope Hall suggested that wartime evacuation shattered this complacency. People learned by direct experience that the 'submerged tenth' still existed and amongst them were, 'so it was said, a number of "problem families", that is "families always on the edge of pauperism and crime, riddled with mental and physical defects, in and out of court for child neglect, a menace to the community of which the gravity is out of all proportion to their numbers" '.[13]

What was meant by problem families changed from Victorian times to the first half of this century and then again post-war. But whenever such a term is used, it is questionable whether it really points to any coherent group with common characteristics. In the late 1940s and early 1950s, according to Hall, the phrase denoted 'families with multiple problems whose standards of living, and particularly child care, are markedly low, and who seem to be little

influenced by, or are even resistant to, measures of general social amelioration'.[14] This latter point should perhaps be emphasized because it reflects the
picture emerging from much of the literature at that time, that here was a
minority whose problems and behaviour marked them as a group distinct from
the rest of society. However, she also pointed out that such a characterization
could conceal both the projected views of those making the judgement and a
wide diversity of lifestyle and outlook amongst the families so labelled.[15]

Who loves you baby?

As has been said, the idea of the existence of a distinctive problem group is a
recurring one, though its precise definition and ascribed membership may
vary over time. The reasons given for it have also changed as time has gone on.
After the stress on genetic factors in the 1920s and 1930s, in the 1950s and
1960s, the spotlight turned to psychological factors and, in particular, the
quality of parental care that children received in their earliest years.[16]
'Deprived' in this context came to mean emotionally deprived – starved of
love and security – so that they could not grow up into confident, self-reliant
adults. They were bound to remain immature, unable to control their
impulses, wanting immediate gratification of their needs. As a result they
could not handle money, keep a job or look after a house. This being the case,
the intervention on behalf of society that was most appropriate was 'treatment' for the families in the form of casework to help the individual to
function better and enhance family relationships.

It is a truism that psychological factors play an important part in everyone's lives and that emotional damage in early childhood can have long lasting
consequences. However, as Bob Holman says, 'The poor cannot be dismissed
as the psychologically sick. Nor can the problem of poverty be confined to a
core of problem families.'[17] Such a diagnosis is dubious in a number of ways.
Childhood deprivations do not necessarily lead to malfunctioning adults. Nor
do a few particular instances where immaturity is evident provide an adequate
basis for making general observations about the large number of people living
in poverty.

There is no necessary association between emotional and material deprivation. On the one hand, in many families experiencing a multiplicity of material
needs, children are brought up in a loving and secure environment. On the
other, children in the most affluent of homes can nevertheless grow up feeling
unloved and insecure. But, in any case, where there is a link between them, it
is more likely that the stress of poverty and social disadvantage has triggered
the emotional disturbance than the other way around. This is borne out by
research which showed the 'improving' effects of better housing conditions,
better education, higher incomes, and more congenial neighbourhoods on the
younger generation of a group of 'problem families'.[18] Other studies show that

for most people in poverty, the main problem is lack of income, which is not necessarily – and perhaps is surprisingly seldom – accompanied by emotional or behavioural problems.[19] Only a very tiny minority of people who are poor become so as a result of personal inadequacy.

POVERTY TRANSMITTED BY CULTURE

After emotional deprivation came cultural deprivation. A different – sociological rather than psychological – slant on the proposition that poverty is handed down from one generation to another in families came with the theory of a culture of poverty. Culture in this instance refers to the entire pattern of living in a given society and the body of learning required to fit into and conform to that way of life. It embraces the values, standards, institutions, relationships and forms of behaviour which characterize and make up its common way of life. At its most basic, its culture is a society's way of coping with the problems of survival. The American anthropologist, Oscar Lewis, developed the idea that within one culture, another could exist, brought into being by a particular group's need to develop its own survival techniques.

In studying poor people, Lewis concluded that they were so alienated from the rest of their society that they had to develop new ways of coping and that these coping mechanisms came to constitute a culture within a culture. It was not just different from, but in some ways inimical to, the dominant culture. The poor tended not to be integrated into the major institutions of society and to mistrust representatives of authority. They did not share, or at least did not observe, social values and accepted practices. They displayed feelings of helplessness and resignation, so that they were not motivated towards work or achieving change and advancement. Although this fatalism meant that they did not rail against their plight, it also ensured that poverty for them remained inevitable and, as a result of their socialization, inevitable too for their children. Acceptance of poverty was passed on from one generation to another rather than any urge or capacity to escape it.

> The culture of poverty insists in its simplest form that the poor are different not primarily because of low income but because they have been habituated to poverty and have developed a sub-culture of values adapted to these conditions which they pass on to their children.[20]

It is a short step from seeing people as different to seeing them as dangerous. This step was perhaps precipitated in the US because the culture of poverty thesis became prominent just at the time when more notice was being taken of the problems of America's black population. Some commentators explained the persistence of poverty amongst black people in terms of

perceived characteristics of their lifestyle, such as an unstable family structure, irresponsible male behaviour, an acceptance of illegitimacy.[21]

The cycle of deprivation

In Britain, Sir Keith Joseph, while he was Secretary of State for Social Services
in the early 1970s, popularized a variation of the culture of poverty theory –
cultural deprivation.[22] This does not place the poor outside the bounds of the
prevailing culture but says instead that the socialization of the young in poor
families is such that they are not equipped to benefit from what that culture
could offer them. His emphasis on parenting connects his thinking closely
with those who adopted a more psychological approach but he advanced his
views in the context not of a diagnosis of individual pathology but a perceived
common pattern amongst whole groupings of families. A. H. Halsey summed
it up, saying, ' . . . the sub-working class family is held to be the major villain
of the piece, failing to provide the early training in literacy, numeracy, and
acceptance of work and achievement habits which constitute the normal
upbringing of the middle class child . . . .'[23]

Joseph talked about poor people having 'problems of maladjustment'.
These problems could be transmitted inter-generationally, setting in motion
a cycle of deprivation. Inadequate parents use inadequate child-rearing
practices which lead to children deprived emotionally, socially and intellec-
tually who fail at school, then become unemployed or are only able to get
unskilled jobs which do not provide enough money to lift them out of poverty.
They embark on unstable marriages and unsatisfactory family lives and in
their turn become inadequate parents. And so the wheel goes round again.

Sir Keith promoted a large-scale research programme to follow up his
theory that poverty persists because social problems reproduce themselves
from one generation to another and, specifically, that inadequate parents rear
inadequate children. However, one of the main findings of the programme was
that there is no such simple continuity. There is no general sense in which like
begets like.[24] The evidence of this and other research shows not that poor
people are alienated or that they behave very differently – allowing for the
impact of poverty on behaviour. Rather it shows their surprising degree of
assimilation of the prevailing values and aspirations of British society and
remarkable resilience in the face of repeated disappointments, for example, in
looking for work.

Creating an underclass

'Underclass', therefore, is a symbolic term with no single meaning, but
a great many applications . . . It represents, not a useful concept, but a
potent symbol.[25]

The current term which perpetuates this age-old distrust of the poor is the 'underclass'. It has a beguiling sociological ring to it, but it should be handled with care by those who would press for social justice. The Swedish sociologist, Gunnar Myrdal, first used the term in the 1960s in his critique of the American economy, *Challenge to Affluence*. He recognized that though the US economy was booming, there was a distressing amount of unemployment and its nature had changed. It was not merely cyclical or amenable to an upturn in demand. The elimination of the need for certain categories of labour was creating an underclass 'of unemployed and gradually unemployable persons and families at the bottom of a society in which for the majority of people above that level the increasingly democratic structure of the education system creates more and more liberty ... '.[26] 'And now in the end,' he said, 'it threatens to split off a true "underclass" – not really an integrated part of the nation at all but a useless and miserable substratum.'[27] Myrdal saw that not only was their political participation and representation minimal, but that the institutions intended to protect the poorest actually tended only to benefit the stratum above them. In his writing, Myrdal was addressing this as a problem born out of the economic system and exacerbated by public policy which failed – in contrast to that in his own country Sweden – to assert other political and social objectives alongside economic ones and so avert such an outcome.

William Julius Wilson, writing in America in the second half of the 1980s, developed the use of the term underclass, notably looking at the position of black people in ghetto areas.[28] He is still analysing the situation in structural terms, looking at the process of exclusion and the reason why certain people are more likely to be excluded than others. He sees social isolation as a key factor leading to a concentration of problems. Young blacks lack the qualifications for available jobs. The few successful ones move out of their old neighbourhoods, thus removing local leadership and positive role models and leaving behind the least skilled, least successful. The young no longer see the value of work, nor the link between education and employment. Living on state benefit is taken for granted as the norm.

Frank Field, in his book *Losing Out*, focuses on the condition of those poorest whom he suggests have been separated even from other low income groups and the working class in general. 'The main thrust of *Losing Out* is that the 300-year evolution of citizenship as an incorporating force in British society has been thrown into reverse ... '[29] He argued that

four forces have brought about this reversal: the record post-war levels of unemployment; widening class differences; exclusion of the very poorest from rapidly rising living standards; and a significant change in public attitudes towards those people who are seen to have failed to 'make it' in Mrs Thatcher's Britain. These four forces . . . have combined to produce an underclass that sits uncomfortably below that group which is referred to as living on a low income.[30]

His underclass consists of the long-term unemployed, single-parent families and the poor elderly.

Ralf Dahrendorf wrote an article at the time of the 1987 General Election in which he looked at the factors that he considered were leading to the emergence of an underclass in Britain. He pointed to unemployment, low pay and low income, saying that

> one of the characteristics of this new underclass is that it suffers from a cumulation of social pathologies. Members of the underclass have a low level of educational attainment; many have not finished school; there is much functional and even absolute illiteracy. Incomplete families are the rule rather than the exception. Housing conditions . . . are usually miserable; to some extent this class is an inner city problem . . . it is also a phenomenon of race both in the US and in Britain.[31]

In these analyses, we see people becoming surplus to the needs of the labour market, particularly amongst the young and ethnic minorities, who then exist outside the normal social contract of citizenship and have little stake in society itself. But even in this brief review, it can be seen that the term underclass is very imprecise. It has no real empirical base and the relative significance of the varying criteria used to define it is unclear.

Defining an underclass by behaviour

However, there is even greater reason for being sceptical about its use when it is deployed in relation to people's behaviour and when the symptoms of poverty are used to personalize its causes and enable the victims to be blamed. A parallel can be drawn with racism. Ken Leech refers to

> the assumption that black people are intrinsically problematic, by the very fact of their existence. They are responsible for increased racism. (In a similar vein Sir Oswald Mosley had said that the Jews were the cause of anti-Semitism.) If they were not present, there would be no racism.[32]

The American theorist, Charles Murray, when writing in 1989 about 'the emerging British underclass', embarked on his thesis as follows:

> 'Underclass' as used in Britain tends to be sanitised, a sort of synonym for people who are not just poor, but especially poor. So let us get it

straight from the outset: the 'underclass' does not refer to degree of poverty, but to a type of poverty.

It is not a new concept. I grew up knowing what the underclass was; we just didn't call it that in those days. In the small Iowa town where I lived, I was taught by my middle class parents that there were two kinds of poor people. One class of poor people was never even called 'poor'. I came to understand that they simply lived on low incomes, as my parents had done when they were young. Then there was another set of poor people, just a handful of them. These poor people didn't lack just money. They were defined by their behaviour. Their homes were littered and unkempt. The men in the family were unable to hold a job for more than a few weeks at a time. Drunkenness was common. The children grew up ill-schooled and ill-behaved and contributed a disproportionate share of the local juvenile delinquents.[33]

This description of his childhood town contains strong echoes of the 'problem family' thesis. Murray chooses illegitimacy, violent crime and labour market drop-out as identifying features of members of the underclass. In substantiating his claim that Britain has an underclass which, though still small and largely out of sight, is growing rapidly, he generalizes misleadingly from his analysis of the United States, which is itself questionable. In his argument that there is a different type of poor person who behaves differently from other people, he uses, at best, evidence which is anecdotal and couched in the language of social sickness and moral hygiene. No reasoned justification is given for his choice of defining criteria. In essence, the message is that these poor are to blame for their poverty because they choose to act in certain deviant ways or are brought up to do so.

As Alan Walker says, in direct response to Murray, 'his thesis is at best misleading and, at worst, a dangerous diversion from the major problems of poverty and deprivation facing Britain'. Walker points out that in this, Murray is part of a long-standing tradition.

... the belief that some poor people are poor because they do not conform to prevailing social values and therefore need to be disciplined may be traced from the repression of vagrancy under the Elizabethan Poor Law, to the workhouse test of the 1834 Poor Law Amendment Act, to the 1930s' genuinely-seeking-work-test, to the voluntary unemployment rules, YTS [Youth Training Scheme] and Restart programmes of the 1980s.[34]

Walker also sees Murray as the natural heir of Sir Keith Joseph.

Charles Murray's work is a very clear recent example of a long academic and political tradition of looking at poverty as pathological. What all the examples have in common is that they use *symptoms* of poverty as an explanation for it. This explanation then very often provides a defence or justification for particular policy responses. William Ryan, in a book called *Blaming the Victim*, recounts the usual sequence of events:

> First, identify a social problem. Second, study those affected by the problem and discover in what ways they are different from the rest of us … Third, define the difference as the cause of the social problem itself. Finally, of course, assign a government bureaucrat to invent a human-itarian action programme to correct the difference.[35]

The concept of the underclass is based upon assumptions that are very dubious both empirically and morally. Even when it is used by people like Frank Field without any intended blame, its implicit logic is still that the cause of the underclass somehow lies in its composition. ' … the reflexive effect of the underclass concept is not to define the marginalized but to marginalize those it defines.'[36] That this is so is not of solely academic interest or of concern just because it will feed the tabloid press with new variations on old stereotypes. It is an example of the way the definition and analysis of poverty is vital to an understanding of policy responses to it. Such explana-tions form policy, justify policy and distract from the outcomes of policy. There *are* people deprived and excluded from the full benefits of their citizenship. There *is* a need to talk about them and their situation. But we also need to be clear precisely who and what we are talking about. We must be aware that the language of our discourse will usually be serving specific interests. Its terms are not neutrally descriptive but explicitly or implicitly perform social functions. In this case, they generate heat not light and further the process of marginalization and stigmatization.

In talking about the debate in America, Wilson states:

> If the liberal perspective on the ghetto underclass is to regain the influence it has lost since the 1960s, it will be necessary to do more than simply react to what conservative scholars and policy makers are saying. Liberals will also have to propose thoughtful explanations of the rise in inner-city social dislocations. Such explanations should emphasise the dynamic interplay between ghetto-specific cultural characteristics and social and economic opportunities. This would necessitate taking into account the effects not only of changes in American economic organisa-tion but also of demographic changes and changes in the laws and policies of government as well. In this connection, the relationships between joblessness and family structure, joblessness and other social dislocations (crime, teenage pregnancy, welfare dependency, etc) and

joblessness and social orientation among different age groups would receive special attention. However thoughtful explanations . . . depend on careful empirical research.[37]

DEPENDENCY CULTURE

What is surprising, really, is that in the middle of pain and in spite of the burden of oppression that the poor experience, they continue to resist.[38]

Another pathological explanation of poverty identifies dependency as the determining characteristic and uses this not only to attack the poor, but also to undermine policies which are purported to have caused or reinforced it. In the nineteenth century, 'the Victorian Poor Law made no bones about the fact that its primary objective was to punish poor people who asked for state help . . . '.[39] The keynote of the post-war welfare state was the relief of poverty rather than regulating the lives of the poor. However, mounting welfare budgets and a change in political and economic philosophy have once again caused the pendulum to swing back to a more repressive government stance. Welfare policies, it is said, have made things too easy for people, destroyed the incentive to work, encouraged irresponsibility in family life, undermined moral fibre. As a result, people no longer mind living 'off the state'. They live according to a different set of norms and standards and have jettisoned values such as thrift, hard work and self-sufficiency.

Mitigating the effects of market forces or encouraging fecklessness?

The free market does not now exist – if it ever did – in a pure form in this country. Private enterprise co-exists with public sector services, including ones specifically intended to protect people against the vagaries of capitalism. The cross-party consensus about the role of the welfare state has broken down since the 1970s and the view that welfare provision undermines personal responsibility has re-emerged more strongly on the right. This swing was influenced by people writing at the end of the 1960s about what they diagnosed as the impact of the growth in social security, social services and public sector housing and education.[40] They feared that state aid interfered with the incentive to work and to meet family responsibilities, discouraged thrift and the exercise of personal initiative. Individuals no longer had to find their own routes to avoid poverty. Welfare dependency could then lead to other deficiencies of relationships and behaviour within families and, ultimately, encourage family breakdown. In particular, there was no longer the impulsion for fathers to work to support their families and, it was said, male children had no role model of a hard-working man as an example to follow.

Further, the growth in welfare provision wasted valuable national assets and it put a burden on taxpayers and transferred money 'from the energetic, successful and thrifty to give to the idle, the failures and the feckless'.[41] This in turn sapped the motivation of those in work as they see their money taken in tax and, in Rhodes Boyson's words, ' . . . the general sense of responsibility and personal pride declines. National economic strength and personal moral fibre are both reduced'.[42] In both cases a connection is made between the social and economic effects of the welfare state and moral malaise. It is asserted that people remain morally immature.

These arguments can be countered in a number of ways. First, there is no evidence to support the contention that the advent of the welfare state has undermined people's wish to work or be free from dependence on state benefits. Its operation is certainly open to a variety of criticisms, some of which will be considered in a later chapter. Some of its provisions can have unintended consequences. Sometimes the main beneficiaries are not necessarily those most in need. But it remains true that it has substantially reduced social deprivation. In fact, it can be argued that collective social provision does not go far enough – and is now being further whittled away – rather than that it has contributed to more impoverishment. The welfare state could not remove choice from those who already had no choice nor limit the freedoms of people whose only freedom was to doss down in a doorway or live on the breadline or queue up at the jobcentre.

Setting forward their catalogue of the distorting effects of the welfare state, its opponents imply that the free market worked well as an arena for all to exercise their economic talents to escape poverty prior to state intervention. They suggest that under a system dominated by private enterprise, the individual could control his or her own destiny. This, of course, is far from true. At the end of the nineteenth and beginning of the twentieth century reformers such as Booth and Rowntree identified a more complex situation. While both criticized a minority of individuals whom they perceived as not wanting to work, nonetheless they pointed to a far larger number who either wished to work but for whom there was no employment, or whose earnings were so low that they could not make ends meet. It is clear, too, that it was not just the unskilled who were pushed into poverty by lack of job or intermittent employment and irregular earnings. Highly skilled craftsmen could also face penury as was demonstrated by a Registrar General's Report in 1910.

The other side of the picture was that then – as ever is the case – achieving success in a free market was no guarantee of ability or desirable moral qualities. ' . . . amongst the rich and powerful in the nineteenth century were some who appeared lazy, feckless, immoral and lacking in talents. But market forces did not bring them to poverty any more than take Booth's hard workers out of it.'[43] Neither rich nor poor are exempt from human defects so that trying to account for poverty solely in these terms is to build on a far too flimsy structure. 'No doubt effort, initiative and drive may help some persons out of poverty, just as laziness and apathy may push others down. But these virtues or vices cannot account for all affluence or all social deprivations.'[44] Such an explanation, too, will inevitably rebound to the detriment of the poor because, in effect, it is a defence of the *status quo*. Success becomes its own justification; failure condemns itself.

Dependency or captivity?

David Ellwood has reviewed and assessed three models of behavioural dependency, which for shorthand he sums up as choice, confidence or culture.[45] First, there is the *rational choice* model. This assumes that people will evaluate the options open to them in relation to their tastes and preferences and decide accordingly. The *expectancy* model looks on dependency as resulting from an individual's loss of confidence or feeling of helplessness in the face of outside forces. The *cultural* model sees dependency as behavioural deficiency and/or the result of aberrant social mores.

Ellwood tried to explain long-term welfare dependency in the United States using these models. He concluded that the rational choice model best fitted the data. For example, the economic and marital choices open to single mothers on benefit posed only unreasonable alternatives to long-term welfare.

Dean and Taylor-Gooby quote research in this country which points to similar no-win situations.

> Similarly, for 18 to 24 year old young people in the north east of England in 1987, among whom almost one in three had never had a full-time job, the real choice even for the relatively well educated was between 'shit jobs, govvy schemes or the dole'. Research indicated that a clear majority of these youngsters were 'non-political, pragmatic young adults ... eager for employment, even on modest wages' and 'far from advancing a rebellious morality, they were conservative on most social issues.'[46]

> The Fourth World families' hopes are revealed by the fact that they keep going. In spite of the perpetual drain on their mental and physical strength, they continue to get up in the morning, face the criticism of neighbours, live without heat and light, manifest their love for their children, present themselves for job interviews, cope with chronic illness on a poor diet and raise children in decaying and dangerous housing.

These families' daily struggle is generally not seen in this positive light. They are referred to as 'that mother who can't cope', 'that lazy father' or 'that child disturbing the class'. Their fight to keep going is not given any weight or significance and is not supported by people who can help them. Too often, their way of doing things is ignored, misjudged or condemned.[47]

We (the Conservative Government) have a different vision of what it means to 'protect and promote economic and social welfare in this country. We believe that dependence in the long run decreases human happiness and reduces human freedom.'[48]

Welfare has been blamed for producing the 'wrong' sort of dependency though, as Dean and Taylor-Gooby suggest, a captivity culture might be a more apt phrase to express the way the social security system 'constructs, isolates and supervises a heterogeneous population of reluctant dependants'.[49] Again the emphasis is on the wrong part of the equation. The focus is on the outcome of what is essentially a power relationship – whether or not masquerading as a welfare one – rather than on the network of structures, policies and actions, which bring the dependency about. Aspects of these structures and policies will be discussed in later chapters.

The use of dependence as a pejorative term in relation to people on benefits somehow suggests that the rest of us are independent. Rather, we just have other sorts of dependencies – on families or on wage relationships – which are equally socially embedded and determined. All individuals are dependent on other individuals and social structures for work, for goods, for services. Interdependence is inherent in the human condition. In a modern society, our inter-connectedness has become more intricate and more indirect but also more pronounced. The object of social policy should, therefore, be about constructing and ensuring mutuality of interdependence rather than pretending there is such a thing as individual independence and pursuing illusory autonomy.

Social policy will be examined later in the book. The next chapter goes on to look at the way economic and social structures frame our lives and thus constrain the opportunities and choices open to people. It addresses structural explanations of poverty.

NOTES

1. Liz Spencer and Dawn Snape, *The Gospel, the Poor and the Churches* (Christian Aid, 1994), p. 38.
2. Robert Holman, *Poverty: Explanations of Social Deprivation* (Oxford: Martin Robertson, 1978), p. 61.
3. *Access and Achievement in Urban Education*, Report from the Office of Her Majesty's Chief Inspector of Schools, Office for Standards in Education (Ofsted) (London: HMSO, 1993).

4. Jeremy Paxman, *Friends in High Places: Who Runs Britain?* (London: Penguin Books, 1991), p. 156.
5. R. Bremner, 'Shifting attitudes', in P. Weinberger (ed.), *Perspectives on Social Welfare* (Collier-Macmillan, 1974), p. 64.
6. F. Hayek, *The Road to Serfdom* (London: Routledge, 1962 edn), M. Friedman, *Capitalism and Freedom* (Chicago: University of Chicago Press, 1963).
7. Friedman, *op. cit.*, p. 5.
8. Con Harty, Principal Careers Officer, Knowsley, *Education and Unemployment*, Merseyside Churches Unemployment Committee conference paper (February 1986).
9. John Atherton, *Christianity and the Market* (London: SPCK, 1992), pp. 68–9.
10. R. Titmuss, foreword to A. Philp and N. Timms, *The Problem of the 'Problem Family'* (Family Service Units, 1962), p. v.
11. M. Penelope Hall, *The Social Services of Modern England* 2nd edn (London: Routledge & Kegan Paul, 1965), p. 158 (first published 1952).
12. *Ibid.*, p. 158.
13. *Ibid.*, p. 159, quoting *Our Towns, a Close Up*, a report by the Women's Group on Public Welfare as a result of a resolution from the National Federation of Women's Institutes deploring the conditions of English town life disclosed by evacuation.
14. *Ibid.*, pp. 159–60.
15. *Ibid.*, p. 160.
16. John Bowlby was one major influence, in particular through *Child Care and the Growth of Love* (Harmondsworth: Penguin Books, 1953). See also the work of Elizabeth Irvine, 'Research into problem families', *Journal of Psychiatric Social Work* (May 1954).
17. Holman, *op. cit.*, p. 95.
18. C. Wright and J. Lunn, 'Sheffield problem families: a follow up study of their sons and daughters', *Community Medicine*, 26 November 1971 and 3 December 1971.
19. See M. Rutter and N. Madge, *Cycles of Disadvantage: A Review of Research* (London: Heinemann, 1976) and for supportive material from America, M. Rein, *Social Policy* (New York: Random House, 1970).
20. A. H. Halsey, *Educational Priority*, Vol. 1 (London: HMSO, 1972), p. 16.
21. N. Glazer and D. Moynihan, *Beyond the Melting Pot* (Cambridge, MA: Harvard University Press, 1963); D. Moynihan, *The Negro Family* (US Department of Labor, 1965).
22. Keith Joseph, 'Cycles of Deprivation'. Speech to the Pre-School Playgroups Association, 29 June 1972.
23. Halsey, *op. cit.*, p. 17.
24. See M. Brown and N. Madge, *Despite the Welfare State* (London: Heinemann, 1982).
25. Hartley Dean and Peter Taylor-Gooby, *Dependency Culture: The Explosion of a Myth* (Harvester/Wheatsheaf, 1992), p. 44.
26. Gunnar Myrdal, *Challenge to Affluence* (London: Gollancz, 1963), p. 40.
27. *Ibid.*, p. 41.
28. William Julius Wilson, *The Truly Disadvantaged: The Inner City, the Underclass and Public Policy* (Chicago: University of Chicago Press, 1987).
29. Frank Field, *Losing Out: The Emergence of Britain's Underclass* (Oxford: Basil Blackwell, 1989), p. 2.
30. *Ibid.*
31. Ralf Dahrendorf, 'The erosion of citizenship and its consequences for us all', *New Statesman*, 12 June 1987, p. 13.
32. Kenneth Leech, *Care and Conflict: Leaves from a Pastoral Notebook* (London: Darton, Longman and Todd, 1990), p. 95.
33. Charles Murray, *The Emerging British Underclass*, with commentaries by Frank Field, Joan C. Brown, Alan Walker and Nicholas Deakin (Institute of Economic Affairs Health and Welfare Unit, 1990), p. 1.
34. *Ibid.*, p. 50.
35. William Ryan, *Blaming the Victim* (Orbach and Chambers, 1971), p. 8.
36. Dean and Taylor-Gooby, *op. cit.*, p. 44.
37. Wilson, *op. cit.*, p. 18.
38. Julio de Santa Ana, Konrad Raiser and Ulrich Duchrow, *The Political Economy of the Holy Spirit* (WCC Commission on the Churches' Participation in Development, 1990), p. 15.
39. Dean and Taylor-Gooby, *op. cit.*, p. ix.
40. See A. Seldon, 'Welfare by choice', in A. Lochhead (ed.), *A Reader in Social Administration* (London: Constable, 1968); M. Bremner, *Dependency and the Family* (Institute of Economic Affairs, 1968).
41. Rhodes Boyson, *Down with the Poor* (Churchill Press, 1971), p. 5.
42. *Ibid.*

43. Holman, *op. cit.*, p. 79.
44. *Ibid.*, p. 79.
45. 'The origins of "dependency": choices, confidence or culture?' in 'Defining and Measuring the Underclass' (special issue), *Focus*, 12(1) (University of Wisconsin/Madison Institute for Research on Poverty, 1989), quoted in Dean and Taylor-Gooby, *op. cit.*
46. Dean and Taylor-Gooby, *op. cit.*, p. 47.
47. *The Wresinski Approach: The Poorest – Partners in Democracy* (ATD Fourth World, 1991), p. 43.
48. John Moore, Speech to Conservative Constituency Parties' Association, September 1987.
49. Dean and Taylor-Gooby, *op. cit.*, p. 125.

CHAPTER 5

Organized and Imposed –
Structural Explanations of Poverty

The exclusion of the poor is pervasive and not accidental. It is organised and imposed by powerful institutions which represent the rest of us. (Quoted in *Faith in the City*, p. 360)

Poverty does not develop of its own accord. People do not become poor because they are idle; they become idle because they are poor. (Conraad Boerma, *Rich Man, Poor Man and the Bible*, SCM Press, 1979, p. 15)

> They go about naked, without clothing;
>   hungry, they carry the sheaves;
>   among the olive groves of the wicked they make oil;
> they tread the wine presses, but suffer thirst.
>   (Job 24.10–11)

What is not accepted, and indeed is little mentioned, is that the underclass is integrally a part of a larger economic process and, more importantly, that it serves the living standard and the comfort of the more favoured community. (J. K. Galbraith, *The Culture of Contentment*, Sinclair-Stevenson, 1992, p. 31)

God stands at every time unconditionally and passionately on this side and only on this side: always against the exalted and for the lowly, always against those who have rights and for those from whom they are robbed and taken away. (Karl Barth, *Church Dogmatics*, II, Chap. 1, p. 386)

FROM SOLIDARITY TO SOCIAL DIVISION

The last chapter looked at the way people and governments have sought to explain poverty in terms of individual or family shortcomings or misguided welfare policies which have created dependency and undermined people's capacity to cope. What so many of these explanations lack is a realization of the constraining effects of the circumstances of people's lives. This is not just a matter of shortage of income. It extends to the way the whole warp and weft of society give people differential access to society's goods – education, employment, housing, health and social care. This chapter seeks to outline some of these structural factors and then show how this sort of analysis is consistent with a biblical understanding of poverty and inequality. It looks at poverty as injustice.

In his profoundly disturbing book *Bad Samaritans: First World Ethics and Third World Debt*,[1] Paul Vallely, having journeyed through Africa, wanted to find out what lay behind the scenes of naked and starving children that he encountered. Going later to Asia and Central America also, he 'began to discern common threads in the economic and political difficulties under which poor people laboured all over the world'.[2] He then spent years looking 'into the structures in which those hapless children were trapped, reporting on the activities of the IMF and World Bank and on the direct effects these were having in Asia and in South America, as much as they were in Africa'.[3] Many Christians and others now know about, and deprecate, the dubious basis and consequences of First World–Third World trade and aid arrangements. They accept the validity of the sort of analysis Vallely applies and the conclusions he draws. Yet are we as willing to adopt the same approach to exploring the structures which may trap the teenagers we see begging in our streets or the millions of unemployed or those who are homeless or inadequately housed?

FROM TRIBAL SOLIDARITY TO A DIVIDED SOCIETY

When the Israelites settled in Canaan around 1200 BC, many things changed about their lives, culture and values. Their previous semi-nomadic existence had been based on the tribe. Tribal solidarity was important for immediate survival. Rich and poor existed and there were slaves. But they were members of the family. There was still apparently a sense of social integration – strengthened by Mosaic law – a feeling of a unified people.[4] Poverty was a material circumstance but it was not a disgrace. Poor people were not disparaged. Their dignity was left intact. After the settlement, the Israelites became small independent farmers. They then became rivals. The fortunes of someone with bad land soon declined and he could be forced to sell himself and his family into slavery. Possession of property started to assume a greater significance. People wanted to accumulate wealth. The basic social unit became the family instead of the tribe.

A distinction grew up between those who owned land and the poor. To be poor meant not to have land. The economy which developed was based upon dealing in trade and land. A divide opened up between rich and poor families. Eventually central state control took over from the loose affiliation of tribes. A hereditary monarchy was established, an army formed, a diplomatic service set up.

The social climate changed. The frugal atmosphere of communal life gave place to pomp and ceremony, with palaces and international alliances, in which trade, waging war and making treaties played a significant role. In both Judah and the kingdom of ten tribes . . . there came into being a prosperous aristocracy, which contrasted with an ever-increasing marginal population.[5]

Archaeological excavations have demonstrated increasing disparity in standards of living. In the tenth century BC houses were of similar size and furnishings. Two hundred years later in the same city, neighbourhoods showed marked differences. Fragmentation had set in. Social groups with conflicting interests had developed. Poverty was now a sign of inferiority.

Conraad Boerma points out that the problem did not stem from the poor man's laziness, but from the changed situation. Poverty was directly connected with the structures of social and economic life. Different perspectives on it are evident in Old Testament writings. In contemporary texts – the Pentateuch and the Prophets – the poor man is not seen as the cause of his poverty. It is only in later wisdom literature – deriving from court circles – that blame is attributed to the poor themselves. In that, a continuing theme is that the poor man was despised because his poverty was his own fault. 'Since riches are a blessing, poverty must be a curse. Men bring this curse down on themselves. The book of Job is written as a protest against this theme.'[6] But for those who believed in the covenant, poverty was a violation. Social divisions were the result of injustice.

The structures of injustice today

For the Israelites over those few hundred years, the shift was from a nomadic society to first an agricultural and then a money economy. An upheaval of comparable proportions has taken place over as many decades in advanced industrial – moving to post-industrial – societies. The nineteenth century saw Britain's transformation from an agrarian to an industrial society. By 1900, 10 per cent of land and 75 per cent of the population could be defined as urban. Only about 10 per cent of people worked in agriculture and the proportion today is under 2 per cent. During this century – aided and abetted by the private car – urbanization gave way to suburbanization, with a greater dispersal of people to smaller towns, suburbs and the urban fringe. The distinction between urban and rural became less pronounced. But during the second half of this century, technological, economic and social developments have taken place which are again changing the character of society and which introduce new considerations about the relationships between rich and poor, 'comfortable' and uncomfortable Britain. [7]

It is now estimated that there are in excess of 52 million people – out of 340 million – in the European Union living in poverty, that is, with incomes less than half the average for their member state. More than 17 million are unemployed, nearly half of whom are long term unemployed and with a high rate of youth unemployment. Of course, all these figures are debatable, but they are more likely to be understating the position than exaggerating it. For example, it is estimated that the official unemployment level in Britain of 2.78 million is about one million below the real figure, because it does not pick up certain groups of unemployed people, such as those who no longer receive unemployment benefit but are not eligible for means-tested benefits because their spouse is working; unemployed men over 60; most 16- and 17-year-olds. The financial cost of unemployment to member states in 1993 was about 210 billion ECU. Its cost in terms of human suffering and social waste is incalculable. The second report of the European Observatory reckons that there are 2.6 million homeless people and if those living in unacceptable conditions or temporarily accommodated by relatives or friends are taken into account, that number rises to 10 million or about 3 per cent of the population who have no personal, decent and secure home.

Whilst there may be some resistance in this country to admitting the existence of poverty, this is not the case in the European Union (EU). Statements, programmes and structural funds all testify to recognition that it is a problem endemic throughout the EU. 'Poverty on such a scale is patently unacceptable at the end of the twentieth century when so many of us in Western Europe enjoy such high levels of comfort and prosperity.'[8]

Alongside this acknowledgement there is a changed understanding of the nature of poverty today. It is not something which can be resolved by economic growth alone. We know this, in any case, from experience in Britain over the past fifteen years. Through boom as well as recession the position of people in poverty has if anything worsened, certainly in relative terms and sometimes also in absolute terms. Nor is this poverty merely a matter of individuals and families trying to get by on too low an income or too few resources. Rather, it has many faces. Long-term unemployment, an upsurge in homelessness, urban crises and disorder, growth of inter-racial tension are all expressions of poverty. The mechanisms which bring these about are similarly multi-faceted. They result in processes whereby individuals, groups, neighbourhoods, and sometimes whole regions are shut out of the mainstream of social and economic life. They are denied the opportunities for participation and improving their quality of life.

For this reason, over the past five years the concept of 'social exclusion' has gradually replaced that of poverty at Community level and increasingly also in most member states. It introduces a fresh image. With financial poverty, society is portrayed as a line from top to bottom with people ranged along it according to their income. Social exclusion brings out the idea of social distance within society – in and out, rather than up and down – between those who are thoroughly active and integrated in the centre and those who are being forced to the margins. This is a more dynamic concept 'highlighting the effects of the way society is developing and the concomitant risk of social disintegration and . . . affirming that, for both the persons concerned and society itself, this is a process of change and not a set of fixed and static situations'.[9]

Exclusion suggests forces at work which are beyond the control and responsibility of the individual. It is a far cry from attributing poverty to personal deficiencies. Instead, it recognizes that the structures and processes of a society go a long way to shaping the situation, opportunities and standard of life open to specific groups and individuals.

The origins of exclusion lie in the structures of a society's economy. In December 1992, the Commission adopted a Communication, *Towards a Europe of Solidarity – Intensifying the Fight Against Social Exclusion and Fostering Integration*.[10] It set out the challenge that social exclusion represents for the member states and the Community. It underlined the impact of structural changes and indicated that a large percentage of the population is increasingly vulnerable to social exclusion mainly because of changes in employment and in family life. A variety of groups whose social and economic integration is fragile, experience periods of, or recurrent, poverty with resulting disruption to their social ties.

The roots of exclusion – analysis and experience

What then are the causes of social exclusion? As poverty has mounted over recent years in the UK, many of us have tended to blame government policies – or even individual politicians – as though they were uniquely culpable. Yet, what we see in this country is mirrored to a greater or lesser extent elsewhere. When people from Ancoats in Manchester and Barcelona met at the Church Action on Poverty Conference in 1993, their experiences were instantly recognizable to one another. As the stories were told, members of each group were exchanging glances and nodding – 'just like here'. The fellow feeling was very evident.

At Pentecost 1992, eight hundred people from 52 countries, representing about five hundred small groups and organizations, met in Strasbourg for a People's Parliament. It was an event which was part of a process under the title *Kairos Europa*. Adopting the Greek word *kairos* meaning 'moment of truth, a decisive time' – to echo the South African and South American Kairos Documents – two symbolic moments were referred to here. One was the completion of the European Single Market in 1992. The other was the five-hundredth anniversary of Columbus. The *Kairos* process aimed to make room for those whose voices are not heard at present in decision-making bodies and who go largely unnoticed elsewhere.

> Europe is at the crossroads. The effects of 500 years of European colonial history are scandalous. People are becoming poor and marginalised in Europe and in the 'Third World'. They are losing their jobs and social status ... We say 'The time has come to stand up for a just, ecological and open Europe, based on solidarity. We cannot leave Europe to the business people.'[11]

As in Manchester, so it was in Strasbourg. Hearing similar stories from different places enabled people to start to see their personal experiences in a wider context, to appreciate more that what they were experiencing was the impact of wider economic forces and policy trends.

The significant themes of *Kairos Europa* were like a checklist of the causes of social exclusion. First, the process of economic internationalization is both quickening and deepening. Nation states have to be players on a global stage nowadays. The very motivation behind the EU of establishing a larger trading bloc is a response to this situation not a cause of it. International money markets and multi-national companies have assumed much greater power. There is growing competition not only between companies, but between regions and nations to establish themselves as favoured industrial and commercial locations. Social exclusion is the flip side of the drive towards economic competitiveness.

In 1994 in *The Empty Raincoat*,[12] Charles Handy looked back on the views he had expressed in a book he published five years earlier, in which he had discussed the way that work was being reshaped and the effect this might have on people's lives.[13] Much of his prognosis had come to pass in the intervening period, but in a way that had dented his earlier optimism about how institutions might cope. As a result – though speaking from a very different perspective and experience from that of the *Kairos* participants – he also talks of disappointment with capitalism.

> Capitalism has not proved as flexible as it was supposed to be. Governments have not been all-wise or far-seeing. Life is a struggle for many and a puzzle for most. What is happening in our mature societies is much more fundamental, confusing and distressing than I had expected ... Part of the confusion stems from our pursuit of efficiency and economic growth, in the conviction that these are the necessary ingredients of progress. In the pursuit of these goals, we can be tempted to forget that

it is we, individual men and women, who should be the measure of all things, not made to measure for something else.[14]

A 1992 study for the European Commission looking at European cities showed the differential impact of economic restructuring and the unevenness of economic growth and decline in cities across Europe.[15] The clearest evidence came from urban labour markets. The major trend during the 1980s was growing unemployment. But urban unemployment levels, as well as shadowing respective national rates, reflected the continued magnetic appeal of metropolitan areas for mobile labour so that rates, in many major cities were up to twice the national averages. In some urban neighbourhoods and within particular groups figures were often set at a much higher level. Youth unemployment will remain a key issue for many areas throughout the 1990s.

> I come from the former East Germany and lost my job two years ago. In all, over 50 per cent of people in my town have no work. The official statistics are all lies. I was shocked to meet many unemployed people here. So they exist in Western Europe too![16]

The old core industrial area of Europe has been worst affected by the restructuring of traditional manufacturing industries. Not only have there been absolute falls in job opportunities, but new and different skills are demanded. The labour market has changed drastically. Between 1979 and 1993 in the UK the percentage of employment accounted for by all production and construction industries fell from 41.4 per cent to 26.9 per cent. Service sector employment now accounts for 73 per cent of all employment. This has also altered the type of employment, the balance of full and part time and the balance of jobs for men and women. Most badly hit have been the skilled, semi-skilled, unskilled full-time manual jobs hitherto occupied by men. Jobs in manufacturing have tended to become more specialized, highly skilled but non-manual. Some service sector employment – such as in the financial sector – is highly skilled and well rewarded, though not necessarily very secure as the 1991/2 recession showed. However, many others in retail, leisure and personal services are unskilled, part-time, low-paid and short-term. Between March and September 1993, there was a 94,000 growth in jobs in Britain. However this net figure obscures the fact that full-time jobs fell by 96,000 in this period while part-time jobs grew by 190,000. The same trends are occurring elsewhere. A two-track labour market has developed.

Marginal labour market groups are often concentrated in their own areas of cities, physically as well as economically segregated from the mainstream. This tendency is driven by market developments but also supported by public policies. High- and low-income communities develop. Often adjacent to city centres or on the periphery of towns and cities, the latter tend to get caught in a vicious spiral of decline. The absence of spending power deters potential investors and drives existing businesses out, so that there is very poor quality consumer services and often a low standard of social housing and public amenity. Whilst housing tenures and conditions vary across Europe depending upon the tradition of state involvement in housing markets, there has been a general trend towards reduced social housing expenditure by member states during the 1980s and 1990s which has exacerbated housing problems.

> When Jesus was born, his family could not find shelter. That was 2000 years ago and we have still not done our homework . . . we have been gathering stories from Naples, from Brussels, from Paris, from Manchester. Everywhere in Europe, homelessness is on the increase and the quality of housing for the poor is decreasing. Many live in ghettos, which the authorities then neglect, because there are no votes there. Miserable housing leads to an atmosphere of violence and fear and then to racism.[17]

On the other hand, city centre developments have often resulted in the twin processes of gentrification and displacement. Public policies supporting private sector development have led to an upsurge in office accommodation and upmarket residential and retail provision, forcing out lower income residents. London Docklands is an example of a central city development which has had negative as well as positive spin-off. In Liverpool, the waterfront was transformed while physical decay and economic marginalization still prevailed in surrounding neighbourhoods. At the same time as Frankfurt has flourished as a financial centre, low-income groups have been displaced to outer areas with inadequate social facilities and higher travel-to-work costs. The development of Brussels as the EU centre has been accompanied by an uprooting of some communities to make way for roads and offices and increasing slicing up of the city into spatially divided quarters. These are just a few of the numerous examples that could be given. Areas become increasingly segregated and socially monochrome and the seeds of social division are sown.

In some metropolitan centres, the position has been magnified by population loss. Liverpool's population has halved since 1945 and fell by 12.5 per cent in the decade 1981–91. In part this has resulted from the slum clearance policies of the 1950s and 1960s when people were moved to peripheral estates often outside the city boundaries. However, there has also been more selective migration. Some of the more affluent moved house to the suburbs beyond the city boundary. Others who moved further away were the more mobile physically and economically who could market their skills elsewhere. Thus the city had a shrinking income base with the left-behind ageing population comprising a higher proportion of those who were more dependent on the public purse in some way – whether for benefits or services. Yet at the same time, the infrastructure still had to be maintained and service levels upheld. They were left behind in more than one sense as the city tried to break out of economic decline. Unemployment is higher and is longer term than in the country as a whole.

Some groups are affected more than others. For Europe's ethnic minority communities, general problems arising from pressures towards exclusion are compounded by personal and institutionalized racism. Originally drawn by the promise of employment at a time of national labour shortages, ethnic minority groups came largely to the larger cities and subsequent generations have remained. So, for example, 40 per cent of France's ethnic minority population lives in the Paris metropolitan region with most of the rest in Lyon or Marseilles. In the Netherlands, 60 per cent live in the four largest cities where they constitute up to 30 per cent of city populations. In all these situations, ethnic minority groups are more likely to be trapped in unemployment or unskilled jobs and in the worst housing. In Britain, the average unemployment rate for black people in the late 1980s was 32 per cent compared with 13 per cent for whites. As disparities grew, there were also increasing tensions during the 1980s continuing into the 1990s expressed in rioting, racist incidents and the growth of racist political parties.

Varieties of capitalism

> The new conservatives would have us believe that all the measures introduced over the past 100 years to provide social cover were in fact anti-economic aberrations; they would ask us to accept that the industrialised nations must now become jungles of dog-eat-dog competition and naked greed if they are to be fit for the twenty first century. No sector will be spared, and no-one will be 'nannied' in this harsh new world. Incredibly, there is almost no argument over this assertion! It has somehow already taken root and displaced 'passe' notions of solidarity and social justice.[18]

People from Eastern Europe at *Kairos Europa* were coming to terms with the fact that some of the promises of Western capitalism which fuelled the overthrow of communism proved hollow ones. Of course, the free-market economy is very good at delivering certain things, but it notably fails in others and lets down some sections of the population. At the beginning of the 1990s, Michel Albert, a French economist and President of Assurances Generales de France, wrote a book about different models of capitalism. He saw capitalism as having gone through three main phases. From the end of the eighteenth century, it grew up to counter the power of the state. The state became subordinate to the rule of law and 'above all the prerogatives of the state were rolled back as market forces began to prevail'.[19] It was an age of exploitation and hardship for the working class.

By the end of the nineteenth century, capitalism started to be disciplined by the state. From then on and throughout a large part of this century, reforms were enacted to regulate capitalism, control its excesses and arbitrary operation and offset the hardships it induced. However, the state began to be seen as a deadweight. The 1990s, according to Albert, ushered in a phase of 'capitalism instead of the state'. It was initiated by the election of Margaret Thatcher in 1979 and blossomed with Ronald Reagan's election as US President in 1980. But it took a decade to realize that these events were more than routine changes of government.

> This time, a whole new ideology of capitalism had come to power. Its essential features . . . can be summed up in a few words: market is good, the state is bad; social welfare provision, once a sign of progress, is blamed for encouraging laziness; taxation, once an indispensable means for reconciling economic development and social justice, is accused (not without reason) of discouraging talent and initiative.[20]

There has been a parallel development recently. Much of Albert's book is taken up with distinguishing between the neo-American model of capitalism, which also holds sway in Britain, and the Rhine model practised in Germany, Northern Europe and Japan. The former is based upon individual achievement and short-term profits. The latter relies more upon collective achievement and social consensus to build long-term success. Albert sees the Rhine model as superior in economic and social terms.

> The Austrian economist summed it up in a famous metaphor: it is only because they have brakes that cars can go faster. And so it is with capitalism. Because the authorities and the citizenry set certain limits and intervene to correct certain faults in the machinery of market forces, capitalism can be made to perform more efficiently.[21]

However, ironically, just at a time when the defects of the neo-American model are being exposed, countries which have hitherto followed the Rhine model are moving nearer to the 'superficial glitter of its casino economy'.[22] This is demonstrated by a number of trends. There is a shift away from the ideal of equality which made social consensus so important. In Japan for example, conspicuous and flamboyant consumerism is escalating amongst some – land owners, property developers and stockbrokers – while for the majority the old goal of home ownership becomes less a dream than a mirage. Traditional values are rapidly being eroded. Events in Sweden provide another example. The priority which had been given there to the protection of collective interests is being superseded as, on the one hand, social protection budgets decline and, on the other, individuals are taking more personal advantage of the system and abuses are becoming more widespread.

In business, firms in countries which have hitherto operated the Rhine model are being sucked into the greater short-termism by the deregulation and globalization of finance.

> . . . the American example has proven too strong even for the sober German financiers to resist; it is as if an order of monks had woken up one day to find that their austere chapel had been turned into the Crazy Horse Saloon. In Frankfurt, as in Tokyo, finance is plotting its revenge.[23]

Albert poses this as a contest between the American hare and the Rhine tortoise. The message seems to be that the hare might well run itself into the ground and the tortoise win the race – on long-term economic viability and social justice grounds – but if no one notices or upholds the result, the tortoise may not survive to race again. Money will have triumphed. Individualism will have triumphed.

INTERRELATIONSHIPS AND INTERDEPENDENCE

Some of the themes in this chapter will be taken up again later in the book, but perhaps enough has been said to indicate the interrelated strands which make up our social and economic framework. It is multi-layered – government legislation and policies or absence of policies, the activities of multinational corporations, the consequences of technological advance, through to local planning and housing management and company employment practices and again through to individual decisions about how we vote and where we live or shop or send our children to school. Priorities, values and actions in all these spheres and at all these levels interweave to make up the social fabric of the country. They go a long way to determining life chances.

It was a deliberate decision to widen the discussion beyond Britain in this chapter. This was partly to show that trends that have been evident here are also occurring elsewhere. Some developments are transnational – the world is becoming smaller and there is no possibility, even if we wanted to, of metaphorically pulling up our drawbridge to shut out wider influences. The

Christian Aid study showed that although people are now seeing more links between the UK and the economies of developing countries in terms of trade, there is less realization of the extent to which UK problems are replicated in other developed countries.[24] This suggests that there is also little understanding of international trends and pressures resulting from the operation of the global economy. Even where people do see structural problems to do with poverty and unemployment, they tend to focus on local causes rather than wider systemic ones.

Another aim of extending the range of the discussion was to indicate that government policy is not the whole story. For the people from Britain who attended *Kairos Europa*, the discovery of common problems and experiences lessened the tendency to blame a specific government for everything. Of course, governments are significant and their actions can ease or exacerbate problems such as unemployment, yet here were these same problems occurring in France, Germany, Spain and elsewhere, without benefit of Mrs Thatcher! The solutions, therefore, also have to be more complex than a change of government.

> The Lord builds up Jerusalem;
>   he gathers the outcasts of Israel.
> He heals the brokenhearted,
>   and binds up their wounds,
>
> The Lord lifts up the downtrodden,
>   he casts the wicked to the ground.
>   (Ps 147.2–3 and 6)

To recognize that poverty is a consequence of the way society is organized and run is also to acknowledge our interdependence. We cannot escape either our mutual reliance or our mutual responsibility. Another reason for looking at the European debate on social exclusion is that the concepts and language of exclusion and solidarity resonate strongly with the message of the prophets and the Gospels. Exclusion suggests that someone or something is doing the excluding. It makes a definite connection between rich and poor, the included and the excluded. It is not a passive state. It is not self-generated. Rather it has the same sense of active forces at work as in the biblical idea of the outcast. Barriers have been erected – physical, economic, social or psychological – to keep certain people out.

Active steps have been taken – whether knowingly or deliberately or not – to bring about and perpetuate a state of estrangement. But they have been supported by apathetic, negligent or ignorant *in*activity. There is no neutral ground here, no way of opting out, no hiding place for Christians wanting to escape the political implications of the gospel.

Any preaching of the gospel that tries to remain neutral with regard to issues that deeply affect the lives of people, like the issue of the rich and the poor, is in fact taking sides. It is taking sides with the *status quo*, even if that is not its intention, because its neutrality prevents change.[25]

In the Old Testament, the prophets clearly invoke God's justice as demanding special care for those with least power. 'Central to the religious consciousness of the prophets are the *anawim*, the poor of God, the little ones ostracised by others in the community.'[26] The Israelites' experience of captivity, exile and foreign control brought a deeper understanding of suffering and dispossession. The later chapters of Isaiah speak of God's kingdom being one of justice, compassion and mutuality rather than oppression and manipulation. They contain a confession of national wickedness. It is not just personal sins that are taken on by the Suffering Servant, but the plight of the nation. And Isaiah contrasts worldly power which is exercised through domination with God's power which is exercised through love.

Jesus was to die as one of the poor and outcast, precisely because his teaching and his life were contrary to the accepted values of his day. His good news to the poor inevitably had implications for others too. It would upset the *status quo*. So he was silenced by being put to death. But the Church carried forward his message. In Acts, we are told,

> no-one said that any of the things which he possessed was his own, but they had everything in common ... There was not a needy person among them, for as many as were possessors of land or houses sold them, and brought the proceeds of what was sold and laid it at the apostles' feet; and distribution was made to each as had any need. (Acts 4.32 and 34–35)

Luke, the author of Acts, clearly felt 'the need to remind his readers of this response of the earliest Christians to the radical challenge offered by Jesus to the accepted views and structures of the society of the day'.[27] It was an experiment based on the false assumption that the Second Coming was imminent, but that same challenge has remained within the Christian tradition ever since.

Promoting the common good

Catholic social teaching over the last one hundred years or so has reiterated themes on the social dimension of Christ's teaching.[28] For example, the idea of the common good is underlined. The human person achieves his or her potential as a member of society. Individuals and groups therefore have to set their own interests in the context of the good of all. But also governments and other institutions have to safeguard and promote the common good as well as the good of society's constituent parts. The right to private property has to be seen in relation to God's gift of the earth to all humanity.

> Whatever the forms of ownership may be, as adapted to the legitimate institutions of people according to diverse and changeable circumstances, attention must always be paid to the universal purpose for which created goods are meant. In using them, therefore, people should regard their lawful possessions not merely as their own but also as common property in the sense that they should accrue to the benefit not only of themselves but of others.[29]

The relationship between capital and labour is another theme. 'Catholic social teaching has consistently opposed the concentration of ownership and control of the means of production in the hands of those who invest money, while those who invest skills and labour are excluded.'[30]

It was with reference to industrial relations that Pope John XXIII introduced the concept of solidarity.[31] Vatican II took it up and since then it has often been used to summarize the idea of the mutual obligations attached to social justice. It is the natural extension of the second great commandment, lifting the injunction to love your neighbour as yourself (Mark 12.31) from the individual to the social plane. Solidarity according to Pope John Paul II is 'a firm and persevering determination to commit oneself to the common good; that is to say, to the good of all and each individual, because we are all really responsible for all'.[32] It applies on every level of human behaviour from personal to international relations. It entails regarding

> the other – whether a person, a people or a nation – not just as some kind of instrument . . . to be exploited at low cost and then discarded when no longer useful, but as our neighbour, helper, to be made a sharer, on a par with ourselves, in the banquet of life to which all are equally invited by God.[33]

Today, the application of the principle of solidarity needs to be thought through in terms of our changed economic and social structures.

Relevant to the divine–human encounter

Another strand of Christian social thought has directly addressed the relationship between Christianity and capitalism. Tawney looked at the rise of capitalism and addressed the seeming inability of Christian theology to get to grips with economic processes and develop a critique of the outworking of the capitalist system.[34] Later the foundation of the welfare state by the post-war Labour Government led V. A. Demant to assume the end of capitalism was near.[35] He saw the new order as promising much greater conformity with Christian principles. By the 1970s, it had become clear that any announcements of the death of capitalism were premature. R. H. Preston began then a fresh attempt to appraise its strengths as well as its weaknesses.[36]

In *Christianity and the Market*, John Atherton examined three traditions of Christian social thinking: the conservative, the radical, and the liberal.[37] Tawney and Demant stand in the radical tradition, repudiating capitalism. It is where Ken Leech stands today. Atherton profiles Ulrich Duchrow, the German theologian who was also one of the main moving spirits behind *Kairos Europa*, as one of the most outspoken contemporary critics of the global market economy.[38] Preston is in the liberal tradition as was William Temple.

William Temple is unusual in this list in so far as he was a senior member of the Church establishment. He was used to bishops being taken to task by politicians for 'interfering' in matters that did not concern them.[39] Some of today's bishops would no doubt sympathize with him. But he argued strongly against the possibility of compartmentalizing religion or of treating politics and economics as though they were self-contained, autonomous systems.

> We all recognise that in fact the exploitation of the poor, especially of workhouse children, in the early days of power-factories was an abomination not to be excused by any economic advantage thereby secured; but we fail to recognise that such an admission in a particular instance carries with it the principle that economics are properly subject to a non-economic criterion.[40]

Temple rejected *laissez-faire* capitalism on the grounds that it was based on a principle of selfishness, if not hatred. For him, economic management should seek wider social goals. His approach was along four lines:

- *The claims of sympathy for those who suffer.* The three main causes of suffering that he identified were bad housing, malnutrition and unemployment.
- *The educational influence of the social and economic system.* 'The social order at once expresses the sense of values active in the minds of citizens and tends to reproduce the same sense of values in each new generation.'[41]
- *The moral challenge to the existing system.* 'The charge against our social system is one of injustice. The banner so familiar in earlier unemployed or socialist processions – "Damn your charity; we want justice" vividly exposes the situation as it was seen by its critics . . . Why should some be in the position to dispense and others to need that kind of charity?'[42]

• *The duty of conformity to the 'Natural Order'* in which is to be found the purpose of God. 'If what has true value as a means to an end beyond itself is in fact being sought as an end in itself, the Church must rebuke this dislocation of the structure of life and if possible point out the way to recovery. It is bound to "interfere" because it is by vocation the agent of God's purpose, outside the scope of which no human interest or activity can fall.'[43]

Atherton also highlights the contribution of J. Philip Wogaman, the American Christian social ethicist. He quotes Wogaman as saying that economics, like politics, is an 'inescapable aspect of human existence, with direct relevance to the divine–human encounter'.[44] Wogaman has constructed a typology of economic approaches, evaluating them in terms of social priorities, including adequate production, equity and security, employment and educational opportunity, conservation, and a new world order. It is significant that 'adequate production' is included because the defenders of the free-market economy – those classified by Atherton as in the conservative tradition – frequently accuse its critics of not taking wealth creation sufficiently seriously. For people like Brian Griffiths,[45] for a time an adviser to Margaret Thatcher, and for Michael Novak[46] in the United States, market economies are superior both for their efficiency and their underpinning of human freedoms. This latter proposition has already been challenged in the discussion of equality in Chapter 3.

Critical theology: between loneliness and alignment

If particular strands of Church teaching have retained an understanding of the social roots of poverty and inequality, so different schools of theology, also influenced by social scientific thought, have come to question the individualism which has permeated other aspects of Christian thought. Political theology, for example, has recognized that theology has to be embedded in both faith and life, in both theory and social practice. Orthodoxy is correspondingly turned into *orthopraxis*. It locates theology in a particular historical reality. It is not that political theology wants to support particular political systems or make political questions central to its concerns. Rather it is designating 'the field, the *milieu*, the environment and the medium in which Christian theology should be articulated today'.[47]

One of its functions is to provide alternative explanations of that reality. A topic common to both sociology and theology is that of human 'boundedness'.[48] In sociology this refers first to the straitjacket which external structures place around an individual – points of social control extending from face-to-face interactions to remote megastructures that affect the person in 'abstract and barely comprehensible ways'.[49] Society, in other words, is experienced as an objective reality. But the individual also has a subjective experience of society 'whereby the "objective" structures "out there" are internalised within consciousness'.[50] To examine either aspect threatens the taken-for-granted quality of society, so that debunking or critique of the *status quo* has been a persistent theme.

Theology can provide an ideological justification for the structure of social life as it is, obscuring the domination of one group by another, providing a false consciousness. In other words, it can allow us to believe what it is convenient for us to believe. Political theology aims to demythologize and deprivatize theology. According to Metz, it 'seeks to make contemporary theologians aware that a trial is pending between the eschatological message of Jesus and the socio-political reality'.[51]

Similar themes are taken up by Jürgen Moltmann.

> The psychological hermeneutics of life in the situation of the crucified God came up against a limit where psychological suffering becomes the suffering of society and suffering in society, and it is determined by that. It therefore remains incomplete, if it is not supplemented by a corresponding political hermeneutics.[52]

'Responsible theology', he says elsewhere, 'can no longer self-forgetfully screen out its own social and political reality as the old metaphysical and personalistic theologies did.'[53]

To that extent, he is agreeing with Edward Said's definition of the role of the intellectual:

> Politics is everywhere; there can be no escape into pure art and thought or, for that matter, into the realm of disinterested objectivity or transcendental theory. Intellectuals are of their time, herded along by the mass politics of representations embodied by the information or media industry, capable of resisting those only by disputing the images, official narratives, justifications of power circulated by an increasingly powerful media – and not only media, but whole trends of thought that maintain the *status quo*, keep things within an acceptable and sanctioned perspective on actuality – by providing what Mills calls unmaskings or alternative versions in which, to the best of one's ability, the intellectual tries to tell the truth. This is far from an easy task: the intellectual always stands between loneliness and alignment.[54]

Like Said's intellectual, the theologian should be one 'whose place it is to raise embarrassing questions, to confront orthodoxy and dogma (rather than to produce them), to be someone who cannot easily be co-opted by governments or corporations, and whose *raison d'être* is to represent all those people and issues who are routinely forgotten or swept under the rug'.[55]

A question of liberation

Liberation theology also puts forward a radically different sort of theology. 'The theology of liberation presupposes the liberation of theology,' says Alistair Kee who goes on to say, 'until theology ceases to identify with the values, interests and goals of those who benefit from structural injustice, then theology can have nothing to contribute to the liberation movement.'[56]

Liberation theology originated in Latin America in countries where even after decolonization, the dominance of richer nations persisted, and within which a tiny minority grew wealthy while the mass of people starved. The emergence of an exploited class provided the mainspring for the theme of liberation and for a reading of history which led to the politicization of the traditional Christian concern for the poor. Insofar as the existence of the poor is 'not socially innocent or politically neutral',[57] but comes about as a by-product of the economic system, the need is not for relief but the construction of a new social order.

Set as it is against centuries of advance in which humankind has shown its capacity to transform the world, the position of the poor and oppressed is the more bitter because the benefits have been appropriated by a minority at the expense of the many. This happened within national economies in the first industrial revolution. In the second, there has been a progressive displacement of human labour by technological advance. Division of labour is now being played out on an international stage. Economic colonialism perpetuates the dependence thought to have been shed with the ending of colonial rule. Poverty is accompanied by powerlessness and hopelessness for those on the margins of the main economic life of the country. Transformation, then, requires both a change of society and a change of nature. More than a new awareness of the meaning of economic and political action, it entails a new kind of authentic personhood. The route to this transformation is solidarity with the poor.

Other forms of liberation theology also begin from two basic assumptions. The first is that a theological understanding of the human condition must include cultural, economic and social perspectives. It must be rooted in a given history, time and place. It must, in other words, be contextual. However, secondly, theology traditionally purported to be a-contextual – to have universal application – though in reality it reflected the existing power structures of its cultural milieu. Thus, writing in America in the 1970s, James Cone said, 'The task of theology is to show what the changeless gospel means in each new situation.'[58] But at a time in the United States when black people were generally awakening to their enslaved condition, theology was found to be silent about their situation. 'Consequently there has been no sharp confrontation of the gospel and white racism.'[59] Even black theologians had tended to accept a Christianity shaped by the dominant cultural ethos. They had received without dissent the definition of problems advanced in white terms.

Feminist theologians would similarly argue that life has been defined in male terms. They would agree with a definition of power given by a black American talking about the struggles of black Americans to go beyond the achievement of civil rights to gain positions of influence in their society: 'Power is the ability to define reality and get other people to respond to that definition as if it were their own.' What feminist theologians are seeking is to 'include in' – not to exclude – the real situation and experiences of women and to allow these to shape our theological understanding. 'Not only is man not the normative human being, but likewise a male God is not the normative God.'[60]

A new agenda for theology in Britain

> There remains a romantic spirituality of the Third World poor and their theologians that, in many ways seems like a linear descendent of the Victorian hero worship of missionaries and their converts.[61]

Christians in Britain cannot appropriate Third-World liberation theology. The context from which it has developed is very different from the British one. To take it 'off the shelf' as a model for our situation is at best escapist, at worst a trivialization of experience here. It avoids the unpleasant necessity of facing the dark side of our own reality. To borrow other people's strategies would be 'the product of a vicarious Church that believes it can speak for the poor while being distant from them, and which believes itself able to accompany the poor without confronting the levels of conflict and moral ambiguity that is their daily lot'.[62]

Nevertheless, there are lessons to be learnt. One is the imperative of doing theology in the context of our own society – our political and economic changes – and to do it with those people who are the main victims of these changes. A serious theological exercise from the perspective of the poor and excluded will inevitably entail unmasking the ideology which legitimates the *status quo*. It will ask 'naive' questions about why things are as they are – in the Church and in society. And it will say that 'there is a better way'.

The next section moves on to looking at the arenas of people's lives in which they encounter poverty: the family, work and unemployment, the neighbourhood. It will start to raise the issues which are the stuff of contextual theology.

NOTES

1. Paul Vallely, *Bad Samaritans: First World Ethics and Third World Debt* (London: Hodder and Stoughton, 1990).
2. *Ibid.*, p. 3.
3. *Ibid.*, p. 75.
4. Conraad Boerma, *Rich Man, Poor Man and the Bible* (London: SCM Press, 1979), chapter 2.
5. *Ibid.*, p. 19.
6. *Ibid.*, p. 24.
7. David Sheppard, Dimbleby Lecture, BBC, 1984.
8. Padraig Flynn, European Commissioner for Employment, Industrial Relations and Social Affairs (DG V) in his opening address to the Commission of the European Communities Conference 'Combating Social Exclusion: A Challenge for the 1990s', Copenhagen, 3–4 June 1993.
9. *Medium-Term Action Programme to Combat Exclusion and Promote Solidarity: A New Programme to Support and Stimulate Innovation (1994–1999) and Report on the Implementation of the Community Programme for the Social and Economic Integration of the Least Privileged Groups (1989–1994)*, Commission of the European Communities, COM (93) 435 final, Brussels, 22 September 1993.
10. *Towards a Europe of Solidarity – Intensifying the Fight Against Social Exclusion and Fostering Integration*, COM (92) 542 final, 23 December 1992.
11. *Kairos Europa:* A report of the People's Parliament, Strasbourg, 5–10 June 1992.
12. Charles Handy, *The Empty Raincoat: Making Sense of the Future* (London: Hutchinson, 1994).
13. Charles Handy, *The Age of Unreason* (Business Books Ltd., 1989).
14. Handy, *The Empty Raincoat*, p. 1.
15. European Institute for Urban Affairs, Liverpool John Moores University, *Urbanisation and the Functions of Cities in the European Community*, Commission of the European Communities Directorate-General for Regional Policies, Regional Development Studies 4, Luxembourg, 1992.
16. *Kairos Europa*, Heinz Ludwig, Magdeburg.
17. *Ibid.*, Dara Molloy, Inismore.
18. Michel Albert, *Capitalism against Capitalism*, Whurr Publishers, 1993 (first published in France 1991), p. 256.
19. *Ibid.*, p. 252.
20. *Ibid.*, pp. 253–4.
21. *Ibid.*, p. 167.
22. *Ibid.*, p. 169.
23. *Ibid.*, p. 180.
24. Liz Spencer and Dawn Snape, *The Gospel, the Poor and the Churches*, a research study conducted for Christian Aid by Social Community Planning Research (Christian Aid, 1994).
25. Albert Nolan, *God in South Africa: The Challenge of the Gospel* (London: Catholic Institute for International Relations, 1988), pp. 13–14.
26. Australian Catholic Bishops' Conference, *Common Wealth for the Common Good: A Statement on the Distribution of Wealth in Australia* (Collins Dove, 1992), p. 5.
27. *Ibid.*, p. 12.
28. See for example: Pope Leo XIII, *Rerum Novarum* (On the Condition of the Working Class) 1891; Pope John XXIII, *Mater et Magistra* (Christianity and Social Progress), 1961; Second Vatican Council, *Lumen Gentium*, the Dogmatic Constitution of the Church, and *Gaudium et Spes*, Pastoral Constitution on the Church in the Modern World, in W. M. Abbott SJ (ed.) *The Documents of Vatican II* (London: Geoffrey Chapman, 1965); Pope John Paul II, *Laborem Exercens* (On Human Labour), 1981 and *Sollicitudo Rei Socialis* (On Social Concerns), 1987; *Economic Justice for All*, Pastoral Letter of the US Bishops on Catholic Social Teaching and the US Economy, 1986.
29. *Gaudium et Spes*, paragraph 69.
30. *Common Wealth for Common Good*, p. 22.
31. *Mater et Magistra*.
32. *Sollicitudo Rei Socialis*, paragraph 38.
33. *Ibid.*, paragraph 39.
34. R. H. Tawney, *Religion and the Rise of Capitalism* (London: John Murray, 1926).
35. V. A. Demant, *Religion and the Decline of Capitalism* (London: Faber and Faber, 1952).
36. See, for example, R. H. Preston, *Religion and the Persistence of Capitalism* (London: SCM Press, 1979) and *Religion and the Ambiguities of Capitalism* (London: SCM Press, 1991).
37. John Atherton, *Christianity and the Market: Christian Social Thought for Our Times* (London: SPCK, 1992).

38. Ulrich Duchrow, *Global Economy: A Confessional Issue for the Churches?* (Geneva: World Council of Churches, 1987).

39. 'When a group of Bishops attempted to bring Government, Coal-Owners and Miners together in a solution of the disastrous Coal Strike of 1926, Mr Baldwin, then Prime Minister, asked how the Bishops would like it if he referred to the Iron and Steel Federation the revision of the Athanasian Creed, and this was acclaimed as a legitimate score.' William Temple, *Christianity and the Social Order* (Harmondsworth: Penguin Books, 1942; 3rd edn, London: SCM Press, 1950), p. 9.

40. *Ibid.*, p. 13.

41. *Ibid.*, p. 18.

42. *Ibid.*, p. 19.

43. *Ibid.*, p. 21.

44. J. Philip Wogaman, *Christian Perspectives on Politics* (London: SCM Press, 1988), p. 3.

45. Brian Griffiths, *Morality and the Market Place: Christian Alternatives to Capitalism and Socialism* (London: Hodder and Stoughton, 1982), and *The Creation of Wealth* (London: Hodder and Stoughton, 1984).

46. Michael Novak, *The Spirit of Democratic Capitalism* (American Enterprise Institution/Simon and Schuster, 1982).

47. Jürgen Moltmann, *The Experiment Hope* (London: SCM Press, 1975), p. 102.

48. P. L. Berger and Hansfried Kellner, *Sociology Re-interpreted* (Harmondsworth: Penguin, 1981), p. 92.

49. *Ibid.*, p. 92.

50. *Ibid.*

51. Johannes B. Metz, *Theology of the World* (Burns and Oates, 1969), pp. 113–14.

52. Jürgen Moltmann, *The Crucified God: the Cross of Christ as the Foundation and Criticism of Christian Theology* (London: SCM Press, 1974), p. 317.

53. Moltmann, *The Experiment Hope*, p. 102.

54. Edward Said, Reith Lectures 1993, No. 1.

55. *Ibid.*

56. Alistair Kee, 'Liberation theology', in Alan Richardson and John Bowden (eds), *A New Dictionary of Christian Theology* (London: SCM Press, 1983).

57. Charles Davis, *Theology and Political Society* (Cambridge: Cambridge University Press, 1980), p. 4.

58. James Cone, 'The Gospel of Jesus, Black People and Black Power', in Alistair Kee (ed.), *A Reader in Political Theology* (London: SCM Press, 1974), p. 118.

59. *Ibid.*, p. 118.

60. Lavinia Byrne, *Women Before God* (London: SPCK, 1988), p. 30.

61. Ian Linden, 'Models and Myths', in *Poverty Network* (Church Action on Poverty, Autumn 1988), p. 7.

62. *Ibid.*

PART III

The Experience of Poverty – Exclusion and Expectations

Poverty is not difficult to define. Poverty is a state of want or deprivation that gravely interferes with someone's life. Those who want to work but can't; those who want to feed their families adequately but can't; those who want to clothe themselves and their children decently but can't; those who want to live in habitable housing conditions but can't; those who want to educate themselves or their children but can't; those whose lives are made smaller by lack of money. These people are poor. They're poor. That's what they are. (Robert Wilson and Donovan Wylie, *The Dispossessed*, Picador, 1992, p. 7)

A factory closes its doors, casual workers are laid off, management is 'thinned out' – unemployment looms. A woman works a 50 hour week doing two jobs to scrape together a living. A lone mother struggles on benefit to meet the costs of her child – the only employment on offer would barely pay for her childcare. A man, prematurely retired because of chronic sickness, lives on invalidity pension which fails to cover the costs of his disability and his ordinary needs. *All these are instances of poverty*. (Carey Oppenheim, *Poverty the Facts*, revised and updated edition, CPAG, 1993, p. 54 [italics in the original])

THIS SECTION looks at where poverty is found, the situations which give rise to it and the many ways in which it affects people's lives. Poverty is a spatial problem. There are parts of all cities, towns and rural areas which have not shared in the fruits of the country's economic growth. Poverty is an occupational problem as labour-market changes have reduced the chances of many either of finding work at all or gaining employment which will afford them a decent living. It is a social problem. There are sections of the community – specific social groups – who are more at risk of poverty than others. It is a personal and psychological problem affecting people's health in all senses of the word.

CHAPTER **6**

Jerusalem or Scar City?

Seek the welfare of the city . . . pray to the Lord on its behalf, for in its welfare you will find your welfare. (Jer 29.7)

> *Scar city* is the brief: the null slogan
> that underwrites the ad men
> who've put up huge billboards
> by the side of the expressway,
> screening off the derelict houses
> and patches of wasteground from view.
>
> Near the industrial district, half
> a street's worth of wire fence
> surrounds a building site: trenches
> and wooden crosses in the mud.
> The contractor's logo on a red sign
> declares the enterprise: MEND-A-CITY.
> (Joel Lane, 'Saving Face')

> When the Stranger says: 'What is the meaning of this city?
> Do you huddle close together because you love each other?'
> What will you answer? 'We all dwell together
> To make money from each other'? or 'This is a community'?
> (T. S. Eliot, Choruses from 'The Rock')

Under such mounting pressure as the people of the inner city have had to endure, social values take on a new reality and the delusion of individualism is exposed for the sham it is. (Margaret Simey, *Government by Consent: The Principle and Practice of Accountability in Local Government*, Bedford Square Press, 1985, p. 44)

THE GEOGRAPHY OF POVERTY

There is a geography – distinctive regional patterns – of poverty and wealth. Although the recession of the early 1990s particularly affected the South-east, it was not enough to alter the deep regional divide. Any number of poverty indicators – the proportion on income support, receiving free school meals, low gross weekly incomes, low car ownership – give a consistent picture of regional disparity. Within England, the North and North-west fare worst; East Anglia, the South-east and West do best. Wales, Scotland and Northern Ireland all compare badly with England as a whole, matching or not even attaining the levels of the worst English regions. The main losers in the 1980s were parts of the largest urban areas and former coal-mining areas.[1] The main winners were parts of middle England on the fringes of a greater 'South-east' region, plus some mixed urban–rural localities in Northern England and North-east Scotland. Poverty is more widespread in areas with a narrow industrial base in long-term decline. Its incidence is greater in larger cities and its localized severity is more evident in large metropolitan areas in northern Britain and in inner London.

Cities of dreams or nightmares?

> The future of humanity lies in the city and qualities of urban living in the 21st century will define the qualities of civilisation itself. Judging by the present state of British cities, future generations will find civilisation a very unkindly configuration.[2]

By the year 2000 there could be up to 500 cities in the world with over a million people. Yet, in this country at least, we still seem unable to come to terms with urban living. Cities can represent life at its most civilized, creative and exciting or at its most horrendous, crippling and oppressive. Cities have always had problems. They have attracted displaced people from elsewhere. They housed often dirty and unsightly industries. Their high population density brought social and environmental problems. But the root of current problems has been the shift in the nature of Britain's economic base. Some cities have come close to losing their economic rationale. There has been a massive loss of jobs in manufacturing – over a million were lost in the inner areas of Britain's six largest urban areas between 1951 and 1981. The compensating growth in the service sector did not necessarily occur in the same places nor on the same scale. Most service sector employment growth was in small and medium sized towns, with the inner areas of large cities losing these jobs also. Unemployment has had a very varied impact both between regions and within them. Vast tracts of vacant and derelict urban land, some so contaminated that reclamation is too difficult and expensive to be worth carrying out, provide physical indicators of a malfunctioning urban economy.

Regeneration presents enormous challenges to cities and their key players. All want to diversify their economic base and redefine their identities. As part of this, they put a lot of effort into renewing the city centre. However, there are limits to what can be achieved given their constrained resources. In many cities, too, the local authority boundaries have been drawn so as to exclude large suburban areas in the conurbation. So they may be unable to harness the wealth of the whole region to the regeneration task, even though these suburban residents are also dependent upon the city for their own income and well-being.

We have developed two-speed cities. Some neighbourhoods have become *relatively* poorer as service and commercial sectors have grown and city centres 'regenerated' with glitzy shopping malls and leisure complexes. 'Britain's most squalid urban areas are now oases of hopelessness sandwiched between the nine-to-five affluence of the regenerated centre and the defensive prosperity of the suburbs beyond.'[3] *Absolute* poverty in many areas has also increased. 'The physical fabric has continued to deteriorate and many people who are able to leave have done so, either to follow the jobs or to avoid the stigma which becomes attached to deprived neighbourhoods.'[4]

Symptom, warning and symbol

> The inner city is now, and is likely to remain, Britain's most dramatic and intractable social problem ... a microcosm of deprivation, of economic decline and of social disintegration in Britain today. It is not only a particular place on the map, but a symbol and summation of the dark side of a whole society ... [5]

In 1983, Paul Harrison said, 'The state of the inner city in the early 1980s is ... a warning of what much of Britain's urban future may look like unless there is a radical change in policies.'[6] Having just spent four years looking at poverty around the globe, he had turned to looking at it on his doorstep in Hackney because he had come to realize that Britain, too, was 'underdeveloping'. What he saw were events and processes which were not new, but had been brought to a head by the combined pressures of global recession and monetarist policies. Nor were they peculiar to Hackney. They were symptomatic of what was happening in many other areas, and a portent of what would become a more general scenario unless positive action was taken to avert it. Not just a symptom and a warning, the inner city is also a symbol. 'It is the place where all our social ills come together, the place where all our sins are paid for.'[7]

The term 'inner city' is used not just with reference to defined areas. It signifies a quality of urban problems which may be found literally in inner cities but which also characterize outer estates and parts of some small towns. A Conservative MP referred to 'areas ... so weighed down by their disadvantages that they have continued to decline against the national trend.

Their residents have watched from the sidelines as an economic renaissance has unfolded around them in which they have had little part.'[8]

Bombardment chamber

> The inner city is . . . of far more than local interest. It is the bombard-ment chamber where the particles generated and accelerated by the cyclotron of a whole society are smashed into each other. It is therefore a very good place to learn about the destructive forces inherent in that society.[9]

Inner London is the extreme example of a concentration of problems. It contains seven out of the top ten materially most deprived boroughs in England,[10] and has a similarly high level of housing stress. It is very densely populated and there is widespread dereliction, pollution and overcrowding. Problems of transport, schooling, employment and crime are seen here at their most acute. Yet local government is fragmented with no one body having overarching authority. Some neighbourhoods have been sacrificed to commer-cial developments which stand in sharp contrast to nearby streets of shuttered shops, peeling paintwork and littered pavements. Here as in other cities, chain-link fences, security cameras and patrolling guards protect office blocks, retail or residential enclaves, marking their physical and symbolic separation. The problem is less one of lack of investment than misconceived commercial investment in developments which lack any sense of scale or place, empty areas of much of their traditional activity, and alienate local communities. 'Billions and billions of pounds are being spent in transforming our city, our history and our ways of life. Yet most of it does little for the majority of Londoners – except to make the quality of life worse.'[11]

It is also in London that the racial dimension of deprivation is most clearly seen. All over the country, black and Asian people are highly clustered in particular regions and urban areas. This spread originated when many first came to Britain in the immediate post-World War II period. But its persist-ence – the fact that few have joined the drift to the suburbs – implies strong social and economic forces operating to maintain the concentration.

'In London in particular, constantly and increasingly, the problems of the racial minorities expose, and present in magnified forms, problems that are present throughout the capital.'[12] Ken Leech points out that, although most poor people are not black and many black people are not poor, as poverty has grown in Britain as a whole, so have the numbers of black poor. 'The proportion of black poor has increased as black communities in all inner cities have been hard hit by unemployment.'[13] The way that the causes and symptoms of poverty are magnified for black people by racial discrimination will recur in later chapters. Ethnic minorities are marginalized by a double dose of stigma and shoulder the blame for ills that really belong to us all. There are

> varying ways in which the presence of black and Asian people in the UK has been constituted as a threat, shattering national unity, denying white people access to resources, and threatening law, order and social stability. This threat has been used to justify immigration control and, at times, intensify and strengthen policing in inner-city areas.[14]

Although it is clear that economic and social problems are more prevalent in some areas than others, some commentators would argue that the concept of the inner city is a 'fundamentally ideological category'.[15] While often used more innocuously, in Mrs Thatcher's social policy, Suzanne MacGregor sees it as 'part of a move to a more conservative and punitive set of social practices and attitudes'. As a public issue, it represents a constellation of social issues to do with urban decay, deprivation, crime, social disintegration and polarization. But the core issue is urban poverty.

Poverty was redefined as to do with the inner city. This process has, argues MacGregor, involved associating it with crime and violence, decay and backwardness. It is a short step from this sort of association to talking in terms of the pathologies of areas and their residents, to seeing problems as self-generated, and giving an individualist explanation of poverty. This redefinition of poverty in spatial terms also justifies focusing policy responses and targeting public expenditure. 'However, reality intrudes on such constructions, as indicated by the gradual widening of the category "inner city" to refer also to "outer estates" and then to whole cities . . . '[16]

Defending and controlling space was the outward manifestation of the urban unrest of the early 1990s as estates erupted into battlegrounds. Yet 'the riots invited no reply, no conversation, only slogans and stereotypes: "unemployed . . . hooligans . . . single parents . . . " '.[17] The very word 'estate' has now come to evoke lawlessness and all who live there are tarnished by the label even though most residents are victims rather than perpetrators of crime. This is the irony. Ram raiding, 'joy riding', street fighting, drug abuse and the like, may all be screams of pain or non-politicized revolt against a system which has sidelined these young men (it is largely men) and against an economic crisis which has become for them an identity crisis.[18] However, it is their own communities that pay the price, their own parents or partners who suffer the anguish, their own neighbours who have to barricade their shops and houses. And it sometimes feels as if it takes a riot to get the outside world to take any notice. 'What always surprises is how little social disruption there has been during a period of cataclysmic economic and social change: most of the vulnerable do not thieve or beg, but show a daunting ability to come to terms with bleak and jobless environments.'[19]

> The riots of the summer nights of 1981 in Liverpool were our French Revolution. The cracking of breaking glass, the roar of the flames, the beating of the bin lids, dramatised for us the collapse of our way of life. The burning of the Racquets Club symbolised the end of an epoch of merchant autocracy of which it was the product. The power of the explosion of feeling reduced not only the physical environment of our daily lives to rubble. Startled and shocked, we realised that the very structure of our society was crumbling about our ears. That which had seemed so permanently enduring was suddenly revealed to us to be no more than a worm-eaten facade, its authority open to question, its adequacy to meet our needs challenged, its very existence threatened. The riots blasted away the trappings which had concealed from us the desperate deterioration of the democratic way of life on which we had so completely relied. No longer could we evade the reality of what had befallen us.[20]

Flight from cities to a rural idyll?

There is some corner of the English mind that is forever Ambridge.[21]

One solution being attempted to make cities as a whole more liveable is to turn them into urban villages. But people are also running away from cities to 'real' villages, voting with their feet for a life they think will be cleaner, safer, quieter and more 'natural'. The 'complex web of urbanisation'[22] has crept out into the countryside. If it is hard to give a precise spatial definition of the inner city, so it is with rural areas. Here too the label has heavy symbolic overtones, it is overlaid with value judgements, but in this case the connotations are favourable not negative ones. For some it harks back to some supposed golden age of 'real' community life. It is imagined as possessing all those desirable attributes which a city lacks and which have been crowded out of urban living. In other words, it conjures up a quality of life as much as a specific locality.

Yet it is hard nowadays to draw a dividing line between city and country. Of course, there are major contrasts between the extreme forms but equally striking is the extent to which they merge and interact. Thirty years ago, the American sociologist Kingsley Davis wrote,

> One can imagine that cities will cease to grow and may even shrink in size while the population in general continues to multiply. Even this dream, however, would not permanently solve the problem of space. It

would eventually obliterate the distinction between urban and rural, but at the expense of the rural.[23]

The trends revealed in both the 1981 and 1991 Censuses bear out this prediction as do the developments which have accompanied population movement.

International and national factors which have changed life in cities have also impacted on the countryside. Economic changes have affected the mix of activities. Although agriculture is still the dominant rural industry, less than 2 per cent of the country's labour force now work in agriculture. The run-down of the coal industry has hit many villages. On the other hand, the availability of land for expansion and the preference of many companies for green-field sites has meant rural areas having a larger share of manufacturing jobs (at least if a fairly loose definition of rurality is used). New technology is further assisting the growth of some service industries in rural areas. Increasing population in some rural and semi-rural areas is accompanying these more diverse economic activities.

It is a little misleading to refer to the 'rural economy' for there is not one but many rural economies. And they are not all changing at the same rate. What we are seeing most strongly is a growing dichotomy between areas of affluence and accessibility, and areas of remoteness and vulnerability. The former category is no better illustrated than by the M40 corridor in Oxfordshire, where the opening of the motorway has had a dramatic effect on new development – and land prices. At the other extreme are many upland areas and coastal resorts, operating on the margins of economic viability. And within rural areas there are also signs of a growing split between the affluent and the vulnerable.[24]

It is debatable whether a spatial dimension can be given to rural poverty in the same way as urban. The intensity and scale of deprivation make a qualitative difference. Villages are not microcosms of inner cities but, if anything, of the social spread of entire cities and their suburban hinterland. They are not whole concentrations of people vulnerable to poverty. Only some of their members are at risk. Even though about 25 per cent live in poverty and, in the poorest areas, it is nearly 40 per cent,[25] the problem is less obvious. However, rural circumstances influence the impact of wider socio-economic issues. Some of the themes for the Archbishops' Commission on Rural Areas (ACORA) demonstrate the results of changes in their social and economic composition: 'competition for rural housing; the loss of village-based services; the problems and tensions associated with observable differences in wealth . . . '.[26]

In some ways, rural life is now less centred upon local employment, less organized around its occupational structure. Part of the population growth reflects the counter-urban trend as city dwellers move out to, or acquire second homes, in rural areas, seeking something suburbia cannot provide for them but bringing many urban attitudes, values and expectations with them. According to Lord Shuttleworth, Chairman of the Rural Development Commission, Nimbys (not in my back yard) have been joined by Notes (not over there either).[27] Having retired from the city, bought a holiday home and/or somewhere within commuting distance, Notes are very resistant to change. 'Local people are there to be tolerated and humoured; any attempts to create jobs or build homes for their children are to be discouraged. A Big Brother mentality has descended over the once peaceful dales, moors and lakes as Notes have made their presence, and feelings, felt.' Some villages are 'being dragged towards museum status' while in others, villagers can have difficulty in finding somewhere to play football, yet planning permission is given for a golf course.

Some demographic changes in the countryside match those elsewhere – smaller families and households, more lone parents, more living alone. And it is an ageing population, living longer. But there are some characteristics specific to the countryside reflecting the movement in and out. 'Incomers out-compete locals for housing, and subsequently influence the availability of jobs and services.'[28] 'They tend to be wealthier, to be overwhelmingly middle class, to have attitudes and mores that are different from the indigenous population.'[29] The consequent pressure on housing combined with the shortage of jobs pushes traffic in the other direction as local people uproot in search of more promising conditions elsewhere.

Low income is one side of the picture. Jobs are being shed in traditional rural industries such as farming and forestry. Unemployment figures for rural areas are misleading, because people have left to look for work elsewhere. Those who remain are often low paid. Any jobs in new sectors tend to be either high tech ones taken by suitably qualified people migrating into the area, or more unskilled, low paid, insecure ones, for example in tourism, more open to women than men. Contrary to the myth that what rural workers may lack in wage levels, they make up for in fringe benefits, a study in the early 1980s found this to be largely untrue.[30] Poverty is also proportionately a greater problem amongst the elderly, especially elderly women, partly reflecting the knock-on effects of their fragile incomes earlier on.

The other side of the picture is a high-cost economy. Poorer households are comparatively worse off because basic items of household expenditure cost more. Weekly shopping bills were higher than the national average even while there was still a village shop. Ironically, the better-off could go elsewhere to shop around more cheaply. The loss of village shops and service outlets is costly to poorer households in money and isolation. Options become very limited especially for those without cars. Transport is needed for access to distant public and commercial services, yet deregulation 'has not delivered the transport revolution in rural areas that was promised'.[31]

'In the owner-occupied sector, rural housing has somehow moved from being "shelter" to an "investment" and with the on-going repopulation of many areas of rural Britain by people with city money, the result has been a considerable increase in the "affordability gap".'[32] Directly, this mainly hits middle-income locals because those on low incomes could never afford to buy, but the distortion of the housing market has wider repercussions. There has always been a smaller proportion of council housing in rural areas. Often, too, the type of properties did not match housing need, with little for families with children. However, that stock has been considerably eroded following the Right to Buy legislation. The private rented sector used to be larger, much of it tied housing. This is now shrinking as owners capitalize on their assets either by selling their properties or letting them for the holiday trade. With the erosion of public and private rented sectors, there is a major shortage of affordable housing.

Poverty may be less visible in rural areas, but it is there. Changes which originate in decisions, trends and events far away have reshaped country living and have particularly damaged those who are least able to counter or resist them. Here as in cities, we see a vulnerable minority whose voices, if they are raised at all, are drowned out when decisions affecting their communities are being taken.

Multiply deprived

If you want to see how stark the rundown of services can be in a declining area then consider this comparison of Bracknell with the Easterhouse district of Glasgow. Both have a population of around 50,000, but Bracknell has six times more shopping floor-space, 23 post offices to Easterhouse's five, 15 banks compared with one, and eight public libraries to Easterhouse's two.[33]

For the residents of deprived neighbourhoods, the result of this process of decline is a cluster of problems often put under the heading of 'multiple deprivation'. Its features are ones which will emerge in the next two chapters but can be summarized now as including the following:

- very high unemployment levels – probably at least twice the city-wide average and three times the national average;
- low income for those in or out of work because of the loss of jobs and the poor job prospects;

- consequent dependence upon public support systems for those on the margins of the employment market;
- pressure on family life not only from the low income but also the changed pattern of daily living associated with male unemployment or insecure work;
- low qualifications, a lack of basic skills and under-achievement;
- lower health standards whether because of hard and often dirty work, a restricted, low-income diet, or the effects of loss of confidence and general despondency on physical and mental health;
- a sometimes bleak environment with restricted and poor quality neighbourhood facilities for shopping and leisure, and in some cases, public services;
- often also isolated with poor transport links;
- high crime rates and fear of crime;
- being stigmatized and subject to blanket criticisms to the extent that local people themselves can begin to accept these negative judgements.

Even in attempting this analysis, that last point should be a warning against stereotyping or drawing a wholly depressing picture. Many communities remain resilient. Many individuals and families within multiply deprived neighbourhoods lead fulfilling lives, provide a stable loving environment for children and, in innumerable ways, surmount local problems, resisting negative influences. It is not the characteristics of the neighbourhood – inner city, peripheral estate, high rise, low rise, ethnic composition – that are the determinants of its deprivation. Nor are the residents. The central problem remains poverty caused by economic restructuring.

Angles on deprivation

The Metropolitan Borough of Knowsley, one of the Merseyside local authority areas, illustrates the trends and forces which contribute to area deprivation. Created in 1974, it is a collection of individual communities. Apart from one town pre-dating Liverpool, much of the development is post-war, small towns and suburbs planted in the countryside to accommodate housing overspill and industrial expansion from Liverpool. Knowsley is a designated Urban Priority Area and, on a social deprivation index using data from the 1991 Census, ranked as the most deprived in the country.[34]

Knowsley has suffered from national economic restructuring.[35] Having been heavily reliant upon manufacturing industries and, notably, having many branch plants, it was squeezed by the decline in manufacturing, industrial rationalization and by the disinvestment to which branch plants are especially vulnerable. The effects were more severe because in the late 1970s, 90 per cent of employees worked in firms employing more than 200. Major factory closures alone between 1978 and 1989 meant a loss of 13,735 jobs. Overall the number of jobs fell from 68,088 in 1978 to 49,152 in 1987. In the rest of the UK, the decline in traditional industries was partly offset by growth in the service sector, but it was not until the mid-1980s that, while total employment continued to fall, Knowsley began to see some growth in the service sector.

During the 1980s, there was a widening gap between the employed and the unemployed. But, in addition, many of the employed are in low-paid, insecure work and the dearth of worthwhile jobs is a disincentive to training. Such a low-wage, low-cost economy easily goes into a downward spiral. Not much spending power goes back into the local economy so that shopping and leisure facilities decline, then those with secure, higher incomes, who are also more mobile, take themselves or their custom elsewhere, and so the decline goes on.

A profile of Knowsley's population shows a high level of deprivation widespread throughout the borough as measured by unemployment rates, eligibility for free school meals, receipt of housing benefit, car ownership, standards of health, single-parent families, educational attainment. All of these are well documented. Knowsley's disadvantage has been heavily emphasized in order to obtain all possible funding to which it might be entitled. The social problems associated with these levels of deprivation are also well known, if only because they have featured so often in the media. Less often portrayed are the positive qualities and strengths of the borough and its people as expressed, for example, in the extent of practical community action; the commitment of many of the firms and agencies connected with the borough; the track record of the council in bringing resources into Knowsley; the extent of renewal being achieved in the physical environment.

Negative stereotypes have predominated in both (allegedly) factual and fictional presentations of this region. They operate as self-fulfilling prophecies in a number of ways. Outsiders develop exaggerated or inaccurate opinions about the region and are less likely to want to invest or move here when 'an unremittingly bleak picture of Merseyside's performance and prospects' is so frequently painted. There is a depressing effect too on the morale of people within the area because they start to believe the negative things said about them.

Cantril Farm – an estate in decline[36]

In the early 1980s, one of Knowsley Council's housing estates, Cantril Farm was, in the words of the then 'Minister for Merseyside', Michael Heseltine, 'a disaster which looked beyond retrieving'.[37] Costing Knowsley about £1 million a year, the bill was rising all the time. Yet the same problems existed to only a slightly lesser extent on other estates around the borough.

The estate, begun in 1967, was tenanted by people displaced by Liverpool slum clearance. Even at the start, it was less popular than anticipated. Many went unwillingly and criteria for tenant selection did not operate for long.

> People resented having been moved and then resented the lack of facilities. When more provision came, it was below par. For example, the shopping deck never took off commercially or socially. Food prices were excessive and it was cheaper to travel by taxi and shop elsewhere.[38]

The maisonettes and high-rise flats were particularly disliked. Vacancies grew throughout the 1970s and properties were quickly vandalized. The escalating cost of repairs put an additional strain on the council at a time when central government was starting to subject local authorities to tighter spending constraints. By the end of the 1970s, the council began to demolish the most unpopular maisonettes.

Even where traditional houses were adequate in themselves, they were blighted by the poor design and layout of the estate as well as by outstanding repairs. 'It was a planning disaster of catastrophic proportions in relation to the housing type, especially the linked maisonettes, the way the families were deployed and the layout. People got totally lost – they only knew the way to their own homes and to the shops.'[39] The layout had not lived up to the idealized conception in the local authority brochure which prefigured a pleasant, safe and green environment. The segregation of pedestrians and vehicles was inconvenient and increased the danger to pedestrians. Footpaths did not necessarily follow the routes people required and the maze of alleyways gave scope for various types of anti-social or criminal behaviour. Underpasses were dirty, unsafe and sometimes flooded or otherwise blocked so that, for example, children could not get to school. Where there were no pavements, people walked on the roads and a number of fatal accidents resulted. The amount of unused land around housing areas reduced people's privacy, attracted rubbish and generally added to the sense of bleakness if not dereliction.

In the mid to late 1970s, the estate started seriously to slide downhill. By the 1980s, most enquiries to the Citizens Advice Bureau were about major housing repairs. Similarly, the local solicitor found her work dominated by housing and related issues: complaints of roofs in danger of collapse, chronic damp, doors hanging off, rotten windows and other structural faults as well as major vandalism and muggings. By 1982, there were 9,000 repairs outstanding for a total housing stock of just over 3,000. Twenty families a week were moving out. Some people set fire to their houses in order to be re-housed. The council stopped even trying to let about a third of the stock, including the maisonettes and some high-rise flats. One in eight lettings went to homeless families, and nearly two-thirds of tenants had rent arrears. Only 1 per cent of tenants had exercised their right to buy.

As the number of empty properties grew, so the crime rate increased. Morale also broke down. People were fearful and disillusioned. Some would lock themselves into their houses or flats and would certainly avoid leaving them unattended. Schools suffered an enormous amount of vandalism, with one primary school alone having over 200 incidents in one year. With the progressive depopulation of the estate, they were also experiencing falling rolls.

Spiralling decline affected both the self-image of residents and the quality of services and facilities available to them. One symptom of the massive alienation was a copycat riot which occurred in the shopping centre in 1981, mimicking the Toxteth and other disturbances that summer. For the Anglican vicar on the estate, the whole experience was encapsulated by the message written in 15-foot-high letters on a tower block behind the church saying NO EXCUSES.

That description of Cantril Farm is a scenario which will still be familiar to many from estates in different parts of the country. Compare it for example with Heath Town in Wolverhampton:

> Heath Town estate was built in the late sixties. At first people had to be vetted to come and live here, but it soon became a 'deprived inner area'. The reason usually given for the decline is unemployment and neglect by the local authority in doing repairs. Heath Town is now typical of most inner areas in Britain, where life is bleak for the many who live there. Over 80 per cent are on Social Benefit, and nearly the same percentage are in rent arrears. In our immediate area there are 1400 properties, of which 230 are empty at present. There are nine tower blocks, some 22 storeys high, and the rest are maisonettes, ranging from two to six floors. Increasingly, Heath Town is becoming a dumping ground for people who cannot be housed elsewhere.[40]

Or the following, which describes an estate in Sheffield:

> It is less than a mile from the thriving city centre but this is a place where hardly anyone has money to spare because hardly anyone can find regular work. Of all those able to work, only a fifth of them have jobs, often part-time. All the rest – 76 per cent – are unemployed. Among families with children, it is even worse – 82.3 per cent have no wage earner at all. The jobs which were supposed to trickle down from the new rich of the 1980s never materialised.
>
> Twenty years ago, it was a working-class estate where most people worked and where those who did not were protected by the state. First

the jobs went, draining out of the steel industry and its network of support services. As the money left the pockets of its residents, the local businesses deserted their streets. The high street banks also left, leaving only the TSB behind. Most of the shops went, too. The Studio Seven cinema, one of the working men's clubs, the local authority youth clubs, three post offices, two primary schools – they all fled.[41]

These are the sorts of estates where people may be refused insurance cover. One company allocates certain postcode areas to category R, which means requests must be referred to head office where there is a list of streets or estates in which insurance is not granted. London has the most R-rated areas, followed by Manchester, Liverpool and Bradford.[42] Even when residents can get insurance, premiums are costlier in precisely those areas where house-holders can least afford them.

Cantril Farm became the focus of a high-profile scheme promoted by Michael Heseltine as a trail-blazing model for private sector involvement in urban regeneration. It entailed selling the estate to a private trust to implement a programme of housing development and improvement, to seek greater diversity of tenure, introduce home owners to the estate and thus create a greater social mix. The wish to make a clean break with the past, to symbolize the introduction of a new era and give the residents a chance to slough off the old 'Cannibal Farm' image was expressed by giving the estate a new name, Stockbridge Village. The name change evoked some derision at first. People were not going to be deceived by new wrappings. Real changes would have to take place before they would be convinced. On the one hand, there was cynicism about what change would be effected. Many residents had long memories of past broken promises. On the other, there were fears of gentrification and the displacement of poorer residents.

The Trust was successful in the physical improvement of the estate, though not necessarily more so than the local authority might have been given the same resources. After ten years, a remodelling and refurbishment programme brought transformation, eliminating all the unfit dwellings, achieving a very low vacancy rate, significantly diversified tenure and a high degree of resident satisfaction with the Trust's management.

In these terms, Cantril Farm was fortunate. Its pre-1982 conditions remain on many estates around the country. However, it was clear that the deeper problems of Stockbridge were outside the Trust's remit and beyond its power to solve. Comparing of the 1981 and the 1991 Censuses shows the persistence of high unemployment and low income, and their associated problems. The housing development programme reduced the size of the estate and affected its demography by altering the balance in the size and types of available accommodation so that there were fewer properties for larger families. The demolition of the hard-to-let (hard-to-live-in) housing removed some families with problems who never went back. But, although tenure was diversified, the social mix was not significantly widened. Effectively the Trust created more favourable conditions for public sector housing's traditional constituency to buy their own homes. Similarly the Trust had not been able to remedy the low level of services and facilities on the estate – the narrow range of shops, the lack of a bank or police station, the paucity of provision for children and young people.

The Stockbridge experience provided many lessons, but a key one was that urban renewal needs to be multi-sector and multi-agency. It requires a comprehensive approach. When an area is experiencing the multiplicity of interlocking problems which comprise multiple deprivation, focusing on housing alone is insufficient. However successful it may be in its own terms, its impact will be limited without parallel economic and community development initiatives.

Active resistance and two sorts of common sense

Another part of Knowsley, the town of Kirkby, has also undergone demographic change and a transition from predominantly municipal housing to mixed tenure. Andrew Wilson, a Citizens Advice Bureau (CAB) worker and lay member of the Kirkby Church of England Team, compares the Kirkby of today with that of twenty to thirty years ago.[43] Despite considerable housing improvement, again many of the basic economic and social problems have still not been resolved. But he found there is a marked contrast in the way that residents are reacting. The women have emerged as a force to be reckoned with. Residents are making themselves heard on the management of the estates. They are joining in a range of community initiatives to respond to problems such as homelessness and debt, and to provide worthwhile alternatives to stimulate and use people's talents in the absence of employment.

Elsewhere in Knowsley, community workers for the Children's Society also discovered how people can develop an alternative common sense triumphing over the despair which might have been a more understandable reaction to the very unpromising circumstances.

The Street[44]

Their street had a bad name in that area. They sometimes felt ashamed to live there. The physical state of the street was bad – no adequate garden fences, rat infestation, etc. There were 155 children under the age of ten, but nowhere safe to play. Traffic seemed to have priority over children's safety. There was very little money around, so few families could afford to take their children out of the street for day trips or holidays.

There was a feeling of continuous pressure, to which people some-times responded with violence, family to family, or person to person. The street had some sense of standing together, (if you kick one of us around here we all limp) but it also experienced chronic divisions. A good number of disputes arose because children literally had to fight over play space. The people's experience of 'helping' agencies were uniformly bad. (They don't give us any respect.)

The 'common sense' of the street was that things were bad and that there was no point in doing anything together to change the situation. This commonsense in fact contradicted some of the facts of the street's history. People possessed considerable organizational skills. They had in the past raised funds for, and put on, street parties and outings. They had successfully campaigned for housing improvements. It was as though there were two opposing influences at work. There was the influence of division and despair, represented by one 'common sense', but there was also the influence of unity, hope, and life, represented by the hard evidence of past achievements and also by conversations tinged with possibility. ('Why couldn't we . . . ?' 'If only we could . . . ?') These influences formed an alternative common sense.

WHO OWNS THE STORY?

In addition to describing the conditions in many communities in this country today, this chapter raises the issue of how to tell the story of communities or groups, and in particular how to talk about disadvantage and deprivation. It is a dilemma which arises both in my working life and in my private life. It is one which affects us in Church Action on Poverty and must face anyone who is concerned with campaigning and lobbying with and for particular groups – whether we are seeking to change political policy or fund a project. What stories are we telling? Who is doing the telling? What images are we putting across? If we focus too much upon some aspects of deprivation, are we selling people short, overplaying them as helpless victims, denying the extent to which they triumph over amazingly difficult circumstances? Are we inad-vertently reinforcing stereotypes? Are we talking or using images in a way that allows the listener or viewer to remain detached; reinforces otherness rather than togetherness; appeals for sympathy-at-a-distance rather than understanding and involvement? What follows is a reflection based upon an address I gave at the Annual Service of Industrial Mission in South Yorkshire in 1993.

I remember the poster a few years ago for the Church Urban Fund which showed a couple of urchins – not quite without shoes, but getting on that way. And it said 'this is a scene from the North of England today'. Well, after all, we all know the North is another country! Perhaps if instead it had said, 'this could have been taken within three miles of where you live', people might have thought differently about it, been challenged in a different way, started to think about what connected them with the 'others' being depicted.

Most of my work is concerned with looking at the impact of urban policy of one sort or another. But it is not done just out of academic interest. You quickly learn that there is no such thing as 'telling it how it is'. There are always choices – conscious or not – about what you see and what you say. And often our work is done for clients who may have particular views about the sort of story they want to hear or want to have heard by others. This is not necessarily because they want a whitewash. It may be because they want the positive messages to outweigh the negative ones. They want to start a virtuous circle rather than contribute to a vicious one.

In Merseyside, we have a long history of bad experiences with the media focusing on the downside – strike records, juvenile crime, drug abuse, one parent families – whatever is top of the bill for the day. It may be purveyed through supposedly sharp reporting in the quality papers or through soap operas. But it adds up to the same thing in the end – a picture of somewhere alien that you would not want to move to, where you would not want to bring up your children or invest or move your business to. Some of the things said may be true, but are only half the story, or they may build upon stereotypes or perpetuate an image which is long out of date.

The danger is, that in avoiding going along this road, you get sucked into the world of hype, where the rhetoric bears no relation to reality, where you are so busy playing up the positive that you kid yourself as well as everyone else. The intention may be good – to bring new money into the city, new job opportunities. But while you are thinking about what messages are being conveyed to potential investors, say, you forget those whose stories are being overlooked or even implicitly denied.

Hamburg has more millionaires than any other German city but it also has more people on welfare. Which story do we tell? There is one story to be told about the Merseyside Development Corporation and the difference it has made to the city by regenerating the central dock area in Liverpool. There is quite another to be told about or by people in the neighbourhoods only half a mile away.

A tale of two cities

A few years ago the Merseyside Churches' Ecumenical Department for Social Responsibility held a half-day conference called 'The Good, the Bad and the ?'. A professor gave an account of some of the regeneration schemes and talked about the signs of revival in the area's economy. A parish priest talked about the effects of social security changes and persistent unemployment on his parishioners. Then the theologian Hadden Willmer was asked to make sense of it all. 'I was asked,' he said, 'to say something theological in response to the growing prosperity and continuing poverty in this city. I was asked "neither to disparage the recovering city nor to mask the still devastated city".' He asked 'Is there pressure in this invitation to accept such a state of affairs, the two city theory?'

Certainly, I find there is constant pressure to accept as a truism that if only the recovering city can be got right, then the devastated city too will be restored. Yet we know this is not the case. Trickle down *has* not worked, *does* not work. As someone said, a rising tide does not lift all ships if some are stuck in the mud. But we do not properly face the connections between the two cities. And people can more easily deceive themselves by hiding behind a sense of otherness.

Facing the connections

Beatrix Campbell illustrates this well in her book *Goliath*, which is about the riots that happened on a number of estates from Meadowell to Blackbird Leys in 1991. She says that these tell us something about the country in which we live, 'what people do with their troubles and their anger, who gets hurt and who gets heard'.[45]

But she also points out that, although there have been riots throughout Britain's history, in the popular ideology 'they have been consigned to a rowdy past'.[46] Where there had been exceptions, people coped with them by defining their perpetrators as different.

> There was Belfast and Derry. [But] whatever the Loyalists want to think, the British really believe that Northern Ireland is another country . . . There was Notting Hill in the fifties. But that was black people. There was Grosvenor Square in the sixties, Red Lion Square and Grunwick in the seventies, but that was the reds. There was the Stonehenge rout in the eighties, but they were hippies. There was the poll tax riot in 1990, but that was anarchists. There was Strangeways too, but that was prisoners. Thus was the riot purged from the mainstream of modern Britain. Rioters were others.[47]

As with rioters, so with poor people, unemployed, disabled. Define them as different and it is much easier to cope.

We see this escapism at a national political level. In so many ways, the terms of the debate are illusory. Not only is what is said – say about job opportunities or economic recovery – often far removed from our everyday experience but the words are so dramatically at odds with the actions and outcomes that you need a new dictionary to interpret them – *protecting* the health service, *targeting* benefits, *saving* jobs – what do these mean? There is delusion both in the analysis of the ills of our society and the prescriptions for putting them right. This allows symptoms to be identified as causes and particular groups to be singled out for condemnation and punitive treatment – lone mothers (more so than lone fathers!), foreigners, young offenders, sink estates, benefit claimants, strikers. The vulnerable become scapegoats. Preserving this delusion relies on an equally powerful *self*-delusion, which is that those doing the labelling and scapegoating are immune from responsibility.

Weeping for the city

The prophet Jeremiah has gained, unfairly I think, a reputation as a great whinger. Living around the end of the seventh and the beginning of the sixth century BC, he experienced the last crisis-ridden years of the independent kingdom of Judah. They were turbulent times. Judah had fallen away from the covenant relationship with God; she went through a period of religious nationalism and attempted reformation under King Josiah's 'solemn League and Covenant', then fell away again.

Within twenty-five years of the reformation the power centre had switched from Jerusalem to Babylon and soon afterwards Jerusalem was charred and devastated. For forty years, through these events, Jeremiah proclaims his 'Thus says the Lord' message – and for much of the book we have a sense of the man agonizing over the message. Trying to resist and challenge the religious and political establishment but also suffering doubt and depression. Struggling to deal with this openly and honestly. Isolated and scarred by the hate he aroused in others.

> For thus says the Lord:
> Your hurt is incurable,
>   and your wound is grievous.
> There is none to uphold your cause
>   no medicine for your wound,
>   no healing for you.
> All your lovers have forgotten you;
>   they care nothing for you;
> for I have dealt you the blow of an enemy,
>   the punishment of a merciless foe,
> because your guilt is great,
>   because your sins are flagrant.
> Why do you cry out over your hurt?
>   Your pain is incurable.
> Because your guilt is great,

because your sins are flagrant,
I have done these things to you.
Therefore all who devour you shall be devoured,
and all your foes, every one of them,
shall go into captivity;
those who despoil you shall become a spoil,
and all who prey on you I will make a prey.
For I will restore health to you,
and your wounds I will heal, says the Lord,
because they have called you an outcast:
'It is Zion, for whom no one cares!'
Jeremiah 30.12–17

Jeremiah's whole testimony is one of grief. But his personal grief stems from the public occasion for grief. He is grieving over loss – of his city, his culture and his value system. His sense of sickness stems from the sickness he sees amongst his own people. He is anguished by what he sees. But he is also bewildered by the failure of his contemporaries to see it. Is it a public cover-up or pitiful self-deception? Stupidity or stubbornness? Are they too busy? Have they got too much at stake? Are they too set on particular ideological tramlines to see what is happening?

Apart from the external political events – the rise in the Babylonian empire – Judah had lost her way, in her relation with God and in her social relationships, in care for one another. The story of the people's deliverance was relegated to distant history. Their essential reliance on God was forgotten. What had resulted was increased greed and self-interest, loss of compassion and humanity.

All Jeremiah's grief comes together and is compressed in that thrilling but rather scary poem: 'your hurt is incurable, your wound is grievous . . . there is no healing for you'. There's no mincing words here. No soft soap. No wrapping up the message in some ambiguous economic analysis. And he moves on from a metaphor of sickness to one of betrayal. Judah's allies have melted away because they have seen her unfaithfulness. This is God speaking and he is speaking in judgement.

The theologian Walter Brueggemann in his exposition of this passage asks who are the enemies identified here.[48] He answers:

I submit that the enemies of this poem are the managers of the *status quo* who deceive themselves and others into pretending there is no illness. They are fascinated with statistics. They are skilful at press conferences. They believe their own propaganda. They imagine that God loves rather than judges, that the Babylonian threat will soon disappear, that the economy is almost back to normal, that Judean values will somehow survive, that religion needs to be affirmative, that things will hold together if we all hug each other.

The expression of Jeremiah's sort of grief is treason to them – underselling the country, washing dirty linen, even if you concede it is dirty – in public. They offer superficial solutions to problems which they largely deny. In the earlier words of Jeremiah, 'they say "peace, peace" where there is no peace'.

In contrast, Jeremiah paints a devastating picture of a country that has lost its way and is utterly condemned by God. But then there is a sharp change of direction in the poem. As the depths are plunged – when Judah is called outcast by everyone else – then God is still there at her side. 'I will restore health to you and your wounds I will heal.'

The healing power of grief

Brueggemann says this poem discloses the structure of the gospel. Between the first part of the passage and the second is a great cleft: the breaking point of Judah's mortal sickness and God's utter alienation. What can bridge that divide? It is not just that God loves us no matter what. Rather, movement across the divide comes out of the grief. Only *our* deep participation in God's grief can give newness a chance.

Brueggemann points out that this theme of grief and newness continues in the New Testament. Just as Jeremiah wept over Jerusalem, so did Jesus.[49] He was also in conflict with an established order that was maintaining a facade, denying failure, suppressing grief. Weeping expresses the grief, faces the reality, releases from the grip of death and allows newness.

The theme of grief and newness is taken up again in the Beatitudes (Matt 5.1–12). Here is a description of life in the new Israel. Here is the contrast between present conditions and the future when God's kingdom is fulfilled. But the good news of Jesus is that this is not just a promise for the future but an invitation now. The kingdom is now as well as not yet. It is breaking in on the present.

But what characterizes it is its complete reversal of the world's values. It is not that poverty, hunger, grief and public exclusion guarantee heavenly bliss. Rather that those who recognize their emptiness, who are not distracted by considerations of fame and fortune, status and security, who have not got everything invested in the *status quo* – these will be receptive to the gifts of the new age. Grief – or discontent – with the present world is seeing it, and ourselves, through God's eyes. It signifies an entering into God's perspective, God's vision. It unlocks the way to newness, to a restoration of right relationships, to the fulfilment, consolation and comradeship of God's kingdom. But as we see in the life of Jeremiah, it is not that the one is a prelude to the other. It is an ongoing, integral process with grief and newness interlocked.

Here is another poem, this time a more recent one. It was written by Carol Bialock, an American missionary sister working in Chile and it is given in a book by Sheila Cassidy.[50]

> I built my house by the sea.
> Not on the sands, mind you, not on the shifting sand.
> And I built it of rock.
> A strong house
> by a strong sea.
> And we got well acquainted, the sea and I.
> Good neighbours.
> Not that we spoke much.
> We met in silences,
> respectful keeping our distance
> but looking our thoughts across the fence of sand.
> Always the fence of sand our barrier,
> always the sand between.
> And then one day
> (and I still don't know how it happened)
> The sea came.
> Without warning.
> Without welcome even.
> Not sudden and swift, but a shifting across the sand like wine,
> less like the flow of water than the flow of blood.
> Slow, but flowing like an open wound.
> And I thought of flight, and I thought of drowning, and I thought
>   of death.
> But while I thought the sea crept higher till it reached my door.
> And I knew that there was neither flight nor death nor
>   drowning.
> That when the sea comes calling you stop being good
>   neighbours,
> Well acquainted, friendly from a distance neighbours,
> And you give your house for a coral castle
> And you learn to breathe under water.

Sheila Cassidy says,

> Now the curious thing is that all the time I was in Chile I understood the
> sea in this poem as an image of the presence of God – the way he takes

over our lives. When I showed it to a monk friend, however, he saw the slow advance of the sea as the gradual encroachment of the agony of the world upon one's consciousness. It is only now, ten years on, that I begin to understand what he meant when he said that the great mystery is that the two are really the same.

I think this is saying what Jeremiah was saying and what Jesus was saying – that we *can* be engulfed in the world's discomfiting reality without drowning in blindness, panic or stubbornness. In fact, we can't ignore it. It is the atmosphere we have to live and breathe in. But through Christ's life, death and resurrection we also breathe in new life and can tell our story with assurance and firm hope.

NOTES

1. Anne E. Green, *The Geography of Poverty and Wealth* (Institute for Employment Research, University of Warwick, August 1994).
2. David Harvie, 'Cities of dreams', *Guardian*, 15th October 1993.
3. John Naughton, 'City flyers', *Observer*, 7 August 1994.
4. Stephen Thake and Reiner Staubach, *Investing in People – Rescuing Communities from the Margin* (Joseph Rowntree Foundation and Anglo-German Foundation for the Study of Industrial Society, 1993), p. 17.
5. Paul Harrison, *Inside the Inner City* (Harmondsworth: Penguin, 1983), p. 21.
6. *Ibid.*, p. 25.
7. *Ibid.*, p. 21.
8. David Trippier, *New Life for Inner Cities* (Conservative Political Centre, February 1989).
9. Harrison, *op. cit.*, p. 25.
10. Ray Forrest and David Gordon, *People and Places: A Census Atlas of England* (School for Advanced Urban Studies, Bristol University in association with Bristol Statistical Monitoring Unit, 1993).
11. Drew Stevenson, 'A Vision for London', an address given to the Association of London Authorities Conference, 19 March 1990 and printed in *Christian Action Journal*, Autumn 1990.
12. Kenneth Leech, *Race, Class and Homelessness in Britain and the USA*, The Founder's Lecture given at the Catholic Housing Aid Society, 22 June 1993 (London: CHAS, 1993), p. 5.
13. *Ibid.*
14. Rob Atkinson and Graham Moon, *Urban Policy in Britain: The City, the State and the Market* (London: Macmillan, 1994), p. 251.
15. Suzanne MacGregor, 'The inner-city battlefield: Politics, ideology and social relations', in Suzanne MacGregor and Ben Pimlott (eds), *Tackling the Inner Cities – the 1980s Reviewed, Prospects for the 1990s* (Oxford: Clarendon Paperbacks, 1991), p. 64.
16. *Ibid.*, p. 65.
17. Beatrix Campbell, *Goliath: Britain's Dangerous Places* (London: Methuen, 1993), p. 302.
18. *Ibid.*, pp. 322ff.
19. Brian Robson, 'At the bottom of the heap', *Guardian*, 15 June 1994.
20. Margaret Simey, *Government by Consent: The Principles and Practice of Accountability in Local Government* (Bedford Square Press, 1985), p. 1.
21. David White, 'The Village Life', *New Society*, 26 September 1974.
22. David Harvie, *op. cit.*
23. Kingsley Davis, 'The urbanisation of the human population', in *Cities* (Scientific American/Penguin Books, 1967), p. 32.
24. *Countrywork: A New Review of Rural Economic, Training and Employment Initiatives* (Action with Communities in Rural England and The Planning Exchange, 1990), p. 4.
25. Professor Paul Cloke, report for DoE and Rural Development Commission, 1994.

26. *Faith in the Countryside*, Report of the Archbishops' Commission on Rural Areas (London: Churchman Publishing, 1990), p. 30.
27. Quoted in Chris Blackhurst, 'Notes, the rural taste tyrants', *Observer*, 21 August 1994.
28. Brian McLaughlin, 'Popular images and the reality of deprivation in rural areas', *Christian Action Journal*, Spring 1991, p. 32.
29. *Faith in the Countryside*, p. 30.
30. McLaughlin, *op. cit.*
31. *Ibid.*, p. 31.
32. *Ibid.*, p. 30.
33. John Naughton, 'City flyers', *Observer*, 7 August 1994.
34. Forrest and Gordon, *op. cit.*
35. This section is based upon Hilary Russell, *Towards an Economic Strategy for Knowsley: an Interim Report* (European Institute for Urban Affairs, Liverpool John Moores University, 1993).
36. See Richard Evans and Hilary Russell, *Stockbridge Village: Achievements and Lessons after 10 Years* (University of Liverpool Centre for Urban Studies, 1991).
37. Michael Heseltine, *Where There's a Will* (London: Hutchinson, 1987), p. 174.
38. Quoted in Evans and Russell, *op. cit.*, p. 3.
39. *Ibid.*
40. Margaret Walsh, *Here's Hoping! Heath Town and the Hope Community*, Urban Theology Unit New City Special No.8 (1991), p. 5.
41. Nick Davies, 'Nomad's oasis in a wasteland', *Guardian*, 1 September 1994.
42. Duncan Campbell reporting in the *Guardian*, 25 March 1994.
43. Andrew Wilson, *Beyond the New Jerusalem, Change and Diversity in an Outer Urban Area: Kirkby in the 1990s* (Cross Connections, Merseyside Churches' Urban Institute and European Institute for Urban Affairs, Liverpool John Moores University).
44. Angus Wood, *Pilgrimage in Practice*. Unpublished paper, available from North West Children's Society.
45. Beatrix Campbell, *op. cit.*, p. x.
46. *Ibid.*
47. *Ibid.*, p. xi.
48. Walter Brueggemann, *Hopeful Imagination: Prophetic Voices in Exile* (Philadelphia: Fortress Press, 1986).
49. Luke 19.41ff.
50. Sheila Cassidy, *Sharing the Darkness: The Spirituality of Caring* (London: Darton, Longman and Todd, 1988).

CHAPTER 7

Poverty Earned and Unearned

No man has hired us.
Our life is unwelcome, our death
Unmentioned in *The Times*
(T. S. Eliot, Choruses from 'The Rock')

The Church that largely failed the urban poor in the first industrial revolution will also fail the new 'poor' who will be shaped by equally radical changes unless we seek to understand what is actually going on. (Bob Dew, Introduction to *The End of Work?*, Industrial Mission Association Theology Development Group, 1980)

. . . joblessness snaps the threads of personal relationships and tosses individuals to the margins of society. (Stephen Fineman, *Supporting the Jobless: Doctors, Clergy, Police, Probation Officers*, Tavistock/Routledge, 1990, p. vii)

THE HUMAN NEED FOR WORK

The importance of work figures strongly in the Christian tradition. Adam was to tend the Garden of Eden (Gen 2.15), bringing God's work to fruition. After the Fall, what had been a creative and pleasurable experience amongst 'trees pleasing to the eye and good for food' (2.9) became 'toil' (3.17) amidst 'thorns and thistles' (3.18). However, the idea of work as an opportunity to share in God's activity of creation remained, closely linked with the concept of stewardship of the world's resources. The medieval church saw work as an instrument of spiritual purpose. Work, in tune with the rhythms of nature's cycle and as a means of fulfilling social obligations, contributed to Christian obedience and resignation. Idleness, on the other hand, was spiritually dangerous as was 'business', that is, labour directed solely or primarily to economic ends.

During the Reformation, however, a work ethic emerged which related to the development of capitalism. The Lutheran identification of vocation or calling enabling the individual to fulfil his (as it would have been) duty to God and to his fellows and the Calvinist emphasis on austerity, hard work and thrift could usefully be harnessed to the needs of the Industrial Revolution. 'The engagement of God as the supreme supervisor was a most convenient device; a great part of modern management has been aimed at finding a secular but equally omnipotent equivalent in the worker's own psyche.'[1]

The later secularization of the work ethic began to discriminate further between types of work. For Marx, the need to work was inseparable from the essence of humanity. But capitalism had alienated people from work because the product belonged not to the worker but to the capitalist, and because the profit motive resulted in extended working hours and the division of labour diminished the meaning of work. It had become drudgery rather than fulfilling, creative activity. Industrialization disturbed the natural work rhythms and to that extent became divorced from life within the home. E. F. Schumacher also saw work that is meaningless or boring as a perversion and a sign of a greater concern for goods than for people. William Morris distinguished between useful work which brings body, mind and soul into unity and useless toil.

As Stephen Fineman says, 'We have yet to construct a society in which a job does not provide the major vehicle for achieving personal meaning, status and wealth.'[2] Across very different traditions, work is seen as representing a deep human need. Work is not synonymous with employment. Clearly much employment does not meet the exacting criterion of 'useful work'. Conversely, some unpaid – gift – work, whether within the home or the community better fits the name. Nevertheless, in our sort of society work is largely identified with employment. The need to subsist and the psycho-social needs associated with work are generally regarded as best met within the employment structure. People need employment not only for economic reasons, but also to tie them into society, to occupy them, to give a sense of purpose.[3] William Beveridge recognized this in his comment on unemployment: 'Idleness is not the same as Want, but a separate evil, which men do not escape by having an income. They must also have a chance of rendering useful service and of feeling they are doing so.'[4]

THE CHANGING PATTERN OF EMPLOYMENT

It is important therefore to look at employment opportunities both in terms of people's access to a reasonable income but also their chances of a worthwhile and satisfying occupation. Despite the myth that we live in an egalitarian society, employment opportunities are not evenly distributed. Article 23 of the United Nations Universal Declaration of Human Rights issued in 1948 states: 'Everyone has the right to work, to free choice of employment . . . and to protection against unemployment.' Yet, this right to work, choice and protection does not exist for everyone. We are seeing growing labour market inequality – a widening divide between the employed and unemployed, the skilled and the unskilled. Although much government policy is predicated on the assumption that individuals are equally able to jostle for position or make themselves 'employable', in practice the prospects for many are determined more by the paucity of job opportunities than by factors over which they have personal control.

Although it has other dimensions, the lack of an adequate income, as *Faith in the City* put it, is at the heart of poverty. Unemployment and low-paid employment are key causes of poverty and some people are at much greater risk than others. The distribution of poverty has changed over recent years. It is now the unemployed, the long-term sick and disabled and lone parents who make up the majority of those in poverty. Alongside and overlapping with them are those groups who hover on the margins of the labour market, those for whom unemployment may not be chronic, but who occupy a twilight zone between steady employment and joblessness, in and out of seasonal work, or going from one casual job to another interspersed with periods of unemployment. Amongst pensioners, income patterns and financial security reflect their fortunes during their working lives. Over half have some income from occupational pensions. But those who have been unemployed for long periods, in low-paid or insecure employment or reliant on a partner's income will carry this legacy into old age.

There are a number of ways in which the pattern of employment is changing radically in our society and also affecting the pattern of income distribution. First, there are the effects of industrial rationalization. Three million, mainly male, manufacturing jobs have disappeared since 1979. Labour-intensive 'smoke-stack' industries such as coal, steel and shipbuilding have declined. Technological development has reduced the need for unskilled and semi-skilled labour. But also the newly industrialized countries, especially in South East Asia, are competing for the same jobs and the same markets.[5] This has had a disproportionate impact on the lower paid, because it is unskilled and semi-skilled labour that can most easily be supplied in lower-wage countries. Industries whose labour costs are a high proportion of their total costs can enhance their competitiveness by moving their operations elsewhere.

As well as reducing the number of jobs, this competition has kept payment levels low. Another change over recent years has been the relative increase in rates for skilled workers and decrease for unskilled workers. Wages at the lower end of the market have gone down in real terms as well as relatively. 'The collapse in labour market opportunities at the lower end of the skill distribution has been so drastic that some men can no longer provide for themselves through employment.'[6] Movements in earnings as well as the effects of benefit and taxation policies have reversed the trend of the 1950s through most of the 1970s towards a narrower income gap between rich and poor.

> The job situation down here is dire. A friend of ours, retired at 60, is desperate for some kind of work. He got work, 3 days a week, chopping up salad, and checking vegetables on a conveyor belt. The floor of the factory is washed with hydrochloric acid mixture several times a day for food hygiene reasons. For this he was paid £2.50 an hour, for a twelve-hour day with two twenty-minute breaks. After three days of this he could not stop coughing because of the fumes from the hydrochloric acid solution, and his family insisted on his leaving the job. Apparently people are collected for this job from all over the county. Incidentally, the workers had Christmas Day only off. Dickensian conditions indeed. Nothing like the flexible market is there! One of this firm's customers is a well known High Street store who pride themselves on treating *their* employees well – or did so.[7]

Another significant trend altering the profile of the workforce has been the growing number of jobs for women. Thirty years ago, under a third of the working population were women and it was only just over 40 per cent at the end of the 1970s. At the end of 1993, 10.53 million women had jobs compared with 10.85 million men. If recent growth rates continue, there will soon be more women with jobs than men. In Europe as a whole, whereas the number of men in employment has fallen by a million over the past quarter of a century, the number of women in jobs has risen by 13 million. Women have been entirely responsible for employment growth over the past two decades. This trend is set to continue. A Department of Employment study of the jobs outlook up to the year 2006 suggested that the labour force will increase by 1.5 million people, but expected women to make up almost 90 per cent of the increase.[8]

While the jobs lost have been full-time, traditionally male ones, mainly in manufacturing, most of the new jobs have been part-time. Nearly 30 per cent of employees now work part-time and 80 per cent of these are women, but amongst both men and women more are working part-time. National overall unemployment figures veil the significance of these changes. When the rate was 10.3 per cent in February 1993, male unemployment was 13.2 per cent as against only 5.4 per cent for women. Also when unemployment rates appear to go down, the loss of full-time jobs is disguised. Yet, in 1992 only 40.5 per cent of UK households were headed by a full-time earner, compared with 49 per cent ten years before. As a result, more families are in poverty with the numbers in receipt of one or more means tested benefit having risen from 7.9 per cent in 1979 to 28.2 per cent in 1991.

EARNING THEIR POVERTY

The expansion of service sector work has favoured the growth of part-time work and opportunities for women in areas such as clerical and secretarial, health, retail, leisure, in which pay is comparatively low and there are 'flexible' working conditions. As new jobs are created or as full-time staff leave, the posts go to part-time staff. Of course, there is a demand for part-time work which can be more easily accommodated with family responsibilities. On the other hand, the desirability of working fewer hours outside the home (in addition to all those worked inside) may be offset by not earning enough for a decent living. There still seems to be a deeply ingrained assumption that women work for pin money and to 'get them out of the house'. If this premise is accepted, it matters less if their pay is low because it is only a top-up to the family budget. The irony is that the women in low-paid jobs are more likely to be those whose earnings are an essential or the sole component of the household income.

Women earn less than men, not only in terms of pay but also in occupational benefits and in terms of the hours they work in paid employment and in unpaid domestic work. The pay gap is wider in Britain than in most European Union states. Despite years of equal pay legislation, women in full-time work still earn only two-thirds of men's average wages and the part-time rates lag even further behind. Deregulating the labour market by, for example, abolishing the Wages Councils, makes the position worse – for millions of low-paid workers, but especially for women because 80 per cent of the jobs covered by Wages Councils are done by women.

Very low pay rates can also mean that women (as well as men) are trapped in unemployment. They cannot afford to forego a steady weekly income on benefit and replace it with a very low earned income in a job which is insecure, which may be short-lived and which may entail extra expenses such as travel, especially when there is so much hassle around the transfer between employment and social security.

Women looking for work, but not eligible for unemployment benefit, are not included amongst the registered unemployed. When a trade union commissioned a survey to shed light on the missing thousands,[9] using 1991 Census data, it found that only 65 out of every 100 unemployed women were on the register. This meant the undercounting of women's unemployment amounted to 400,000. Another case of being invisible.

JOB INSECURITY

The National Association of Citizens Advice Bureaux (NACAB) produced a report in 1993 on job insecurity.[10] Recession brought the bureaux an increased volume of employment-related enquiries so that employment problems had become the third largest category after consumer/debt problems and social security. A large number of clients spoke of employers unilaterally changing their terms and conditions, in particular, cutting pay and changing the number of hours to be worked. Individuals were frequently helpless to oppose such changes, either because they had no written statement of their terms and conditions in the first place, or because they feared dismissal. There is no employment protection against unfair dismissal for full-time workers until they have two years' continuous service. Those working 8–16 hours require five years' service and those working less than eight hours never qualify.

Full-time hours may be hugely increased without overtime pay. Shifts may be extended with no extra pay, effectively reducing the hourly rate. Or earnings can be reduced by a cut in hours, sometimes to enable the employer to engage a young person who could be paid at a lower rate. People may also be required to work at different times, for example, supermarkets insisting that they work on Sundays.[11] The most common form of reduction in pay was a cut in the basic pay, but it could also take the form of abandoning overtime pay or shift allowances, or docking pay during sickness.

> A CAB in South Wales reports a client who had his contract changed eleven times. He had already lost his lunch and tea breaks, and his employer then wanted him to change to night shifts. The employee was told that if he did not accept the change, his day job would 'disappear'.[12]

Merseyside Trade Union Community and Unemployed Resource Centre conducted one of its regular JobCentre surveys in June 1994. The majority of jobs were hourly paid indicating part-time work. One-fifth did not stipulate the number of hours or the rate of pay, leaving vulnerable people open to exploitation. A further 20 per cent gave earnings below the National Insurance threshold of £57 so that employees would lose out on all contributory benefits, including Unemployment, Invalidity, Maternity, Sickness Benefits and Statutory Sick Pay. Over 90 per cent of the hourly rates offered fell below the Low Pay Unit's low-pay threshold of £5.51 per hour (1993–4), which is two-thirds of male median full-time earnings for a 37.5 hour week and over 93 per cent were below the European Decency Threshold of £5.75 per hour. As the report says, 'low rates of pay reinforce the weakness of the Liverpool labour market with people having less disposable income to spend on goods and services. This in turn reduces local job creation potential.'[13]

The abolition of Wages Councils in 1993 – after the publication of the NACAB report – has adversely affected pay in a number of low-pay sectors of employment such as shops, hotels, catering, clothing manufacture and hairdressing. Wages Councils covered about 2.5 million workers, about a quarter of whom were from ethnic minorities. The Yorkshire Low Pay Unit found that employers had taken advantage of their abolition to freeze the pay of workers who were already some of the country's lowest earners and to offer jobs at rates well below the previous minimum. Some rely on employees not realizing that slashing their pay rates would be an illegal breach of contract. Young people who would formerly have graduated to adult rates at 21 years have been left on the lower pay level. Another Low Pay Unit survey found that about one-fifth of jobs advertised in JobCentres which would previously have been covered by Wages Councils paid below the old minimum rates. Prevailing low rates can make it hard for good employers to sustain decent wages while remaining competitive.

Even quite small cuts can make sufficient difference to disposable income for it to be no longer financially worthwhile working. A cut of 30p per hour would reduce the income of the poorest tenth of the population after taxes and benefits by nearly 7 per cent. Similarly, for people employed on a casual basis – for example by supermarkets – not knowing from one day to another how many hours they will be asked to work, their income can fluctuate wildly and, at the end of the week, often be lower than benefit rates. It is not as though cutting pay has increased the number of jobs on offer. Other studies have shown that, apart from raising the pay of low earners and narrowing the gap between low- and high-paid workers, Wages Councils had created rather than destroyed jobs.

NACAB also found that some groups of employees experience more job insecurity than others. Women are particularly affected because of their predominance in sectors more acutely affected. For example, Citizens Advice Bureaux have received a lot of evidence about deteriorating conditions for care workers in residential and nursing homes, which in turn can upset life for residents.

A CAB in South Wales reports that a client who worked in a local private nursing home discovered that her employers routinely dismissed staff before they completed two years' service. This means two employees were being dismissed every month. Apart from the consequences for employees, the client was concerned about the residents who were upset by the high staff turnover.[14]

Other groups, such as black people, disabled people, lesbians and gay men, are especially vulnerable to unilateral changes in terms and conditions, because of the general discrimination they experience.

A CAB in the West Midlands reports an Afro-Caribbean client who was employed for 15 years by an industrial welding company. During that period his terms and conditions were continually altered, involving reductions in holiday entitlement, withdrawal of health insurance cover, and failure to provide pay rises.

A CAB in Gloucestershire reports a female client who was dismissed after 12 months. One of the reasons stated for dismissal was that she was a woman.

Another CAB in South London reports an Asian client who had been employed for one and a half years. His employer reduced his wages and had not provided a proper pay slip for a year. The client was desperate to keep his job, so would not go to court or to an industrial tribunal.[15]

Another way of changing employment conditions for the worse is for employers to pressurize people to change from employed to self-employed status. This, of course, reduces the employer's obligations and costs and denies the ex-employee various employment rights, such as redundancy pay or unemployment benefit if the 'parent' firm eventually folds, as well as any guarantee of regular income. For employers, sub-contracting increases their flexibility, enabling them to scale down operations more easily in slack trading periods.

A CAB in Wiltshire reports an employer with a VAT debt, who decided to make all his employees self-employed. The employees concerned had between 4 and 25 years' continuous service. Their hours were to be determined by the 'ex-employer', who would also be altering their conditions. The employees were given one weekend to make their decision.[16]

The requirement for local authorities to put various services out to tender – compulsory competitive tendering – has also led to the erosion of employment conditions for some workers. Some have lost their jobs altogether. For others, new contracts have meant cuts in hourly pay, shorter hours and sometimes only temporary contracts.

HOMEWORKING

This is a group of people completely outside the scope of trade union activity, with no political clout, whose voices in the natural run of things would never be heard; which in itself is a form of poverty.[17]

Having 'a little job' which you do at home so that you can be with the children or in when they get home from school sounds attractive and an ideal solution to combining employment with childcare. The reality of most homeworking is far from this cosy picture. In 1988, Leeds Industrial Mission and Yorkshire and Humberside Low Pay Unit invited homeworkers, community workers and local authority officials to join together to found a West Yorkshire Homeworking Group.[18] The group's main purpose was to overcome the isolation of homeworkers and give them support. It also proved a remarkably liberating experience for those homeworkers centrally involved as they discovered unsuspected talents in themselves through running the group, especially as it developed contacts nationally and internationally.

Women undertake homeworking because they are caring for children and they are in financial need. But for ethnic minority women there may be additional reasons. Their cultural tradition may frown on going out to work. They may have language difficulties. They are liable to face racism when applying for jobs or when at work. People from ethnic minorities have commonly worked in areas of the economy such as the clothing industry which have been particularly exposed to international competition. This is a type of work readily adaptable to homeworking and employers have cut costs by subcontracting and casualization.

One of the problems of homeworking is its hiddenness. The workers themselves are hidden. Their contribution to the economy is hidden. The total number of homeworkers in the country is unknown. But research by the West Yorkshire Group suggested there are probably 5,000 to 10,000 in Leeds alone. They found over a hundred types of homeworking – sewing, knitting, parts assembly, vegetable preparation, packing. The Merseyside Homeworking Group and others have found a similarly wide range of activity. West Yorkshire is evidently a major national centre for the Christmas card and cracker industry. Though the homeworkers may not realize it, these products – for which they earned pitiful wages – may often be retailed through household name firms. Some of the Christmas cards for which workers received less than 50p per hour were for a major producer of charity cards.

Homeworkers are at the bottom of the heap for pay yet often have to pay themselves for the purchase and maintenance of their equipment such as sewing machines. The work is invariably paid on piece rates which the West Yorkshire Group found mainly amounted to an hourly rate of just over £1. They are usually bereft of any employment rights and they and their families are unprotected by health and safety legislation. Homes become workplaces. There is no such thing as a 'working day' or 'working week' as they work all hours every day trying to make a living wage.

A homeworking young mother of two from Leicester:

'No matter how many hours I put in, my wages at the end of the week didn't seem to be over £40 or £50, even working at weekends. I know I am a fast overlocker. I carried on working from 7 in the morning till 9 in the evenings. My wages were still the same. After nearly two years hoping things would get better, I quit my job. My son was diagnosed as asthmatic, not surprising really – the dust was everywhere. On the fireplace, on the television, carpets, nets, on your clothes and definitely in your nose. No matter what you sewed, there was dust everywhere.'[19]

UNEMPLOYMENT

Arguments abound about the 'true' rate of unemployment. Twenty-nine changes in the jobless definition used for the Government count are alleged to have reduced the total figure by as much as a million. In the figures for 1993, the official claimant count amounted to 2.81 million. The International Labour Office (ILO) total of 2.9 million included 1.08 million unemployed non-claimants, but it excluded some benefit claimants. Those it excludes are people who combine low, part-time casual earnings with state benefits to make up a living income, those who have given up hope of finding a job even though they would like one, and about half a million other workers classified as inactive, some of whom may be incapable of working but others are simply 'discouraged workers'. Neither the official tally nor the ILO measure counted in the 306,000 people on a variety of Government work-related training schemes. This number might be categorized as hidden unemployment. John Wells, the Cambridge economist,[20] suggested that combining all these separate elements in a realistic way would bring the 1993 figures to around 4 million.

Then we heard the stories behind the statistics from people struggling with unemployment. One told us of her humiliation when signing on; her fear of the regular inquisition-style approach of Benefit Office staff on whether she was doing enough to search for (non-existent) work; of how at nearly sixty years of age she is still expected to attend Re-Start training. She shared with us how this led to depression and anger as she began to realise that her talents were not wanted.[21]

The structural changes in employment through the 1980s reinforced regional differences in the distribution of unemployment. The north was far harder hit by the decline in manufacturing and industrial rationalization and the worsening position of manual workers relative to non-manual is also reflected. The recession in the early 1990s took its toll of service jobs in areas where these had notably increased in the 1980s so that the balance was slightly redressed, but the disparity remains. In May 1994, when the 'claimant count' unemployment rate was 9.4 per cent for the UK as a whole, regional rates varied from 7.2 per cent for East Anglia and 8.5 per cent for the South-west to 10.8 per cent in Greater London, 11.3 per cent in the North and 13.1 per cent in Northern Ireland.

However, there is also variation within regions, even in areas of generally low unemployment. In general, inner-city areas have the highest unemployment, suburbs and small towns tend to have lower rates. When in June 1994 the rate for the North-west was 9.7 per cent, for one part of the region, Cheshire, it was 7.2 per cent whereas for another, Merseyside, it was 13.8 per cent. And so the analysis can go on, with variations between local authority wards and even within them. Unemployment has a corrosive effect on communities as a whole, not only damaging the infrastructure, but lowering morale and producing whole streets where two and three generations in family after family have little or no experience of work.

It is also damaging a whole generation of young people. Around 1 million under 25-year-olds are not in work. They are missing out on this essential stage on the way to maturity and having a stake in society.

THE CASE OF NORTHERN IRELAND

Northern Ireland's unemployment rate is persistently higher than in the UK as a whole. There are other dimensions which make the problem worse. First, there has been a much higher increase in the proportion of the very long-term unemployed (more than two years) and, the longer people are out of work, the more they are at risk of poverty. Second, the two religious communities have quite different experiences of unemployment which is about twice as prevalent amongst Catholics as amongst Protestants. Predictably, explanations conflict about the reasons for the disparity. On one side, it is seen as the outcome of industrial and employment policies affecting the location of industry and the recruitment of workers, further exacerbated by intimidation of Catholics in the workplace. 'Thus, discrimination can be overt or covert: it can be intentional or the legacy of pro-active policies of the past. Whatever form it takes, it persists, remaining the most significant determinant of religious distinctions in the labour market.'[22] A contrary view looks to factors inherent in the Catholic population itself, higher population growth, lower social status, skills shortage and the misfit between where they are and where the jobs are. However, although some 'supply-side' factors may be relevant, such as lower educational qualification, too heavy a reliance on explanatory factors relating to the character of the Catholic population itself suggests self-deception. Laying responsibility at the door of the victimized community allows a blind eye to be turned to the many forms of discrimination.

UNEMPLOYMENT AS A PERSONAL EXPERIENCE

Unemployment is a negative word and it bestows a negative identity. Some people can surmount this, can retain or even build up their confidence, can use a period of unemployment as a positive opportunity. But the odds are against them particularly if weeks without a job stretch into months and then years. They lose their occupational status and 'the means by which the integrity of self-image is maintained'.[23] Someone who lost his job when his pit closed said, 'I never say I'm unemployed. I always say I'm an unemployed miner.' Official regulations and attitudes are judgemental and restrictive. Getting involved in formal education or voluntary work – not being 'available for work' – can imperil benefits. Public spending cuts have pared down leisure and adult education facilities. Politicians and tabloid newspapers feed social disapproval with stories of scroungers living like lords on benefit.

> Now he isn't even a statistic. He's joined what he calls the army of 'non-workers' on so-called 'dole-plus' – unemployment benefit plus £10 – who are excluded from jobless figures because they attend training schemes, sometimes with a little arm-twisting from officialdom.[24]

The 1980s saw an increasing proportion of people falling into the category of long-term unemployed. Poor labour market opportunities for this group largely explain the extent to which economic recovery or growth leaves unemployment untouched. So far efforts to improve their prospects of reintegration into the labour market have failed and yet policies towards increasing stringency in benefits have still gone ahead as though this can impel them into work.

> 'I was working in a plastics factory that closed 14 years ago – a German firm that has gone back there. I've never worked since. I'm told I'm too old now. I've been active here at the (Unemployed) Centre for the last six years.'
>
> 'I was made redundant 6 years ago when the hospital closed – that was it.'
>
> 'We did a survey of local JobCentres and found there were 29 people for every vacancy. And a lot of them are rubbish jobs, some only paying about £1.80 an hour.'
>
> 'They keep saying "Are you looking for work?" Well, there's no work to look for.'
>
> 'I'm 25 and I've never had a proper job – just been on a few schemes that never lead anywhere.'

'YTS kids are waiting now to go on schemes and it's worse now because they get no dole while they're waiting.'

'Rather than create employment, they tinker with the benefit system – that's not going to solve anything. Unless there is a positive commitment to full employment, messing about with the benefit system isn't going to solve anything.'

'You get that you don't think about the future. Just take things day by day, week by week.'

'You shouldn't be poor because you're unemployed. Just because you're on the dole, your quality of life shouldn't have to sink to rock bottom.'[25]

THE DECLINE OF THE MALE BREADWINNER

. . . joblessness reveals much more than the problems of surviving with little income and no occupational identity. It exposes the deep and unquestioned penetration of employment structures in the individual and social psyche, through which success, solidarity and sanity are defined.[26]

The collapse in unskilled and semi-skilled labour market opportunities has been so drastic that it is unrealistic to expect some men to be able to provide for themselves and their families through employment. This has financial, cultural and personal repercussions. 'Most of the unemployed will tend to go through the confidence-sapping experience of repeated rejection, which undermines the enthusiasm for retraining or relocation where that is a possibility. There will be strains in family relationships and friendships.'[27] The distress of unemployment extends to the rest of the family. For older men especially, losing their role as breadwinner has been a profound culture shock. A man can feel diminished in the eyes of his wife and children. If his wife works, it may relieve the financial problems but heighten other pressures. However, the growth of labour market participation has actually taken place more amongst women with an employed husband. Sixty per cent of them are working compared with only a quarter of ones with husbands out of work. One of the problems is balancing the equation between earnings and benefit eligibility in a way that makes it worthwhile financially to go to work. The increase in 'no-earner' households reflects the disincentive effects of low pay combined with a high rate of benefit withdrawal.

This major change in the position of men and women in the labour market has fundamental implications. It has upset our no doubt long outdated but still persisting notions of men's work largely built around the cash-nexus and women being involved in 'gift work'. The balance between these two forms has been largely protected by the division of sex-roles. Thus the two issues – what is happening to paid employment and the respective roles and identities of men and women – are deeply intertwined.

RACIAL OVERTONES

> People are looking to you for hope, comfort and reassurance, and you have to keep going. It's constantly hitting your head against a brick wall – but what can I do? Jobs, racism and a history of social deprivation – how can I touch all that?[28]

After World War II, Britain was short of manual labour. Economic expansion shifted employment patterns away from blue-collar towards non-manual, white-collar jobs. People from the Caribbean and the Asian sub-continent were then encouraged to come to Britain to take up the 'abandoned low status jobs'[29] in transport and the NHS and in industries such as textiles and engineering. They were recruited into low-paid, unskilled or semi-skilled jobs, often in positions not covered by trade union agreements, in jobs spurned by white workers because of their low pay and status, poor conditions or unsocial hours.

Manufacturing has seen massive reductions in employment which have disproportionately affected ethnic minority communities. Employment restructuring has similarly hit them especially hard. New industries have tended to reinforce the racial division of labour and are in any case often located outside cities in places where ethnic minorities are less likely to live.

A TUC report, which analysed the Government's Labour Force Survey, showed that in 1993, black and Asian people were seven times more likely to lose their jobs than white workers. Unemployment amongst ethnic minorities was 22 per cent compared with 10 per cent for the rest. Of Afro-Caribbean workers, 28 per cent were unemployed, along with 35 per cent of Asian workers. For those of Bangladeshi origin the rate was 48 per cent. Unemployment has always been higher amongst people from ethnic minorities, but as the overall level of unemployment rose, the gap grew wider. It is wider again amongst young people. Even when people from ethnic minorities are better qualified than white people, they are still more likely to be unemployed. For example, a local survey conducted in Kirklees and Calderdale in 1990 showed that the proportion out of work for over a year was almost identical for white and Asian people, but 75 per cent of the Asians had been unemployed over three years, double the incidence amongst white people.[30]

The Gifford Report quotes a church worker talking about the difficulty in persuading black youths to go on training courses. She illustrated the isolation they can feel if sent to an all-white area. 'Maybe the work will be OK,' said one, 'but what do I do in the lunch hour?'[31]

Racism plays a large part. The Gifford Inquiry concluded that 'the situation with regard to racial discrimination in Liverpool is uniquely horrific'.[32] A study carried out by a Liverpool vicar, John Burgess, suggested that this conclusion needed to be taken very seriously. 'I don't think it means that Liverpool people are uniquely bad. I think it confirms that economic factors play a very basic part in the way racism expresses itself. I think tribalism is a large constituent. When an area is in decline you need to feel superior to someone. When jobs are hard you are going to do all you can for your son or niece.'[33]

The pattern is not uniform. It varies according to the specific minority group, gender and whereabouts in the country people live. But the overall message of a deep racial divide is all too evident. So are its roots in racism and discrimination. Research by the Department of Employment amongst young Asian Muslim women brought out themes which have much wider application.

Respondents referred less to overt manifestations of crude racial abuse and more to the subtle and indirect forms of structural and institutional racism. They spoke of the ways in which racialised stereotypes of Asian communities and women in particular served to undermine their own aspirations, and said they were likely to face more difficulties in finding jobs than their white counterparts because of racial discrimination by employers.[34]

HANDICAPS FOR DISABLED PEOPLE

I live with a constant attitudinal barrier – the assumptions regarding what I am unable to do, rather than what is attainable. But I have learnt through periods of alienation and separation to own my distinctiveness; to begin the process of believing in my heart as well as my head that I am 'fearfully and wonderfully made'.[35]

The fiftieth anniversary of the Disabled Persons (Employment) Act fell in 1994. It had introduced a quota scheme requiring all employers with 20 or more workers to employ 3 per cent registered disabled people. It was a requirement never seriously enforced. The maximum penalty of £100 introduced in 1944 had not been increased since and the total amount paid in fines over the fifty years only amounted to just over £400. It was, in other words, a thoroughly ineffectual tool for increasing employment among people with disabilities. This failure at national level reflects more prevalent attitudes which have consequently closed doors to disabled people which could and should have been open to them.

According to the surveys carried out by the Office of Population Censuses and Surveys (OPCS), only 31 per cent of disabled adults below pension age were in paid employment compared with 69 per cent of the general population. This low rate was not the inevitable outcome of disability, but the product of a combination of barriers within the labour market, not least discrimination. Nearly one-third of those actively looking for work had been doing so for three years or more. A national survey in 1989 showed that almost three times the proportion of people with disabilities had gross weekly earnings below £150. A quarter of the people questioned said they earned less than others doing the same job.

UNEMPLOYMENT AND HEALTH[36]

Unemployment is clearly associated with various measures of ill health. It is not just that the sick are more likely to be unemployed, nor that unemployment disproportionately affects people who are poorer who tend in any case to suffer poorer health, though both of these are true. Unemployment itself causes a deterioration in the health not only of the persons out of work but also their families.

As has been said, employment meets various human needs.[37] It imposes a time structure on the day and provides necessary activity. It brings contacts and shared experiences with people outside the family circle. It bestows status and social identity. Unemployment therefore has consequences in all these areas. Often there is an initial period of denial, followed by pessimism and then hopelessness. It can be likened to bereavement except that the loss of work is one that people are not meant to accept or recover from, so that the stress associated with it is aggravated. There are numerous ways in which unemployment can impair mental health. At the extreme, unemployed men are at over ten times the risk of suicide compared with employed men and the risk increases as the period of unemployment drags out from months to years.

Financial worries combine with a loss of control and choice. People very often feel that they have failed, a feeling which is reinforced by repeated unsuccessful job applications. Employers receive so many applications that frequently they are never even acknowledged, which heightens the sense of powerlessness and invisibility. Their environment is more restricted either because of a lack of means or opportunity. They lose contact with people, old routines and social habits. Time hangs heavy. The more anxious a person is to work, the greater is the resulting distress. Middle-aged people suffer in particular, often having heavy financial commitments and losing their role as provider as well as their place in the working community. The threat of redundancy is also damaging. Conversely, getting a job quickly results in improvement.

The psychological and emotional consequences of unemployment can be mitigated either if someone has lost an unrewarding or stressful job, or they have a strong commitment to some 'work' which is not employment such as political, community or church activity or the acquisition of some new skills, which may fulfil some of the psychological functions of employment.

> The evidence that unemployment kills – particularly the middle aged – now verges on the irrefutable.[38]

In part, an increase in physical ill health is more likely to be associated with the wider effects of poverty on such things as nutrition, heating and housing. However, numerous studies also show higher mortality amongst the hitherto 'well' unemployed and their wives. For example, in a group of men who had had stable employment, its loss was associated with an increased risk of mortality even after the findings had been adjusted to take account of socio-economic variables and health-related behaviour such as smoking. Similarly, studies have shown that mortality amongst the wives of unemployed men was higher than that for other married women even when allowance was made for their own economic activity and housing circumstances. Over three-quarters of the regional variation in the number of prescriptions supplied per head of population is associated with regional differences in levels of unemployment.[39]

UNEMPLOYMENT AND CRIME

> ... perhaps the biggest single intervention affecting the level of crime and criminality might be the ability to offer the next generation of young people better prospects of realistic full-time employment.[40]

Most unemployed people do not commit crimes. Further, it would be very difficult to prove that unemployment *causes* an increase in crime. Nevertheless there is a strong association between crime and unemployment. David Dickinson, a Cambridge economist, found that from 1970, there was approximately a quadruple increase in both official unemployment and recorded crime. There was an especially strong link in the 1980s between unemployment amongst young men of 17–25 years and the number of domestic burglaries. Criminal offences dropped when joblessness fell during the late 1980s' boom, only to soar again in the next recession. For Dickinson, unemployment is probably most potent in eroding the social restraints of those with fewest educational and economic opportunities. Nearly 70 per cent of convicted offenders referred to probation officers for pre-sentence reports in 1993 were unemployed. Unemployed ex-offenders are three times more likely to re-offend than those with jobs. It is a particular problem amongst young people. It seems that the link is not just with joblessness. Rather we should look for reasons in the wider economic, social and cultural context. We have a manifestly consumer society, with private property on show everywhere. 'Luxuries' are advertised as necessities – certainly a must for any self-respecting citizen. Goods have become the measure of the person. And they are supposed to be available to everyone. Although social class is still significant and social background still an important determinant of sub-sequent prospects, nevertheless our social philosophy is a meritocratic one. Theoretically the way to the top is open to anyone. Individual responsibility is the key, so if you do not get on, whose fault is it? Set this ethos alongside deep-seated and long-term unemployment and it becomes a recipe for discontent, both personal dissatisfaction and resentment against society. One option is to find some alternative route to success, and crime can be one such route.

> They've got time on their hands and nothing to do. No money to do things while the TV is telling them to do this and buy that. They're keen to work. They're not thickies, but they've come out of school with little or no qualifications. They become very bored and look for ways of escape. They'll never be able to afford a car on the dole money or Youth Training Scheme money. I'm sure some of them do convince themselves that it's borrowing not stealing.[41]

In a supposedly egalitarian society, social goals are assumed to transcend class lines. The same success symbols are held out to all as though they are equally available to all. Yet social and economic organization is such that access to them varies enormously. When poverty and associated disadvantage are linked with a monetary success as a dominant cultural goal, high rates of criminal behaviour are the normal outcome. Crime may be less in countries where there is more poverty or opportunities are even more restricted, but where expectations are also lower. For Robert Merton, it is the full configuration of poverty, limited opportunities and the assignment of the same cultural goals for all which explains the correlation between poverty and crime. It produces 'victims of this contradiction between the cultural emphasis on pecuniary ambition and social bars to full opportunity'[42] even though these victims may not themselves be fully aware of the structural sources of their thwarted ambitions.

BACKSTOPS TO THE HUMAN CONSEQUENCES

At the end of the 1980s, Stephen Fineman made a study of four groups of professionals – doctors, clergy, police and probation officers – who encounter in the course of their work people who are unemployed and whose unemployment is relevant to their relationship.

> All the people I met saw themselves as back-stops to the human consequences of social forces which they, the helpers, were powerless directly to influence. That left them frustrated and resentful. It was a familiar experience for them to feel remote from the sources, or causes, of the problems they addressed: structural problems in society, such as poverty, homelessness, or poor education, often ended up as their problems. But now the dearth of employment exacerbated many of the longer-standing social deprivations. It also created new ones, such as a generation of youngsters who had never experienced ordinary paid employment, and perhaps never would.[43]

As Fineman tells the story of these different professional worlds, and quotes a range of views from practitioners in each of them, there is an echo of the 'coping mechanisms' described in the Christian Aid research (see Chapter 2). He talks of how they reduce their own feelings of helplessness through 'processes which protect the helper's position and reduces the threat to their customary ways of coping'.[44] They all see people through their professional lens and the experience of those without jobs – the pain, friction, and poverty – will be seen only as well as the lens is focused. There can be dramatic differences in the way in which the unemployed person is defined and labelled. 'An individual's concern about unemployment can be transmuted into a "problem" of internal emotional adjustment, drug taking, drinking, family strife, moral corruption, or anti-social behaviour, depending on the eye of the particular helper.'[45] The professional's power to label can be accepted by the person concerned so that he or she becomes what the professional wants them to be.

None of the professionals Fineman met felt themselves adequately prepared to understand and respond to the individual and social effects of unemployment. For inner-city clergy there are a number of dilemmas. Where does a response to unemployment fit within his or her overall ministry and the life of the parish?

To remain viable a church has somehow to be both *of* current society and *apart* from it. Excessive movements in either direction risk a loss of credibility: to its members if it can offer nothing which addresses their real-life distresses; to its ministers and its members if it departs too far from fundamental religious principles.[46]

To use shorthand, how should the elements of prayer, practical action and protest be combined? Taking on employment schemes, for example, apart from requiring a major commitment of time and energy plus different skills, can in the end seem to involve too many compromises. As Fineman says,

> he now begins seriously to doubt whether he can live with his growing unease about providing for the unemployed through the offices of a government which he considers bears much of the responsibility for bringing about the problem in the first place. He is loathe to participate in what appears a political face-saving operation.[47]

There follow two examples of the ways in which the Church responds to unemployment and economic change. The first was initiated by local churches, the second by Industrial Mission. It is no accident that both stories concern mining communities. They were chosen deliberately to illustrate the different but complementary ways in which Christians try to live out an authentic gospel response to the social realities around them.

Maltby Rainbow Projects[48]

A young cancer sufferer in the South Yorkshire mining township of Maltby in the early 1980s drew rainbows to assert her hope in the face of life-destroying illness. At the same time a small group of Anglicans and Catholics were beginning to meet to focus on the future of their community in the face of recession and massive, potentially destructive, changes in the local economy. The girl's defiant hope became linked in their minds with the promise of God to Noah – that the Lord would never allow his people to be overwhelmed and destroyed – and Maltby Rainbow Projects was born.

We believe our life as Christians can scarcely be authentic if we do not allow the love that God has for all his creation to show through us. That love is not a patronising concern by the wealthy for the poor, it is the solidarity of those who live, work and belong together. Evangelism is the sharing of that love with others so that they may choose to respond to it.

The group owns next to nothing. It has set up and set free: a community programme scheme (latterly employment training), starter workshops for self-employment, a housing co-operative, a credit union, a new housing development, a good neighbour scheme and a register of voluntary organisations. The current project focuses on self-building housing for rent by young unemployed people. To create an empire would be to destroy our freedom to follow wherever the Spirit leads us. To cling to control of each project would be to proclaim an authoritarian gospel . . . .

We believe that in our community God provides the skills and talents necessary for us to begin to free ourselves and those around us from all that enslaves us. This has been borne out by our experiences in the different tasks we have worked on.

We believe that our role as a Christian community organisation is to identify the needs of the area that the gospel tells us should be met and to build alliances to tackle them. We can work alongside statutory and voluntary agencies not as supplicants but as partners. We do not need to relinquish control of our lives to the experts, however benign.

In 6 years we have come far beyond anything we could have imagined at the start; but are well aware that God will have equal challenges still ahead of us.

The Coal Campaign 1992/93[49]

Michael Heseltine, President of the Board of Trade, announced the closure of 31 out of the remaining 50 deep-mine collieries in October 1992. News of some closures was expected, but this was worse than anticipated. It amounted to a loss of 30,000 miners' jobs and over 60 per cent of the industry's capacity. In South Yorkshire 9 of the 12 pits were to cease production.[50] Mining jobs had already halved from the 26,000 in the mid-1980s. The Rt Revd David Lunn, Bishop of Sheffield, with extensive experience of mining communities, issued an immediate press release reacting to the announcement which registered the 'sheer madness' of wasting a precious natural asset. It soon became clear from the overwhelming opposition to the plans in Parliament and in the country that the Government had under-estimated the depth of feeling that the issue evoked. The demise of the coal industry seemed to symbolize not only the squandering of natural resources, but the loss of the country's industrial strength. There was enormous sympathy for the plight of communities entirely founded on coal.

Within a week, 600 congregations in South Yorkshire contributed to a petition seeking an urgent review of the closure plan, and by the time it reached Westminster the petition had 70,000 signatures. 'Few voices were raised against the involvement of the Church in politics.'[51] The announcement of a review allowed time to campaign during the 1992/93 winter, targeting especially the areas with Conservative MPs opposed to the plan. Information was provided for local church leaders to use in their lobbying. The Coalfields Chaplains' Network met Tim Eggar, Minister for Coal, but 'the two discourses never met'.[52] The Minister put across the Government's view about the reality of the coal market, while the chaplains argued along several lines: the human impact of the policy; long term energy policy; the waste of investment through the premature closure of pits; the need for additional aid to communities where closure was inevitable because the pits were exhausted.

It was also necessary to stop concern flagging in the churches and keep the issue high on their agenda. Industrial Mission in South Yorkshire (IMSY) built links with church groups in mining areas nationally and produced a briefing and action pack. The 'ten things you can do' included lobbying, local action and suggestions for worship and prayer. In January 1993, a national Coalfields Churches Conference was convened jointly by IMSY, Church Action on Poverty, the Coalfields Chaplains' Network and the Diocese of Sheffield Social Responsibility Committee. The Bishop of Durham, David Jenkins, and Richard Caborn, MP, Chairman of the Trade and Industry Select Committee, addressed the conference.

In the end, the closures went ahead despite all the campaigning. 'Nevertheless the dispute had exposed a sea-change in the relationship of the Churches to their political role.'[53] The campaign had been effective in mobilizing the churches. It had been founded upon IM's knowledge of the issues, their implications and their human and theological significance. It depended upon the capacity to integrate Christian belief with social and economic analysis and with effective organisation 'to galvanise the prayers and genuine concern into action that had the passion and vitality of an effective response'.[54] For Tony Attwood, 'the coal crisis showed the Church at its best because the importance of having a Christian presence in every community and at significant points in our social and economic life was widely recognised' and 'the heightened awareness of a political context for ministry provided a situation in which the dynamics of Church life were seen to operate effectively'.[55] Christian presence in the communities, at the pit gates, talking with management and with union officials, lobbying MPs, 'had a sharp, practical, human edge . . . It was spirituality at work.'[56]

NOTES

1. P. D. Anthony, *The Ideology of Work* (London: Tavistock, 1977), p. 43.
2. Stephen Fineman, *Supporting the Jobless: Doctors, Clergy, Police, Probation Officers* (London: Tavistock/ Routledge, 1990), p. 1.

3. See A. G. Watts, *Education, Unemployment and the Future of Work* (Milton Keynes: Open University Press, 1983), in which he cites various American and British surveys indicating that most people would want to work even if it were not an economic necessity.

4. William Beveridge, *Full Employment in a Free Society* (London: Allen and Unwin, 1944), p. 20.

5. Howard Davies, Director General of the CBI, 'Good News, Chancellor, the Rich are Getting Richer?' Address to Manchester Business School, 10 March 1994.

6. Amanda Gosling, Stephen Machin and Costas Meghir, *What Has Happened to Wages?* Institute for Fiscal Studies, June 1994, p. 12.

7. Example given in the Campaign Against Poverty Action Sheet 62, May 1994.

8. Robin Ellison, 'British Labour Force Projections: 1994–2006', *Employment Gazette* (April 1994), pp. 111–121.

9. GMB *Working Woman Magazine* (September 1993).

10. *Job Insecurity: CAB Evidence on Employment Problems in the Recession.* National Association of Citizens Advice Bureaux (NACAB), March 1993.

11. The 1994 Sunday Trading Act includes protections for workers against dismissal, redundancy or being subjected to any other detriment for refusing to work on Sundays, enforceable through industrial tribunals.

12. NACAB, *op. cit.*, p. 9.

13. Merseyside Trade Union Community and Unemployed Resource Centre, *Liverpool Job Centre Survey*, 1994, p. 10.

14. NACAB, *op. cit.*, pp. 22–3.

15. *Ibid.*, pp. 15–16.

16. *Ibid.*, p. 17.

17. Dian Leppington, 'Home Truths about Homeworking', in Elizabeth Templeton (ed.), *A Woman's Place . . . ? Women and Work* (Edinburgh: Saint Andrew Press, 1993), p. 136.

18. See the account by Dian Leppington, *op. cit.*, which also gives a helpful bibliography.

19. From *The Clothes Trade – Rags or Riches?*, produced by Shopping for a Better World, a project of NEAD/ Third World Centre, no date.

20. Reported in the *Guardian*, 10 January 1994.

21. David Cross's report on the Church Action on Poverty Manchester Poverty Hearing in *Poverty Network* (Autumn 1994).

22. Frank Gaffikin and Mike Morrisey, *The New Unemployed, Joblessness and Poverty in the Market Economy* (London: Zed Books, 1992), p. 169.

23. J. Hayes and P. Nutman, *Understanding the Unemployed* (London: Tavistock, 1981), p. 86.

24. Peter Hetherington, about a man who was a Wearside welder for 37 years, made redundant and out of work for two years, though officially on the dole, in 'Despair on the Tyne as yard's last hopes sink', *Guardian*, 10 September 1994.

25. Participants in a discussion with the author in Merseyside Trade Union, Community and Unemployed Resource Centre, 18 August 1994.

26. Fineman, *op. cit.*, p. vii.

27. Robbie Gilbert, *Employment in the 1990s* (London: Macmillan, 1989), p. 271.

28. Fineman, *op. cit.*, p. 129, quoting a probation officer.

29. See Kaushika Amin and Carey Oppenheim, *Poverty in Black and White: Deprivation and Ethnic Minorities* (London: CPAG and the Runnymede Trust, 1992).

30. Chris Hasluck, *People and Skills in Calderdale and Kirklees: An Audit of the Education, Training and Work Experience* (Calderdale and Kirklees Training and Enterprise Council, 1991).

31. Lord Gifford, Wally Brown and Ruth Bundey, *Loosen the Shackles: First Report of the Liverpool 8 Inquiry into Race Relations in Liverpool* (London: Karia Press, 1989), p. 72.

32. *Ibid.*, p. 83.

33. John Burgess, *Isolation, An Investigation into the Life of Isolated Black People in Britain* (Churches Anti-Racist Enterprise, no date), p. 23.

34. Amin with Oppenheim, *op. cit.*, p. 6, referring to A. Brah and S. Shaw, *Working Choices: South Asian Young Muslim Women and the Labour Market*, Department of Employment Research Paper No. 91 (London: HMSO, 1992).

35. Jane E. Wallman, 'Fearfully and wonderfully made', *Poverty Network*, September 1993. Revd Jane Wallman is a partially sighted, guide-dog owner, an Anglican curate and a Research Fellow at the University of Birmingham.

36. This section draws mainly upon an Office of Health Economics briefing No. 29, July 1993, *The Impact of Unemployment on Health*. Standard work has been done on this subject by Richard Smith, for example, *Unemployment and Health* (Oxford: Oxford University Press, 1987).

37. For a discussion of the psychological experiences associated with employment and the consequences of unemployment, see M. Jahoda, 'The impact of unemployment in the 1930s and the 1970s', *Bulletin of the British Psychological Society*, 32 (1979), pp. 309–14.
38. Richard Smith, 'Unemployment: here we go again', *British Medical Journal*, 16 March 1991.
39. *British Medical Journal*, 30 April 1994.
40. Sir Clive Whitmore, senior Home Office civil servant, in a document leaked to the *Independent*, April 1994, quoted in the *Independent on Sunday*, 10 April 1994.
41. A police constable quoted in Fineman, *op. cit.*, p. 98.
42. Robert K. Merton, *Social Theory and Social Structure* (Free Press, revised edn, 1962), p. 147.
43. Fineman, *op. cit.*, pp. 3–4.
44. *Ibid.*, p. 153.
45. *Ibid.*, p. 154.
46. *Ibid.*, p. 169.
47. *Ibid.*, pp. 168–9.
48. David Walker, Secretary of Maltby Rainbow Projects 1987–91, an extract from an article in *Poverty Network*, No. 18 (Autumn 1992).
49. See Tony Attwood, 'The Coal Campaign 1992/3: the interaction of faith and economics', a paper given to the Industrial Mission in South Yorkshire (IMSY) Jubilee Conference, September 1994; Paul Bagshaw, *The Church Beyond the Church: Sheffield Industrial Mission 1944–1994* (IMSY, 1994), Chapter 6, 'Mission to the Coalfields'.
50. In fact, the three pits designated to survive closed, but four others remained to operate independently with much smaller workforces.
51. Bagshaw, *op. cit.*, p. 123.
52. *Ibid.*
53. *Ibid.*, p. 124.
54. Attwood, *op. cit.*, p. 9.
55. *Ibid.*, p. 8.
56. *Ibid.*

CHAPTER 8

Public Issues, Private Troubles[1]

> The other gods were strong, but Thou wast weak;
> They rode, but Thou didst stumble to a throne;
> But to our wounds God's wounds alone can speak,
> And not a god has wounds but Thou alone.
> (Edward Shillito)

The two aspects of poverty – the physical and the relational – are both theologically important. But they raise different kinds of questions. The problem of physical deprivation translates into suffering and lost potentialities. But relational poverty translates into broken relationships, unfulfilled community, loss of self-esteem on one side and inflated pride on the other. Physical poverty represents a frustration of the intentions of creation; relational poverty undermines the purposes and possibilities of covenant. (J. Philip Wogaman, *Economics and Ethics: A Christian Enquiry*, SCM Press, 1986, p. 71)

It was clear from our discussion that they were not looking for an 'easy ride', but that the combined effects of limited opportunities and an inflexible and bureaucratic benefits system acted as a deterrent to their efforts to seek employment or to improve their prospects through training. They were quite angry that their positive aspirations to become self-sufficient were being frustrated. They also resented the sense of degradation brought about by their enforced dependency on families, friends and the State. (Amanda Allard, Graeme Brown and Roger Smith, *What People Want: Families Making Family Policy*, The Children's Society, 1992, p. 34)

THE BROAD SWEEP OF POVERTY

The findings in the government report *Households below Average Income*,[2] published in 1994 covering the years 1979–1991/92, reflect the combined effects of economic, social and demographic changes on the composition of income distribution. In 1979, the proportion of the population below half the average was 9 per cent. By 1991/92, it was 25 per cent – 11.6 million people.

For the population as a whole, average net income rose by 36 per cent in real terms before and after housing costs (BHC/AHC). Looking at the population in 10 per cent groups (deciles), in the lower half of income distribution the top three deciles (20–30 per cent, 30–40 per cent, 40–50 per cent) still saw a rise in real income but it became progressively smaller going down the income distribution. In the second lowest decile, the 1991/2 income was 6 per cent higher than the 1979 figure BHC, but unchanged on the AHC measure. For the bottom decile, on the BHC measure the real median income was unchanged, whereas on the AHC measure, it was 17 per cent lower. This marked a worsening of the position since the last *Households below Average Income* report in 1993 when the fall since 1979 was 14 per cent.

The share of income for all the lower income groups in the bottom 50 per cent of population fell during this period from 33 per cent BHC and 32 per cent AHC of total income to 27 per cent and 25 per cent respectively. Right at the bottom in the lowest 10 per cent, the group's composition changed. There were proportionately fewer pensioners in 1991/92, more unemployed and self-employed and more lone parents. This meant that substantially more children were included. Whereas in 1979, 10 per cent AHC of children lived in households with less than half average income, by 1991/92, the proportion had gone up to 32 per cent.

PERCENTAGE LIVING IN POVERTY
(below 50 per cent average income after housing costs)

	1979	1991/92
Pensioner couples	21	28
Single pensioners	12	40
Couples with children	8	24
Couples without children	5	12
Lone parents	19	59
Single people	7	22

Source: CPAG/Government statistics

As we have seen, much of the impact of poverty is mediated through the structures of community life and the labour market. This chapter focuses on poverty within households. Poverty arises out of people's employment or family circumstances over which they may have little or no control. Social class, gender and race all influence the risk of poverty. People are more or less vulnerable at different stages of their life. Public policy fails to counter the problem and even exacerbates it. Poverty is, therefore, avoidable. It permeates all aspects of life. It is confining. People have to go short on essentials. They become isolated, may get into debt, suffer stress and lose confidence. Their physical health suffers. During the 1980s, the long-term fall in mortality rates among 15- to 44-year-olds stalled. That there is a link between relative deprivation and mortality rates has been demonstrated by an international comparison. Between 1970 and 1990 Britain slipped from twelfth to seventeenth position among the 24 Organization for Economic Cooperation and Development (OECD) nations in terms of average life expectancy. Life expectancy increased fastest in those developed countries where income differentials narrowed.[3] People in poverty are more exposed to all forms of deprivation – from run-down schools to poor housing, from polluted or dangerous environments to deteriorating deregulated bus services.

Thus the story of poverty can be traced in the fortunes of certain social groups, in the extent to which they are at risk and in the character of poverty as it affects them. The subject is a vast one. It is only possible to skim the surface and try to give one or two glimpses into the scale of the problem and the way that people experience it. In attempting to describe a problem, there is a danger of drawing too negative a picture. Not everyone on a low income is subject to all the possible features of poverty outlined here. Nor are people to be seen just as flotsam swept along unresistingly, overwhelmed by economic and social currents. On the contrary. But it is necessary to underline the individual hazards and social waste associated with the increase of poverty and inequality.

FEELING THE EFFECTS IN THE FAMILY

As the basic institution linking the individual with wider society, the family provides continuity but is also subject to change as social and economic circumstances alter. The 'domestic group'[4] is ideally the arena in which we are nurtured, grow into maturity, receive and give love and care. It can provide much of our emotional support but, because it is a human institution, it can also be destructive. Family relationships can be shallow, neglectful, imprisoning or exploitative. Society depends upon family life – or domestic relationships – to serve a wide range of functions. Apart from meeting the physical and emotional needs of its adult members, it has responsibility for child rearing and socialization to produce the sort of adults to meet society's future needs. In many ways the family has proved a resilient institution. But it has also been subject to some bruising over recent years. The growth of a consumer society, economic and labour market upheavals, social and demographic changes: all these have had repercussions within the family unit. The extended family has become more fragmented, affecting the care of the very young and the elderly. Marital breakdown is more common which invariably brings financial hardship in its wake. Changing employment patterns and expectations upset traditional gender roles. Male authority has been challenged.

Since poverty began to be measured, women have been the poorer sex. They made up the majority on poor relief in Victorian times and the majority of those in workhouses. At the turn of the century, 61 per cent of the adults on poor relief were women. Now 62 per cent of those on Income Support are women.[5] But it is only comparatively recently that they have been recognized as a vulnerable group. Over the last decade there has been talk of the 'feminization of poverty'. However, it is less a case that women are more at risk than that their experience was previously overlooked. They were seemingly invisible. Now, gender and the position of women generally are being more widely acknowledged in the analysis of poverty, though whether or not responses are appropriate is much more questionable. The particular character of women's poverty derives from their position in the labour market, which has already been discussed, and in the home, and their treatment in the social security system.

NEW WOMEN – BUT WHERE ARE THE NEW MEN?

Whether in or out of work, the position of women is affected by the allocation of roles and responsibilities within the home. Traditionally the man was expected to be responsible for the financial support of wife and children, and the woman for the emotional support of her husband and children. And often that duty of care extended to other relatives, such as elderly parents. With millions of women going to work – out of necessity as much as choice – the picture is no longer so clear-cut. Yet although the financial support of the household is now more often shared, there has not been a matching realignment of caring and domestic tasks.

As one study put it, 'there are few signs that men had metamorphosed into the caring and labour-sharing breed that the media was trumpeting in the early 1990s.'[6] Although the majority expressed the view that men and women should do the same jobs around the house, in practice women still performed nearly all the household tasks of cooking, shopping, washing and cleaning. 'Women are service sector workers inside and outside of the family.'[7] It is also probably the case that traditional roles are dying harder in some working-class communities so that the women most burdened by combining roles inside and outside the home will receive least support. Similarly employers are slow in realizing that men are also fathers so that nearly all the care of children pre-school and out of school tends to fall on mothers. Despite their emphasis on the imperative of two-parent families, the Government has resisted legislating for even unpaid paternity leave.

All this has health implications. Women have a higher life expectancy than men but women record higher rates of chronic and acute sickness overall. As with men, rates of illness vary according to differing social circumstances. Again, across the population generally, health patterns tend to indicate a North/South divide with mortality rates and rates of chronic sickness increasing from the South and South-east to the North and North-west. Similarly, there can be large differences between small areas within the same region. Inner cities and outer estates have much poorer health profiles than the neighbouring suburbs. The impact of employment outside the home on health is very dependent upon social circumstances and family responsibility. For middle-class women paid employment seems to be associated with less illness. But for mothers without adequate resources to help with the burden of combining the triple roles of housewife, mother and employee, full-time work can be detrimental. The risk of depression is three times greater for working-class women in urban areas than for professional women.

MAKING ENDS MEET

Individuals and families in serious debt face a complex, multi-dimensional, distressing and destructive problem. To say that such people are just an irresponsible minority is to ignore the evidence given in this report about both the numbers affected and the mechanisms by which individuals and families fall into debt.[8]

Many women have the constant anxiety of trying to make ends meet, often alone, often trying to protect family relationships from being seared by money worries. There are two main reasons for getting into debt. First, there are those households who suddenly experience a drop in income, probably because of unemployment. If their outgoings, such as mortgage payments or hire purchase, cannot quickly be scaled down, then other aspects of the household finances are soon under pressure. Then there are those households living long term on low incomes, for whom the normal expectations of late-twentieth-century life entail one long struggle.

By the end of the 1980s, 75 per cent of households in Britain had access to credit facilities.[9] Habits have changed considerably. Apart from retailers inviting people to 'buy now, pay later', government is encouraging the trend by increasingly using loans as a substitute for grants, for example with the Social Fund and student loans. In fact, low-income families use credit far less than more affluent households. This is partly because they cannot afford credit. They may not be given the opportunity, because potential lenders will see them as an unsafe risk. When they do get the chance, they probably only embark on it to meet an immediate need, in the full knowledge that it is a short-term solution storing up long-term trouble. The lower a person's income and the smaller their material assets, the more expensive credit is and the fewer the resources open to them, because of the greater risk involved as perceived by potential lenders.

If you have a low income, it is very hard to get a low interest loan from a bank or other reputable loan companies. It is very easy however to get a loan from loan sharks, less reputable money lenders and catalogues. Loan sharks and money lenders cause major problems. They don't ask too many questions about your ability to pay, and encourage people to take on more than they can afford.[10]

I think when they are on a very low income every week through the year, people get into a rut and then they see things like Christmas coming, the problems of how they are to buy toys for their children. Then someone comes along and says, would you like to borrow some money and you only pay this back at such and such a week, and you are very, very tempted. I would say that lots of people get involved with these money lenders and they all got into a rut because they had gone from struggling every day to the worry of being able to pay these money lenders, so they had more problems. They were bigger problems because they had the constant worry of the two things – the worry how to pay not just bills but the repayment back to the local company and then the added problem again was if they knew you were struggling to pay they would offer you more money in order to pay up your arrears which meant that you would go deeper and deeper in debt.[11]

A family of four on Income Support is nearly £34 per week short of what is needed for a very basic lifestyle.[12] A Barnardos survey in 1994 showed that the prices of many everyday necessities were higher on housing estates in Liverpool or Bradford than in the more exclusive parts of Kensington. In any case, families often have to use small shops that are more expensive because supermarkets have abandoned estates. They have no car and may be unable to rely on or afford public transport.

Over 1.5 million families in Britain in 1994 could not afford to feed their children on the 1876 Workhouse diet. At today's prices the 1876 Workhouse diet would cost £5.46 per week per child, which is 30 per cent more than the estimated £4.15 that Income Support allows for a child's weekly food. The 1913 Poor Law recommendations would be 70 per cent too dear for families on benefit.[13]

NCH (National Children's Home), the Methodist agency which has the UK's largest network of family and community centres, recently published *Deep in Debt*,[14] the report of a survey of problems faced by low-income families. The findings confirm what would be expected: that 'in addition to the obvious financial hardship, families in debt also experience considerable psychological stress. In many cases this results in the breakdown of family relationships.' In fact, one-third believed that money problems had led to separation or divorce. What was also notable was that in nearly two-thirds of all families women took primary responsibility for ensuring that bills were paid.

Lone mother with two children still at home and two older ones living away

Living on Income Support is a real worry. It's hard to make ends meet, to keep up with the bills, you just get one sorted out and then you have to start sorting another out, you're always 'robbing Peter to pay Paul'! Another thing about that is keeping up with clothing for the children, these days it's all designer names, particular brands, or it has to look good in a certain way, and that's expensive, the kids have to wait until I have got the money; I'm lucky in that I have older children who often help with bigger items, but even so, what if I had nobody? There are lots of people who haven't, and that can cause real friction in families, when you can't give them what they need.[15]

One of the problems of disentangling the reality of women's poverty from that of households as a whole is that the usual measures take no account of the distribution of resources within the family. Yet studies such as *Deep in Debt* and another by NCH on *Poverty and Nutrition*[16] indicate that excessive burdens fall on women and that often they go without for the sake of the rest of the family.

On the other hand, it is also often the women who fight back and who take the lead in strategies to overcome poverty, such as credit unions, housing and food co-operatives or in campaigns to improve their neighbourhoods.

There are many examples of groups of women who work carefully to document their experience of their community. They then use their findings to encourage other members of their community to work with them or to confront people in authority with their responsibilities. One example is of women in Salford who consulted the members of their community and established that their concern about the lack of children's play facilities was shared by others. This led the women to draw up plans for what a safe area would be like and to challenge the local council to release a piece of waste land for the purpose. They were then able to raise money from various sources to pay for it to be fenced, a safe surface laid and play equipment bought.[17]

Teesside Church Action on Poverty undertook a community profile of Port Clarence. They found a high percentage of young men dying of cancer and that the proportion of people with long-term, low-level illness is 62 per cent higher than the national rate, 44 per cent higher than in the neighbouring town of Stockton-on-Tees and 37 per cent higher than in Cleveland county in general. The group wanted to know why this was so. A science research unit in the area is now holding a series of air quality tests in Port Clarence and other parts of the Cleveland area to try to discover the causes.

The Cedarwood Centre, a Church of England community resource on the Meadowell estate in North Tyneside became home to a Church Action on Poverty group which had a 'women's issues' group out of which developed a food co-op and a credit union during the early 1980s. These stood as forms of practical resistance to the accelerating decline on the estate. The women running them who could 'take the temperature' of the estate, became increasingly concerned as they saw the local pain destructively expressed through vandalism and violence amongst local youth. No-one in the Council listened to the women at that stage. It took the tragic eruption of disorder in 1991 for people to start to listen.

ON THEIR OWN

The terms 'one-parent' or 'lone-parent' families cover a variety of circumstances. They include men or women who are widowed, divorced, separated or never married. The terms exclude those who are cohabiting or with spouses or partners temporarily living apart.

The particular problems faced by lone parents make them a legitimate focus for social policy research. Lone parent status does not, however, transform families into some strange or pathologically altered species. Given current trends, increasingly large numbers of parents and children will experience lone parenthood as one phase of their family life cycle.[18]

Tentative estimates suggest the average duration of lone parenthood as between three and five years.[19]

Lone parents constitute one of the main groups in poverty in Britain today. Since 1971 numbers have doubled from 570,000 to 1.3 million lone-parent families with about 2 million children in 1991 – approaching 20 per cent of all families. Figures for 1989[20] show that:

• about 90 per cent of them were headed by women;
• just over half result from separation or divorce;
• a third were single (never-married) mothers;
• 6 per cent were widows.

Single (never-married) mothers

- comprise about 30 per cent of lone parents
- numbers are up from 90,000 in 1971 to 360,000 in 1989
- grew as a proportion of all families with dependent children from 1 per cent in 1971 to 6 per cent in 1991
- tend to be younger (half are under 24), but one survey showed 60 per cent to have been over 20 at the birth of their first child
- tend to have smaller families (75 per cent have only one child) and younger children (60 per cent are under 5 years)
- more are choosing to bring up their children on their own
- but, also, more couples are choosing to cohabit and, if they split up, the resulting lone mother will be classified as a 'single' mother
- most likely to be on Income Support
- less likely than ex-married mothers to be receiving maintenance
- about 56 per cent had given or would give details of the absent parent to DSS; 35 per cent refused
- about 27 per cent employed, 14 per cent full time, 13 per cent part time
- about 10 per cent with children under 5 work full time, 11 per cent part time
- about 27 per cent non-householders and about two-thirds of those living with their parents; 80 per cent of the rest in local authority accommodation; over 90 per cent in rented accommodation; only 6 per cent owner-occupiers

Divorced mothers

- in 1989 one-third of lone parents were divorced
- the number went up 300 per cent between 1979 and 1989 to 380,000
- likely to be mid-30s – 75 per cent are between 30 and 44 years, with an average family size of just under two children, three-quarters of whom will be 5–15 years
- most likely of all lone mothers to receive maintenance at some time – just over half – and to get it regularly
- those on Income Support (IS) less likely to receive maintenance
- about three-quarters will give details of former partner to DSS; 15 per cent refuse to do so
- just over half employed; 31 per cent full time, 21 per cent part time
- less than 10 per cent with children under 5 work full time, 16 per cent part time
- one-third are owner-occupiers mainly with mortgages; about half renting from local authority; 10 per cent in other rented property

Separated mothers

- in 1989 a fifth of lone parents were separated
- the number went up by 23 per cent between 1971 and 1989 to 210,000
- likely to be in their early 30s – 70 per cent between 25 and 39 years, with just under two children, about 70 per cent of whom will be between 5 and 15 years and a quarter under 5
- about 60 per cent received IS in 1986 compared with one-half in 1971
- 40 per cent will have received maintenance payments at some time and about one-third regularly
- about three-quarters of separated women will give details of former partner to DSS; 18 per cent refuse to do so
- about 40 per cent employed; 23 per cent full time, 16 per cent part time
- only 7 per cent with children under 5 work full time; 16 per cent part time
- one-third owner-occupiers, mainly with a mortgage; about half renting from local authority; 10 per cent in other rented accommodation

Lone fathers

- number nearly doubled from 7,000 in 1971 and 13,000 in 1989
- as percentage of all lone parents has remained about the same
- about 25 per cent are widowers
- likely to be in their late 30s or 40s, have relatively smaller families (averaging 1.5 children) and rarely have young children – two-thirds between 10 and 15 years; 80 per cent between 10 and 18
- about 60 per cent in employment, mainly full time
- almost half are owner-occupiers, about a quarter of whom are outright owners

Lone parents tend to live on minimal incomes. Seventy-five per cent are on Income Support; over 60 per cent of the families on Income Support are lone-parent families. But just because the total social security bill is growing does not mean that individuals have lavish lifestyles. Most live below the poverty line and 50 per cent live on less than £100 per week. Lone parents' income averages only 43 per cent of that in a two-parent family. Lone mothers are worse off than lone fathers.

Not only have numbers grown, but their situation has deteriorated. Since 1979, the proportion reliant on state benefits has grown by more than half, and the proportion in employment has fallen. Similarly incomes have declined in both absolute and relative terms. A survey in 1989 showed that 65 per cent of lone mothers working 24 hours or more per week were low paid, that is, on less than two-thirds of male hourly rates.

Disadvantage is also reflected in housing. About half of lone parents are local authority tenants compared with only 20 per cent of two-parent families. Others are mainly in the poorest privately rented accommodation. Fewer live in houses and more in flats and maisonettes than two-parent families. Twice as many suffer from overcrowding. As local authorities sell off their more desirable properties, many are becoming concentrated in the worst housing on unpopular estates.

The National Child Development Study, the world's largest of its kind, followed a set of men and women all born one week in March 1958.[21] The survey found that 18 per cent of women had been divorced by the age of 33 years and that nearly one-quarter had been lone parents at some point, the vast majority of these as a result of marital breakdown. The report showed not only how bringing children up single-handed badly affected their income, but how the seeds of poverty planted now would also constrain their future well-being. Even for those working, the nature of their work would exclude them from occupational pensions later on. 'It appears that female members of this study in their old age will remain dependent either on their male counterpart or the state in order to maintain themselves.'

The increase in teenage pregnancies is a worrying trend. Rates for girls under 20 are six times higher in the most deprived areas than the more affluent and three times higher for those under 16. But those in affluent areas are much more likely to terminate the pregnancy by abortion (two-thirds) than the poorer ones (one-quarter), reflecting parental pressure. Again there is a need to ask why young girls are apparently opting to forego their youth and plunge prematurely into parental responsibilities. Many will themselves have had broken family relationships, either having problems at home or having been in care. They may have few educational qualifications, few prospects of a rewarding training course or job. They are looking for status and affection – the security of being loved expressed above all by a baby. 'Every woman feels she has done the cleverest thing in the world when she has produced a baby.'[22]

But it is no passport to an easy life. Motherhood on welfare entails much battling with authorities to sustain even a meagre existence and barely adequate living conditions. To turn the tide of this growing trend of teenage pregnancies, what is needed is to give vulnerable young women some positive alternatives to motherhood through education, personal development and, above all, employment. As Frank Field says, 'To stress the need for jobs does not mean there are no other policies worth pursuing. It means that other reforms will be less effective until every young woman is given the option to work rather than that of immediately starting a family.'[23]

HIT SINGLES

Some argue for a punitive approach – no council housing for single mums, cut benefits, increase the stigma of divorce and illegitimacy. The increasing cost to the state has prompted questions in which money matters and morality become entwined. So the Child Support Agency has now been established, which is an expression of disapproval about absent parents evading responsibility for their offspring, but which has also been set a target by the Secretary of State of making annual savings of £530 million.

The significance of rising numbers of single mothers has been one of the main themes in the 'underclass' debate. The American, Charles Murray, has influenced the debate on both sides of the Atlantic in arguing that 'the "underclass" does not refer to degree of poverty, but to a type of poverty'.[24] It comprises not necessarily the poorest people but ones who are different – from other poor people as well as from the middle class.

As discussed earlier, the argument that some poor people are poor because they do not conform to prevailing values and therefore need to be disciplined fits in a long tradition stretching back to the repression of vagrancy under the Elizabethan Poor Law. The thesis is not only misleading but a dangerous distraction from the real problems of poverty and deprivation. Much research points to conclusions quite contrary to those of Murray. So too does the experience of people working in hard pressed urban communities. Prevailing values and aspirations of British society survive to a surprising degree. What is remarkable is the resilience shown in the face of repeated knock-backs and disappointments. Of course deprivation has an impact on behaviour, but this is an *outcome* not a cause of poverty.

Murray's choice of illegitimacy as a defining feature is especially relevant here. He calls it 'less ambiguous than other forms of single parenthood . . . the purest form of being without two parents'. However, half of the children who are born 'illegitimate' have their two parents living together at the time of their birth, many of whom will subsequently marry. In any case, the popularity of marriage is no necessary guide to the stability of parental relationships. Scandinavian countries have much higher illegitimacy rates and yet most children are born into two-parent families.

As if coping alone was not enough, lone mothers are being made to feel like outcasts. Many of society's problems are being heaped on their shoulders. For example, a link has been made between the rise in crime and the increase in single-parent families. Beatrix Campbell points out that during the debates about the meaning of the riots on estates in 1991, 'the spectre of the "problem family", the demise of the masters and the rise of the lone mothers was constantly invoked. Implicitly, if not explicitly, the mothers, but not the men, were scapegoated. No political commentators alluded to the reliance and ingenuity of single parents, or to the capricious and often cruel culture created by the men who abandoned and harassed them.'[25]

Research indicates that maladjustment and crime are not linked with being illegitimate or from a 'broken home' but with deprivation.[26] Quality of parenting is also important but just as much so in two-parent families. What is problematic is unpredictability and inconsistency in exercising discipline. This is perhaps more likely amongst parents struggling to survive and suffering the anger and depression of having no worthwhile economic role or rewards.

> Whatever path of family change and diversity the parents of children take, more children are likely to lead lives of transition than they were twenty or thirty years ago. These flows in family life may now need as much attention as the family structures themselves.[27]

Some studies indicate that children of lone parents *are* disadvantaged, but questions remain about whether it is the fact of divorce that is damaging or the bitterness that can surround it and the material consequences that can flow from it. A study charting the progress of children in single-parent families on average incomes compared with two-parent families with the same income found that the children did well and escaped the expectation of failure.

> I left school at 16 years of age with one O-level in music and 5 CSEs. My subsequent jobs as a result of not having been rated highly did not bring in much income. The goal of my life had been to be happily married and have a family. I was not ambitious. I got married at 19, afraid of being left on the shelf. I did not become a mother until I was 25 as I'd had three miscarriages owing to a hormone deficiency. I now have three wonderful children who are all Christians and growing into creative and responsible teenagers. When I was 31, after 12 years of marriage, I finally plucked up enough courage to leave my husband, a policeman, who had been violent and broken every marital vow many times. People say it is too easy to get divorced. This was not my experience. What does a woman with 3 small children do, or where does she go and how does she survive on her own? No indeed, it took a lot of courage and support from my GP, friends and family before I could leave . . .
>
> I had been a Christian by now for many years and had always been active and believed that now I was in a time of need, my fellow Christians would be able to help and support me. This however was not the case. I believe there is much hypocrisy in the church especially in the area of love. Christians will tell you they love you easily, but do they spend time with you or their money on you? I needed some decent human kindness, a phone call or a visit to say in unspoken words that I

was worth bothering with. I needed to talk and be really listened to, to have prayer ministry and help with the children. But instead I received empty promises like 'you must come for tea' – seven years later I'm still waiting! . . . To be frank it's kinder to yourself to be outside the church at a time like this for the sake of self-preservation! That's exactly what I did. For four years I went nowhere. It was interesting to observe that when this happened, Christians managed to call to tell me what a terrible sinner I was. How was it that when I needed a friend they were nowhere to be found? . . . I believe Jesus weeps over the church, His representative body that cannot show love, for real love goes beyond mere words. The church is all too often middle class and can seem a real culture clash to those in trouble, including me. Unfortunately the church is riddled with the world's view of how you are valued.

After four years . . . God challenged me to go back to church . . . to another one, where as soon as I walked in I knew I had come home. The difference? The new church was informal and the children were welcomed and spoken to and so was I, and we were shown practical love and support . . . For the first time in my life I began to like myself because I knew other people liked me too . . .

For two years I began to think about setting up a single parent group to help those who are going through divorce, or bereavement, or are single parents, because Christ commands us to love our neighbour as ourselves and do unto others as you would be done by. Eventually I was approached by my church to set up just such a group which I have done. It is called Pharos, which is Greek for lighthouse. We aim to show the love of God to a dying, hurting world! There are 81,000 single parent families in Leeds out of a population of 730,000. That makes it 11 per cent of the population of Leeds are single parents. We have only been going a short time and in two months have 14 single parents coming to the group. We have specific teaching on issues that concern us – loneliness, unforgiveness, stress, budgeting, benefits, love, how to parent your children, and so on. We still have a long way to go to reach all single parents in Leeds, but at least we started and I know God is delighted. What is more my church are delighted and back us enthusiastically.[28]

YOUNG PEOPLE ADRIFT

In the summer of 1993, NCH surveyed 120 young people across Britain aged between 16 and 26, though two-thirds were 16 to 18 years old. They were individuals the organization had encountered through projects aiming to help vulnerable and low-income young people. Nearly two-thirds had been in care at some time in their lives. Now they lived in various types of accommodation, temporary hostels, rooms they rented with others, at home with their families, on the street or on friends' floors. Less than 10 per cent were working. Most were unemployed; a few were on Youth Training and others had picked up casual work in the recent past. Their average income was £34 per week to cover all expenses except housing. One in five was trying to live on less than £29 per week. That is approximately half the amount (£57.66) that the Family Budget Unit at York University estimates as the true cost of caring for a 16-year-old.

As a result, virtually all these young people were going without meals and living on nutritionally sub-standard diets, including the young women who were either pregnant or already mothers. They visited their doctors more, were depressed and worried about their futures and they sought escape in cigarettes (2 out of 3), drink (1 in 3) or drugs (1 in 6).

In 1992, when the Income Support rate for young single people aged 18 to 24 was £34.80 per week, but the full adult rate was £44.00, the Parliamentary Social Security Advisory Committee said: 'It cannot be right to decrease the level of benefit due to this group if the rate is based on basic "needs". We can see no sensible reason for this and have received no evidence to justify it. Food, clothing and housing are no cheaper for a person aged (under 25) than for someone aged 25 or over.'

A major survey in Scotland found that family stress was to blame for 60 per cent of homeless young people leaving home. A higher proportion had left after rows with a step-parent than where both parents were still at home or it was a lone-parent family.

> I was living with my mum and step-dad until May 1993. I'm 17 now. I haven't lived with my real dad for well over 10 years. After they split up I wasn't allowed to see my dad and I didn't see him for seven years. I was four when they split up. My step-dad gave me one month's notice to leave because we weren't getting on – I wasn't doing anything particularly bad – we just didn't get on. I'm getting on much better with him and my mum now that I'm not living with them. I miss not having my real dad around. I wish my mum would get back together with him but I know that cannot happen. The thing I really miss is eating together and bringing problems out into the open. I really want to have my own family one day. I want to learn from my mum and dad's mistakes. My dad used to come in drunk most nights, I think that's what destroyed their marriage. I would want to make sure that I found the right person before I jumped into a commitment. It would be nice to have kids. I want to be proud of them. I think trust and support are the things that make a good family.[29]

NECESSARY BUT NOT SUFFICIENT

I have frequently quoted reports by organizations like NCH, The Children's Society and Barnardos, all large-scale Christian pastoral agencies with a long respected history of work with those children and young people whom we most fail in our society. It is notable that over recent years these organizations have increasingly recognized that pastoral work by itself is not enough. They are in a position to see the effects of unemployment and poverty, but also to know that the people with the real experience and expertise – those with whom they work – have important insights to convey and messages the rest of us need to hear. The experience of these organizations tells them that preventative work must extend beyond social work intervention with families and communities to more comprehensive action through public policy to raise incomes, for example, and improve education and training. They feel compelled to speak out on policy issues.

The Children's Society is also committed to raising public awareness of issues affecting children and young people and to promoting the welfare and rights of children and young people in matters of public policy.[30]

NCH is committed to campaigning with, and on behalf of, young people at risk and in need, and maintains an active research and campaigning programme to this end.[31]

POVERTY IN OLD AGE

It has long been recognized that people are more vulnerable to poverty at certain times of their life. Old age is one such time. There are over 10.5 million people over pension age in Britain. In 1991, retired households were dependent on social security benefits for 41 per cent of their income.[32] Two-thirds of the elderly population are women, who are also more likely to be poor because of their interrupted patterns of work, their lower earnings and their longer life expectancy. In 1991, three times as many women pensioners as men were dependent on Income Support.[33] Over 40 per cent of pensioners also have disabilities. Tying pensions upratings to price rises has meant that the retirement pension is falling in relation to male average earnings, dropping from 20.4 per cent in 1979 to 17.8 per cent in 1992.

The case of pensioners, however, exemplifies the dangers of statistics. In the 1960s poverty was seen as largely a pensioner problem. Supplementary benefit was introduced in 1966 to overcome the resistance of elderly people to claiming their benefit entitlement. In the 1980s, two trends changed this perception. First, a new group of better-off older people emerged, so that government ministers could talk about the growing number of affluent pensioners. Second, the growth of unemployment swelled the ranks of poorer younger people, masking the fact that although older people accounted for a smaller percentage of those in poverty, their actual numbers changed little. There were no fewer of them, but they became subsumed in a larger problem.

One of the attendant risks of ageing is becoming frail or disabled. Restricted mobility, for example, can lead to greater isolation and dependence on the care of others, whether public services, voluntary agencies or family, friends or neighbours. It can be a frustrating and debilitating experience, especially if others seem to assume that they no longer have anything to contribute to society.

POVERTY AND DISABILITY

In 1975, the United Nations issued a *Declaration of the Rights of Disabled People*. Paragraphs 7 and 8 state: 'Disabled persons have the right to economic and social security and to a decent level of living' and 'Disabled persons are entitled to have their special needs taken into consideration at all stages of economic and social planning'. Can this country be said to have acted upon these principles in the light of the current position of disabled people? They encounter barriers to proper housing in the community, to public transport and to all kinds of public amenities. Efforts to get a bill through Parliament even to give disabled people the same civil rights as others have so far failed.

Reports from the Office of Population Censuses and Surveys show a huge gap between the average incomes of the disabled and non-disabled population under pensionable age: a difference of £56 per week at 1991 prices. Inequity in earnings and access to work have already been mentioned. There is also inequity in benefits, since some needs are not taken into account, such as the real costs of mobility or diet. The benefits system discriminates against certain types of disability and against disabled people who are over 65. The overwhelming picture is of disabled people in a double-bind, getting by on lower incomes than the rest of the population but actually needing higher incomes because they incur extra expenditure as a result of being disabled.

EVEN MORE AT RISK

People of Afro-Caribbean and Asian origin are more likely to have to rely on social security benefits. For them the general strain of surviving on a low income can be compounded by greater difficulties in dealing with DSS officials. The ethnic minority population is a much younger one so they have been especially hard hit first by the withdrawal of income support for 16- and 17-year-olds and the frequent failure to meet the guarantee of a Youth Training place and second by the lower rate of income support for single childless people under 25.

Fewer ethnic minority groups now live in the private rented sector than used to be the case in the 1950s, 1960s and 1970s when squalid and overcrowded conditions co-existed with blatant racism amongst landlords, but they are still more likely to than white people. Housing patterns vary according to ethnic group. Asians are more likely to be home owners or, for Pakistanis and Bangladeshis, rent privately, while two-fifths of West Indians live in council accommodation. Overcrowding is still more prevalent amongst all minority groups than in the population as a whole.

Active discrimination is still sometimes exposed in local authority housing departments. For example, staff in Tower Hamlets, which has areas of the most intense deprivation in the whole of England, were found to show 'suspicion and resentment' and sometimes 'overt racism' towards Bengalis.[34] Elsewhere it has been revealed that black applicants were offered lower quality housing or were much less likely than white families in similar circumstances to be offered a house as against a maisonette or flat. Policies to limit the access of lone parents to council accommodation can also impact more on some groups, such as those of West Indian and African origin, in which there is a higher incidence of lone parenthood. They will also be more at risk in the labour market. And, as they are more likely to be single than divorced or separated, they may have less access to maintenance. 'It may well be that Afro-Caribbean lone parents who are likely to be poorer in general and more likely to be single will find themselves at the very bottom of an already poor pile.'[35]

There has been little systematic study of health amongst ethnic minorities. Inevitably they suffer the consequences of deprivation. They certainly experience higher rates of particular diseases and higher rates of perinatal and infant mortality. Protasia Torkington, who made a study of black health, emphasized the need to analyse the experience of black people not in a vacuum but in the social, political and economic context of class and gender.[36] As she found, there are also ways in which the NHS fails to meet needs, for example:

* poor provision for ethnic minority elderly;
* the limited availability of translating and interpretation services;
* ignorance of cultural matters such as diet amongst health professionals;
* the treatment of black people under the Mental Health Act.

POVERTY AT HOME

When Jesus was born, his family could not find shelter. That was 2,000 years ago and we still have not done our homework. In our commission we have been gathering stories from Naples, from Brussels, from Paris, from Manchester. Everywhere in Europe homelessness is on the increase and the quality of housing for the poor is decreasing. Many live in ghettos, which the authorities then neglect because there are no votes there. Miserable housing leads to an atmosphere of violence and fear and then to racism.[37]

Nicholas Bradbury asked several middle-class parish groups to draw a list of ideal features to do with housing, which came out as follows:

- privacy;
- good views and a setting of natural beauty;
- peaceful surroundings;
- safe play space for children;
- friendly neighbours;
- enough bedrooms to entertain guests overnight;
- a spacious kitchen;
- two bathrooms, if possible.[38]

As Bradbury says, 'From a UPA perspective, this list is striking for what it omits. It assumes that the accommodation will be dry, and that it can be heated, that the fabric will not be in a state of decay and that it is not infested with vermin. In the inner city however these things cannot be taken for granted.' Many people nowadays assume that their house will be comfortable and flexible, for example, that it will be warm everywhere so that children's bedrooms are also their playrooms, often also equipped with stereos and TVs. The list is also revealing about what more people want from their houses over and above physical shelter. It tells us something about people's conception of 'home', which has to do with having

- the right to be a family – or, to use a more neutral word, a household – inside its own living space; to have personal space which cannot be violated, to be free from harassment, to be able to leave belongings safely;
- somewhere to express one's personal identity through the way it is decorated and furnished;
- room and appropriate facilities for all the household's individual and collective needs;
- a place of support from family and friends and a base for one's social relationships in the fullest sense;

- a sense of belonging in a neighbourhood and a stake in the local community;
- a refuge from the external pressures of life, somewhere to relax, 'be oneself'.

In other words, home is not just materially important. It helps defines who a person is. It is the primary context for living, growing, self-expression and personal relationships. Moving out of the parental home is frequently a significant step into adulthood and emotional, if not financial, independence. A home individualizes, but it also signifies belonging. It can express where a person is in the social hierarchy. It gives pointers to other people and it is part of an individual's self-definition and self-expression. (It is said that some architects of high-rise flats were aggrieved when they could not insist on all the residents having the same curtains in order to preserve the symmetry of their creation!)

Questions raised by the Churches' National Housing Coalition in its *Reflections on Faith Statement*:

- What is your own understanding of creation and human creativity? How is this affected by your housing circumstances?
- What do you think are the essentials of a home? What does it mean to have fullness of life in relation to a home and housing?
- What relation is there between personal and social stewardship and housing?
- Do the principles of the Jubilee (Lev 25.8–28) mean anything today? In what senses could they be applied?
- Does seeing Jesus in the poor (Matt 25.31–46) have anything to do with the consequences of the world's sin being borne by Jesus and materially carried by the poor?
- How is the Kingdom of God present amongst the people you know; the people on the edge of society; those who are homeless and in housing need; those in your own neighbourhood? How have you recognized its presence?
- How can we promote and strengthen the values of the Kingdom in our own lives and work?
- Are those with power in our own country being responsible to those in housing need?
- How do we understand what it means to turn away from God in regard to housing policies?
- What are the Church's pastoral and prophetic responsibilities in relation to housing need?

Not to have a home, or to have one over which little control can be exercised because of a lack of resources or the imposition of particular conditions, is therefore demeaning. The homeless may have to rely on the hospitality of others or learn to survive on the streets. They lack even that most basic aspect of identity – an address – which is crucial, for example, in applying for work. People in bed and breakfast – temporary accommodation even though it may go on for a long time – have no stability, no privacy. Those in overcrowded or unfit accommodation find the physical discomforts also interfere with relationships within the household. To lose a home or experience inadequate housing can reveal what is really valuable. Is it the physical comforts and possessions *per se* or are they only valuable insofar as they provide a home base which can fulfil these wider needs?

The pressure of homelessness is seen most acutely in London. Over 20 per cent of council accommodation was sold in the 1980s. But in the late 1980s and early 1990s the number of people in long-term mortgage debt and whose properties have been repossessed has greatly increased. While thousands are living in temporary accommodation, repossessions have boosted the number of empty properties on the market, estimated to be nearly 300,000 across the country in 1993.[39] It is difficult to count how many are homeless. The Shelter report, *Homes Cost Less than Homelessness*,[40] charts the growth and scale of the problem. Homelessness has nearly tripled since 1978. In 1991, 146,290 households (about 420,000 adults and children) were accepted as homeless by local authorities. These are the official homeless. Shelter estimates that the unofficial homeless could be as many as 1.7 million, including people sleeping rough, unauthorized squatters, single people in hostels or lodgings, insecure private tenants or – and this is the largest group – the 'concealed' homeless, living as part of other households who want and need their own accommodation. In 1991 London councils alone estimated that about 70,000 married couples and lone-parent families were hidden in this way, and over 123,000 single people.[41]

MORE THAN A STOPGAP

The shortage of permanent homes has increased councils' reliance on temporary accommodation in hostels or bed and breakfast. In London the cost of temporary accommodation was about £1 million per day in 1991/2 and this was projected to rise to £1.6 million per day in 1995/6.[42] 'Temporary' can be a misnomer as it can last anything from a few days to several years, often also entailing moves from one hostel or bed-and-breakfast establishment to another. Quite often precipitated into homelessness by circumstances beyond their control, by a relationship breakdown, domestic violence or economic ruin, families can be made to feel as though they deliberately engineered the situation. 'They think you do it on purpose . . . I didn't want to be made homeless. I was working, my husband was working. The landlord came and said he was selling the house next week and we had to move.'[43]

It is a demeaning and isolating experience. People are frequently distant from friends and family, unable to travel and sometimes subject to restrictions on receiving visitors or ashamed of their surroundings. It is an expensive way to live. Communal kitchens and the hazards of cooking in one room, which is also the only place for children to play, lead to using more convenience foods or going out for fish and chips. Laundry and travel costs can be greater. For people in jobs, the strain of this sort of living affects their work. It interferes with children's growth and education. Limited play space slows their process of maturing. This is not a home life conducive to quietness and study, and frequent moves can also mean changes of school.

Living in such difficult circumstances exacts a massive emotional toll. Overcrowding is one of the most wearing aspects. There is no privacy, people get on each other's nerves and feel their own identity crumbling. There is no opportunity for adults to be alone without being overlooked or overheard by the children. Relationships are severely tested and not surprisingly sometimes crack under the strain.

This is the story of Barbara, who had become homeless with her husband and 2-year-old son, recounted in the NCH report *Your Place or Mine?*.[44]

Living in one room had been too much of a strain on Barbara's relationship with her husband and after many arguments he had left her – 'I feel resentment, it needn't have been . . . a long time ago Nigel and I came to the conclusion that when we got a flat we would have separate rooms which has got to do with the fact that for so long we have lived in one room.'

One of Barbara's principal concerns was the welfare of her son and the multiple impact living in a bed and breakfast would have upon him. In particular she was concerned about her ability to be the mother she wanted to be. Amongst other things, she described how the lack of space meant that she could not enforce any reasonable child care routines. From past experience she believed he was the type of child who responded well to an established routine – 'what I find most difficult is the actual putting to bed and have time for yourself after . . . He is a very good baby for getting into a rhythm, you just darken the room, he will play for a little while and go to sleep of his own accord. But because I'm in the room I have the light on, I have the telly on.' This had a knock-on effect on her own independence and social life – 'I regret not being able to have friends around, we used to socialize a lot . . . I worry when people come around. My friend came round with her baby and David was asleep, he (the baby) woke David up . . . If I had a normal flat my friend could just come around and we could have been in one room and David could have stayed asleep in another.'

Barbara has been attending the NCH family centre every day since she has been in temporary accommodation. She feels the centre has offered her vital support – 'without the family centre – I don't know, I think I'd have gone crazy . . . It makes an awful difference . . . the people are so friendly here . . . they're very nice. They make you feel welcome, you know, if you have problems you can always talk to them, or if you haven't got enough clothes for your kid they'll always help you out. Everybody here is in the same situation.' She feels the centre has been of particular benefit for her son, providing him with space to play and other children to interact with – 'There's a girl here who's voluntary, and the (children) think she is their teacher, you know . . . and children to play with, things to do. When he is playing, I can sit down and have a cup of tea, and I know he is safe.'

NCH staff have also given her useful practical advice concerning her housing and financial situation. They have helped her to pursue benefit payments which she had applied for yet not received and to chase up the housing department.

THE CLAIMING EXPERIENCE

In 1990, Hartley Dean and Peter Taylor-Gooby talked to a sample of long-term, working-age, Income-Support claimants to see whether there is a 'dependency culture', characterized as Government ministers have said by distinctive behaviour patterns and attitudes. They actually found that 'there is no distinctive "dependency culture" amongst social security claimants and . . . claimants constitute a heterogeneous group which subscribes by and large to the same norms, values, prejudices and aspirations as the rest of the population.'[45] Any departure from the values guiding most people was exceptional.

> People in contemporary Britain tend to follow a value orientation in which material dependency upon the wage relation is seen as natural and necessary to personal identity; emotional dependency within the family is seen as natural and necessary to self-fulfilment; state dependency is seen as perhaps less than natural, but represents an important guarantee of last resort.[46]

Patterns of dependency on paid employment, within the family and on the state, are changing as a result of processes of social and economic change, which have increased not diminished the role of the state. To base policy on the idea of a dependency culture is therefore counterproductive; 'the implication that claimants are "culturally" separated from the rest of society is inaccurate and unhelpful.'[47]

The claiming experience is already one which invades people's privacy and offends their self-respect. Making the social security system more punitive, implying at best scrounging and at worst fraud, restricting entitlement – all these set claimants at odds with the state. They create adversarial relationships. 'Claimants do not need to be discouraged from claiming state benefits, so new obstacles to the establishment of benefit rights may undermine claimants' faith in the guarantees (and perhaps therefore the obligations) of citizenship.'[48]

It is against the backcloth of the manifestations and dynamics of poverty discussed in this section that the next one goes on to look at public policy to see how we are collectively responding as a society and whether we are integrating or excluding those on the social and economic margins.

NOTES

1. C. Wright Mills, *The Sociological Imagination* (Harmondsworth: Penguin, 1970, first published 1959), pp. 14–15, referring to the distinction between 'the personal troubles of milieu' and 'the public issues of social structure'. *Troubles*, he says, occur within the character of the individual and within the range of his or her immediate relations with others and their resolution lies within the social setting directly open to personal experience and to some extent the person's wilful activity. *Issues*, on the other hand, are to do with the organizations of many such milieux into the institutions of the historical society as a whole.
2. Department of Social Security, *Households below Average Income: A Statistical Analysis 1979–1991/92* (A Government Statistical Service Publication, London: HMSO, 1994).
3. Based on a report in the *British Medical Journal* (30 April 1994).
4. Stephen Barton, paper submitted to Board for Social Responsibility Working Party on the Family, *Crucible*, January–March 1993.
5. Carey Oppenheim, *Poverty the Facts* (Child Poverty Action Group, 1993), p. 93.
6. National Child Development Study, 1993.
7. Jane Millar and Caroline Glendinning, *Women and Poverty in Britain: the 1990s* (Harvester Wheatsheaf, 1992).
8. Andrew Hartropp (ed.), *Families in Debt*, Jubilee Centre Research Paper No. 7 (1988), p. 141.
9. Janet Ford, *Consuming Credit: Debt and Poverty in the UK*, Child Poverty Action Group, 1991, p. 1.
10. Charlotte Anderson and Hilary Russell, *Debt and Credit Unions* (Centre for Urban Studies, University of Liverpool, 1988), p. 3.
11. *Women and Poverty*, Report of a European Consultation sponsored by WCC/CICARWS, held in Macclesfield, 24–29 May 1990, p. 5.
12. Nina Oldfield and Autumn C. S. Yu, *The Cost of a Child: Living Standards for the 1990s* (Child Poverty Action Group, 1993).
13. NCH, 'Action for Children', press release on the 125th anniversary of the organization.
14. *Deep in Debt: A Survey of Problems Faced by Low Income Families* (NCH, October 1992).
15. Quoted in Mary Catherine Dunne, *Stitched Up! Action for Health in Ancoats, Voices of Struggle, Hope and Vision* (Church Action on Poverty, 1993), p. 92.
16. *Poverty and Nutrition Survey* (NCH, 1991).
17. *Women and Poverty*, p. 13.

18. Louie Burghes, *One-Parent Families: Policy Options for the 1990s* (Family Policy Studies Centre, Joseph Rowntree Foundation, February 1993), p. 6.
19. Office of Population Censuses and Surveys, *General Household Surveys for 1988 and 1991* (London: HMSO, 1990 and 1992).
20. These and other figures in this section are taken from Burghes, *op. cit.*
21. National Child Development Study, 1993.
22. Margaret Hebblethwaite, *Motherhood and God* (London: Geoffrey Chapman, 1984), p. 94.
23. Frank Field, *An Agenda for Britain* (London: HarperCollins, 1993), p. 94.
24. Charles Murray, *The Emerging British Underclass*, IEA Health and Welfare Unit, 1990.
25. Beatrix Campbell, *Goliath: Britain's Dangerous Places* (London: Methuen, 1993), p. 252.
26. See Louie Burghes, *Lone Parenthood and Family Disruption: The Outcomes for Children*, Family Policy Studies Centre Occasional Paper 18 (January 1994).
27. *Ibid.*, p. 11.
28. From Paul Wilson, 'Bruised reeds', in *Poverty Network* No. 21 (May 1994), pp. 22–4.
29. *Poverty Network* (May 1994), p. 25.
30. The Children's Society, 1992, p. 51.
31. *A Lost Generation?* (NCH 1993), summary.
32. *Family Spending, A Report on the Family Expenditure Survey 1991* (London: HMSO, 1992) quoted in Oppenheim, *op. cit.*, p. 68.
33. Department of Social Security, *Social Security Statistics 1992* (London: HMSO, 1992) quoted in Oppenheim, *op. cit.*, p. 68.
34. Quoted in Amin and Oppenheim, *op. cit.*, p. 23. See D. Phillips, *What Price Equality?* (GLC Research and Policy Report No. 9, 1986).
35. Amin and Oppenheim, *op. cit.*, p. 47.
36. N. P. K. Torkington, *Black Health: A Political Issue* (Catholic Association for Racial Justice and Liverpool Institute for Higher Education, 1991).
37. *Kairos Europa: People's Parliament Strasbourg 5–10 June 1992*, Dara Molloy reporting on the Shelter commission.
38. Nicholas Bradbury, *City of God? Pastoral Care in the Inner City* (London: SPCK, 1989), p. 7.
39. Data quoted from *Your Place or Mine?* Report on Homelessness by NCH, London Housing Unit and SHAC, published by NCH 1993.
40. L. Burrows and P. Walenkowitz, *Homes Cost Less than Homelessness* (Shelter, 1992).
41. NCH, *op. cit.*, p. 7.
42. NCH, *op. cit.*, p. 8.
43. NCH, *op. cit.*, p. 12.
44. NCH, *op. cit.*, p. 28.
45. Hartley Dean, 'Poverty discourse and the disempowerment of the poor', *Critical Social Policy*, 12 (2), 1992, p. 81.
46. Hartley Dean and Peter Taylor-Gooby, *Dependency Culture: The Explosion of a Myth* (Harvester Wheatsheaf, 1992), p. 123.
47. *Ibid.*, pp. 122–3.
48. *Ibid.*, p. 123.

PART IV

Responding to Poverty –
Policies and Prophecy,
Pastoral Care and Protest

Three simple, subversive questions, to be insistently pursued, are: 'who benefits? who suffers? who decides?' (Brian Wren, *Education for Justice*, SCM Press, 1986, p. xv)

One of the most radical disadvantages suffered by the powerless and marginalised of our society is their ultimate exclusion from the *conversation* which creates society. (Austin Smith, *Journeying with God: Paradigms of Power and Powerlessness*, Sheed and Ward, 1990, p. 132)

The 'church of the poor' is not somewhere back in New Testament times nor in some overseas Third World continent. It is here in Britain, where no effort is spared and no encouragement denied to help in the creation of a society where two thirds of the population are incomparably better off than ever before, while the remaining third is pushed aside. (Patrick Logan, *A Life to Be Lived: Homelessness and Pastoral Care*, Darton, Longman and Todd with UNLEASH, 1989, p. 3)

THIS PART OF THE BOOK turns to looking at public policy and poverty. Very often when poverty is discussed, it is assumed that social security is the key to the problem. In practice, the whole range of government policy is relevant in its direct effects on income and quality of life through employment or taxation, or its indirect effects through the extent of provision of free or subsidized services. The vision that a government has of the kind of society it wants will determine its priorities and these in turn will decide its spending and its actions.

Although economic and social policy are inseparable and interdependent, the philosophy which steered policy in the 1980s tried to drive a wedge between them. The economy was regarded as the self-contained engine of society, the driving force encumbered by having to carry the burden of the welfare state. And if the budget is seen as a burden, it is only a short step to seeing the recipients as burdensome. Yet frequently public policy has itself added to the personal costs borne by the most vulnerable and to the financial and social costs carried by everyone.

This book has argued that poverty is a systemic problem. It therefore requires, not just amelioration, but fundamental preventive change *via* a realignment of the major economic and social institutions which determine material wellbeing. This in turn entails a redefinition of citizenship.

For Christians, there are compelling moral and theological reasons as well as pragmatic ones for striving to eliminate poverty. Serving and standing with the poor is to follow and to find Christ. There are signs of hope within the Church. However, as an institution, it requires radical change if it is to become the Church of the poor, which is its proper calling.

CHAPTER 9

The Arteries of the State

Let justice roll down like waters and righteousness like an ever-flowing stream. (Amos 5.24)

... the moral relations that exist between my income and the needs of strangers at my door pass through the arteries of the state. (Michael Ignatieff, *The Needs of Strangers*, Chatto and Windus/ The Hogarth Press, 1984, p. 141)

Do we have a welfare society – that is, one concerned with the well-being of all its members? What are the principles underpinning public policy and how are they expressed in social security and taxation? These are the questions addressed in this chapter.

THE WELFARE STATE

The welfare state flowered after 1945. Although there had been a gestation period for many of its policy strands before 1939, the war provided the right mood for its emergence. War is no respecter of persons. The bombardment of the 1939–45 war brought people together from across the social spectrum in the face of a common danger. This paved the way for the old Poor Law principles, which so rigidly categorized people, to be set aside in favour of a system of mutual assistance and care. The state took on a larger role. Social services were extended to all, without distinction of social or economic class. But also there was a profound change of attitude. These benefits were now regarded amongst the rights of citizenship. Recipients need no longer be ashamed. Nor could administrators withhold benefits on the grounds that the person was undeserving.

The provision included a system of social insurance to ensure a minimum income, as of right, in circumstances of illness, unemployment, injury, retirement. Secondly, there was social assistance, including family allowances, housing assistance and what was then called National Assistance (now Income Support). These were the non-insurance benefits which were nevertheless thought to be national rather than individual responsibilities. Universal education and health services were also introduced, funded through taxation, to be free at the point of use and to be of standard quality for all. Again the assumption was that it was not in the national interest to cut such services according to people's differing ability to pay for them, whether directly or indirectly. In addition there were welfare services, providing goods and personal services rather than cash benefits, such as child welfare, school meals and milk, home helps.

Altogether the premise was that the welfare state should be organized to ensure the well-being of citizens and collectively use resources to that end. This was at the other extreme from the *laissez-faire* tradition which, in its pure form, leaves citizens to pursue their own welfare as well as they can. It was intended to be a means of freeing people from 'poverty, insecurity and inadequate provision for healthy living'.[1] Its organization was not an end in itself. The welfare state evolved from the needs and inclinations of British people at a specific time. As circumstances and needs change so welfare provision must also change to serve the same purpose. For several decades, its development was haphazard. Policy and administration were tinkered with but not thoroughly rethought. Different political emphases held sway in different periods.

After the enormous legislative activity of 1945–48, there was a period of consolidation before the return of a Conservative government in 1951. This saw the beginnings of a shift away from the universalist model which had been introduced. The government set a number of policy reviews in train. For example, it was concerned to limit expenditure on the health service and it wanted to reduce the role of local authorities in housing provision and thereby cut the cost of Exchequer aid to local authorities. But by the end of the decade, there were criticisms of the quality of welfare provision.[2] Many hospitals were in a very poor state. No new ones had been built since the war and capital expenditure was at a very low level. More efforts were made to mobilize opinion. Professional interest groups and local authority associations developed closer links with the relevant government departments. Social scientists came to the fore as departments commissioned research to assist them to push for increased spending. So social spending started to burgeon. There was a massive council house-building programme and the largest hospital building programme in the twentieth century. Personal social services were reorganized. Population growth meant the number of schoolchildren rose and more of them stayed on at school after the minimum leaving age. Higher education expanded, fuelled by concern that the country should keep up with the technological revolution. Now, too, the elderly who had gained pension rights under the post-war legislation were reaching retirement. It was time for the country to pay up.

This was the time, if any, when there was something approaching a bipartisan consensus. But it was not long before political philosophies began to diverge again. The Conservatives in opposition in the late 1960s began to worry again about public-sector demands on the economy and about levels of personal taxation. On return to office, they wanted to focus spending in the major service areas of health and education in which there was no private alternative. In the spheres of housing and income maintenance, on the other hand, they took steps to develop alternatives to public provision, though some of their attempts were thwarted when their term in office ended in the early 1970s.

The Labour Party at this time, on the other hand, was moving from 'espousing a basic citizenship model of welfare to more egalitarian aspirations, abolishing grammar schools, toying with positive discrimination, and introducing measures to re-distribute health-care resources more equally and to abolish tax reliefs for children'.[3] These were all measures that began to hurt middle-income voters, and rising tax rates began to affect lower earners too. A political balancing act was needed to keep taxes at a level which the electorate would tolerate while not having to cut services or public-sector jobs.

The growth of social expenditure in the UK followed a similar pattern to that in other OECD countries between 1960 and 1981, though with the UK falling a little behind the average. However, increased spending on public services was not solely a product of conscious political choices. Social and economic factors also played a part, particularly ones associated with a highly industrialized and urbanized society. Children remained dependent for longer as the school-leaving age rose and, increasingly, post-school training or education was required. Greater social mobility meant that elderly people were more likely to lack the support of extended family networks. A growing proportion of expenditure – about half in the mid-1970s – went on cash payments. These, of course, were then used by recipients to buy goods and services in the market economy. The contribution of benefits to local economies in this way is often forgotten.

By the beginning of the 1980s, the ideological hostility of the new Conservative Government, combined with the economic problems previously encountered by the Labour government, did not promise well for the future of welfare. Since the mid-1980s, although there have been major reforms which have also involved substantial erosion of principle, they have still not been set against any index of social need or related to any explicit new framework of social principle.[4] Two main motive forces have driven the changes which have taken place – an increasing public spending bill and fears about the nanny state.

Attitudes to the welfare state[5]

The New Right is hostile to the welfare state because of its need for levels of taxation which burden companies and individuals and discourage enterprise. By lessening the prospect of economic growth, it is argued, it also reduces the possibility of tackling poverty. Welfare spending creates a dependency culture and weakens the idea of rewarding success and punishing failure. This contrasts with the more traditional Conservative position which sees a need to balance economic and social policy. The welfare state can smooth the sharp edges of the free-market system and public expenditure can be used to help create a healthy economy by investing in people as human capital. For Democratic Socialists, the welfare state is essential to social harmony, giving 'the vital mediating force between political rights provided by democracy and the aspirations which grow out of such rights, and the free market's neglect of considerations other than market power in the distribution of the social product'.[6] It is also key to attempts to reduce inequalities and, in that way, to prefigure what social relationships would be like in a socialist state.

However, others see the welfare state as in one way or another colluding with the maintenance of capitalism – by curbing its excesses without requiring fundamental change; by intentionally or unintentionally perpetuating particular patterns of oppressive relationships as, for example, male domination; or because the welfare state is itself dependent on economic growth which Greens would argue is buying short-term gains at the cost of long-term disaster.

This range of views from outright opposition at the extremes of the New Right and Marxists or Greens to enthusiastic or more qualified support is echoed in the attitudes towards the possibility of achieving beneficial social change through political action. Vic George and Paul Wilding identify four areas in which optimism or pessimism over politics can be expressed:[7]

- whether or not a sense of common purpose can be reached in society or is ruled out by fundamental social conflicts;
- human capacity to plan and implement effective policies;
- whether our social institutions and their professionals are capable of translating policies into good practice or are inherently inefficient and/or self-interested;
- whether the ills which we are seeking to eradicate are so endemic to the human condition that it is an impossible task.

In the ongoing debate about the welfare state all these strands can be detected.

A strategy that has been tried and failed or never been tried?

> Once we recognise that poverty is the product of the operation of social and economic forces, in which individual choices or individual responsibility may be important but can never be decisive, then we must look for the solutions to poverty in anti-poverty policies which take account of and seek to influence these major social and economic forces.[8]

Why has the welfare state not eliminated poverty? In broad terms, it is because there has been no coherence or consistency across welfare and economic policies. Beveridge recognized that even the most comprehensive social security system would be ineffective in isolation. There needed to be a full frontal attack not just on want but on the rest of his 'five giants' – disease, ignorance, squalor and idleness.[9] Social security must be underpinned by the maintenance of something approaching full employment, child allowances and free health care. These goals were not achieved. Full employment was never actively pursued and the national insurance scheme has been unable to cope with the actual levels of unemployment. Family allowances, one-third lower than the rate recommended by Beveridge when introduced in 1945, have been on a downhill slide since then. Finally, despite the NHS introduction of health care free at the point of need, it has not prevented a close association between poverty and ill health. Inequalities in access to, and quality of, provision, as well as in health chances, have more recently been compounded by mounting prescription, optical and dental charges.

> The welfare state that emerged from the extraordinary circumstances of the 1940s was the brain-child of John Maynard Keynes and William Beveridge. When Keynes seemed to have solved the problems of production, Beveridge calculated how to distribute the proceeds fairly. The intellectual authority of the political Right over the last twenty years has in large part come from the breakdown of the Keynsian and Beveridgean legacy.[10]

To address the question of why poverty has not been eliminated more specifically, we need to disentangle the various functions of state welfare. First it has a role in providing major services, such as education and health, essential not just to the well-being of individuals in every part of society, but also to the economic health of the country as a whole. Little mention is made of this function, especially when governments are seeking to cut public spending, but it is of primary importance. It has provided a buttress to avert some of the more radical efforts to dismantle public services.

The second function is to counter poverty. Both defenders and critics tend to emphasize this more. Yet it has largely been confined to first aid and bandaging, an approach which is shown most starkly in means testing for social security. To go beyond this to a preventative strategy would require policies on wealth and income as well as benefits. As Pete Alcock points out,[11] this would entail intervention in the labour market to influence both the availability of employment and the level of wages. It would involve policies on taxation and investment in order to direct wealth into socially productive industrial or service activities rather than allowing it to be accumulated in private pockets. All this amounts to 'intervention in economic forces as well as social structures; it would require the welfare state planning directly for production and distribution, and not only for redistribution'.[12]

Without such intervention, it can be argued that the welfare state's third strategy – that of promoting equality – has never really been attempted. Certainly a number of commentators have given reasons for its failure. According to Julian Le Grand the strategy was never properly developed to achieve equality of outcome as against equality of opportunity.[13] Expenditure on health and education has raised standards for all, but the more active and articulate middle classes have been most able to benefit. This served to reinforce the inequalities of monetary income. But inequalities have also flowed from fiscal 'welfare'. Its significance was pointed out in the 1950s by Richard Titmuss,[14] but it has grown in importance since then to the point where it can almost be said that a strategy of inequality has taken over. At the end of the 1980s, the estimated costs of major tax reliefs were £10.9 billion on mortgage interest relief to home owners, £12.9 billion on occupational and personal pensions, £300 million on support for private schools and £100 million on support for private medical insurance.[15]

SOCIAL SECURITY

The Beveridge Report of 1942 was implemented to introduce a two-tier system of social security. There was state insurance against most contingencies like ill health, disability, unemployment and retirement, which it was thought would cater for the vast majority of people. Then there was a safety net of 'supplementary' benefits for the few who for some reason were not eligible.

Although the social and economic circumstances in which the social security system has to operate have changed and will continue to change, there are some basic aims which social security policy should always seek to fulfil. First it should ensure an adequate level of income for all. In this way it should prevent or alleviate poverty by ensuring that no one falls below an agreed minimum level of income sufficient to maintain a quality of life giving reasonable security and good health. It should redistribute resources over people's lives, recognizing the different financial burdens at different stages in the life cycle and taking particular care to protect the very young and very old. It should give protection against risks and unexpected events such as illness or redundancy.

Second, the social security system should be a way of promoting social cohesion and strengthening community, by enabling recipients to participate and remain active as citizens, by minimizing isolation and stigma. Such a system will then benefit everyone whether or not they receive financial support, because it upholds a strong and balanced community. Third, the system should reduce division and inequality, ensuring incomes and resources for those in need which are sufficient to allow them to keep in touch with other members of the community. It should redistribute from richer to poorer members of society and counter discrimination on such grounds as disability, race, religion, gender or sexual orientation.

There are also important operational principles. The system should be:

- simple and understandable;
- fair in the treatment of equal needs;
- responsive to changes in individual and social needs;
- economically sustainable;
- effective and cost effective.

Types of benefit

Contributory benefits

include National Insurance unemployment benefit, sickness benefit, widow's pension and the retirement pension. Eligibility depends upon having paid enough National Insurance contributions during past periods of employment.

Means-tested benefits

are paid in specified circumstances to those whose income and assets fall below a certain limit. These include Income Support, housing benefit, council tax benefit, family credit and disability working allowance. Those on Income Support are eligible for 'passported' benefits in kind such as free school meals.

Categorical benefits

are paid in prescribed circumstances, but are not based on any test of means or contributions. They include child benefit, industrial injury benefits, disability living allowance, the invalid care allowance, and the occupational benefits of statutory sick pay and statutory maternity pay.

Discretionary benefits

is the term covering the Social Fund. This pays means-tested grants or loans, but even low-income people have no legal entitlement to these.

From solution to problem

The mid-1970s saw some expansion in cash benefits. The basic retirement pension was increased and indexed to changes in earnings or prices, whichever was the greater. A state earnings-related pension scheme (SERPS) was introduced. Child Benefit replaced Family Allowances and Child Tax Allow-ances. National Insurance contributions became almost wholly income related. The theme of all these measures was equity and a reduction in inequality. They aimed to avoid means testing, to achieve redistribution and to offer equality to women. 'Cash benefits were the solution; the only problem was how to pay for them.'[16] However, it was also being recognized that social assistance – that is, means-tested benefits – could no longer be seen as a residual scheme. Although designed only to meet the needs of a minority, it was having to deal with millions of claimants each year. Yet there was no public discussion of the role of social assistance or its relationship with National Insurance.

Antagonism towards claimants had been growing through the 1970s, especially to those groups traditionally regarded as 'undeserving', the unem-ployed and, to a lesser extent, lone parents. In the 1980s, this hostility in effect became government policy. One of the new Government's earliest actions was to break the link between the uprating of long-term benefits and earnings.[17] Since the end of 1980, benefits have only risen in line with prices and have fallen further behind average incomes. The Government had a number of anxieties about the disincentive effects of the high tax levels required to support the social security system and whether the rate of benefit compared to net income from wages would discourage unemployed people from rejoining the labour force. Social security was now perceived as a problem. In the 1985 Green Paper which heralded the Fowler Review of social security, the Government identified the three main objectives which should underlie the reform. First, the system must be 'capable of meeting genuine need'.[18] It is notable that the vocabulary of official reports no longer included the word 'poverty'. It was replaced by expressions such as 'people on low incomes' or 'those in greatest need'. Second, it 'must be consistent with the Government's overall objectives for the economy'. Third, it 'must be simpler to understand and easier to administer'.[19]

In fact, all the signs were that this review, purportedly the 'most funda-mental examination of our social security system since the Second World War'[20] was primarily cost-driven. It had a no-cost remit, so that the scope for any reform which would substantially improve life for claimants was almost nil. Recognizing that, as well as economic growth, restraining public expendi-ture was a key economic objective, the implications were that there would be more means testing, more targeting to reduce the cost of the system and a reduction in the unemployment benefit relative to wages. The proposals in the 1985 review survived virtually intact in the Social Security Act 1986, which mainly came into effect in 1988.

A series of piecemeal policy measures between 1979 and 1988 had already had the cumulative effect of reducing support for the unemployed. The 1986

Act 'paid even less attention to the impact of its policies on the lifestyles of claimants than previous reforms'.[21] The Government had rejected any enquiry into the adequacy of benefits even though research it had itself sponsored, conducted by the Policy Studies Institute, reported that already over half of all unemployed families ran out of money before the time for their next giro. Income Support was introduced to replace supplementary benefit. Means testing was brought centre stage. Knowing this pushes up administration costs, there was also an attempt to simplify the system and computerize it, which made it a much more blunt instrument. Weekly additions and lump sum payments were abolished. Another means of cutting the social security bill was removing the right of 16- and 17-year-olds to benefit. Later most full-time students also lost their right to benefit. On the other hand, the curtailment of SERPS would increase the number of people likely to need assistance in future.

The Social Fund

Prior to 1988, many people were having to claim both insurance and supplementary benefits because most insurance ones were not adequate for those totally reliant on them. The weekly rates of supplementary benefit were also too low by themselves to allow for intermittent items of household expenditure such as beds and cookers. 'Single payments' for larger items of expenditure or to cover urgent need were designed to meet this shortfall. This system of 'single payments' was replaced by the Social Fund which provides budgeting and crisis loans and community care grants.

It's ridiculous isn't it? If you're too poor, you can't get a loan.[22]

These provisions were founded on wholly new principles. First, the concept of entitlement was replaced by discretion. Social Fund officers decide who gets a loan or grant and there is no open appeal system. Second, the overall amount that can be spent is subject to cash limits rather than determined by need. In 1986, immediately before the Social Fund's introduction, £350 million was spent on single payments whereas the national budget ceiling for the Social Fund was only £203 million, not all of which was available for loans and grants for equivalent items. To offset this shortfall, a mere 0.3 per cent rise was given in allowances to provide for these occasional major outgoings.[23] Third, the majority of payments are in the form of interest free loans instead of grants. One of the criteria officers have to consider before allowing a loan is the likelihood of repayment and the period over which it might be made. All too often, people are too poor to be deemed able to repay and are therefore refused. Alternatively, they do not apply because they are conscious of the unbearable pressure repaying a loan would place on an already overstretched budget.

Preventing poverty?

What is the current impact of social security? Are benefits appropriate to meet need and relieve poverty? Various factors indicate that they are not. Nicholas Barr and Fiona Coulter put forward a number of considerations which all amount to poverty being on the increase.[24] Income Support has gone up relative to the Retail Price Index but evidence suggests that poor people probably face a higher average rate of inflation than the RPI measures. More of their income is spent on basic needs and the shift from direct to indirect taxation, which is discussed later in this chapter, disproportionately increases living costs for lower-income families. In addition, Income Support claimants have to draw on this minimum level of benefit to pay water rates. Living standards may therefore have fallen. Certainly average earnings have risen more quickly than benefit rates, so that even though the consumption of some poor households may have risen, the gap between living standards has increased. In any case, some people on incomes below supplementary benefit level may not be eligible for benefit, perhaps because they are in full-time work or full-time education, or they have savings high enough to disqualify them, or because they are unemployed who have failed the 'availability for work' test.

Comparison of low-cost budgets and Income Support
rate at April 1993 prices[25]

	Low-cost budget*	Income Support	Shortfall
2 adults/2 children under 11	£142.56	£108.75	£33.81
1 adult/2 children under 11	£111.73	£88.65	£23.08

* These budgets take maximum housing benefit and council tax benefit into account.

The numbers in poverty relative to benefit have risen markedly. Sometimes it is argued that this is a misleading measure because simply raising the rate of benefit will bring more people into the count. However, because benefit rates have hardly risen in real terms, and on some measures have fallen, 'there is no upward bias on that account in the number of people counted as poor'.[26] As Barr and Coulter say, it is in any case a parsimonious definition of poverty. A poverty line of 140 per cent Income Support level is more realistic.

People are also worse off as a result of the 1986 Social Security Act. The aims of the Act were inherently contradictory. Simplifying provision and improving incentives are expensive and run counter to the overall objective of saving money. A London School of Economics study in 1994 showed that almost half the poorest 20 per cent of households suffered as a result of the shake-up effected in 1988 and that the unemployed and others without children lost unequivocally. Although elderly people, the long-term sick and families with children gained on average, these average gains hid a substantial number of losers. They included half of all lone-parent families and more than one in three couples with children. The effect of the switch to Social Fund loans alone was equivalent to a 2 per cent cut in benefit for pensioners and unemployed couples with children. Judging from a sample of Income Support claimants and a sample of all housing benefit claimants, real incomes after housing costs fell by about 10 per cent between 1987/8 and 1990/1.

A sorry tale

It is slowly dawning on us how we have failed 16- and 17-year-olds, leaving them exposed to a vicious combination of circumstances. It is a sorry tale of how social policy is not made.[27]

The number of young homeless people sleeping rough rose instantly when Income Support for 16- and 17-year-olds was axed in 1988. Centrepoint estimated an increase of over one-third amongst under-19s in its London hostels between 1987 and 1992 apart from the thousands of 'invisible' young homeless in the capital and elsewhere. A high proportion are young people leaving local authority care lacking the personal and financial support to help them en route to adulthood. Others are the victims of a breakdown in family relationships where the 'normal' strains of adolescence compound other problems. They may be households struggling on low incomes and/or in unsuitable accommodation where parents are already operating at the limits of their endurance. Or parents may have divorced and be in new relationships. One study found the number of teenagers with step-parents leaving home was significantly higher than for single parents. Limited prospects in terms of training, employment and pay may also give them little incentive to remain at home. Intervention to arrest the drift into homelessness would also cut crime. Lacking any other source of income, crime can beckon as a substitute career, tempting young people into theft, prostitution and drug dealing.

I look at the question of training elsewhere (in Chapter 11). Other aspects of policy affecting young people reflect wider confusions and contradictions. There is the perennial tension between responding to what is – meeting real and immediate needs – and sticking to some principles of what ought to be. In this instance, the ideology around family life and parental authority has become highly politicized. The Government has sought to hold the line that teenagers (sometimes young people into their twenties) *ought* to stay within the parental home or at least remain the parents' financial responsibility. On this premise, offering them an independent income, apart from being expensive, undermines family cohesion and self-sufficiency. But, however desirable, such family support is not the reality for many young people. Neglecting their needs at this crucial juncture of their lives jeopardizes their capacity to make a successful transition into employment and establish stable adult relationships.

The poverty trap

One of the concerns about benefits is their possible disincentive effect. The combination of low wages and the high rate at which in-work social security falls away as earnings rise means that people are often better off not working. They can face the equivalent to enormous marginal tax rates if, for example, they lose out on Housing Benefit or Family Credit. Apart from discouraging people from looking for work or seeking promotion, the poverty trap is inequitable and makes cheating more tempting. 'The gain from hiding income is much higher for those in the poverty trap than for those only facing Income Tax and NICs [National Insurance Contributions].'[28] The move to make Family Credit more generous as a cheaper alternative to Child Benefit meant that more people were caught in the poverty trap. In 1993, if a family with two children paying a rent of £50 per week increased their income from £100 to £200 they would only be £6.50 per week better off, with the remaining £93.50 disappearing in tax and reduced benefits.

> John and Debbie have children aged 1 and 4 years. They live in a council house with a weekly rent of £37.50. Until recently they were claiming Income Support of £108.75 per week, which meant that after paying their regular bills they had about £70 for food, clothing, household items, travel, social activities, etc. John recently took a job as a security guard. His take home pay is £130 and, with Family Credit, Housing Benefit and Child Benefit, the family have a total income of £169.40. However, John gets the bus to work and they now pay rent and council tax. They are just £7 per week better off than they were on Income Support.[29]

There are no easy solutions. It would probably be impossible to devise a system removing all disincentives for all households. However, the policy of holding down benefits quite clearly drives people into poverty. Instead, two aspects of taxation and income-related benefits could be revised. First, benefits could be withdrawn more gradually as income rises. Secondly, the level of income at which tax becomes payable could be increased.

Being on benefit

> I don't feel as if any of it . . . is a right; it's a privilege. But they actually make me feel dependent . . . I feel that the system is such that it wants to make me dependent by this resentment, this grudging, this second-rate – I put it more than second-rate, it's worse than that, but that's the member of the population that you become. You are a problem . . . [30]

The object of policy reforms has been to reassert the dependency on employers and families by making state dependency problematic. The effect however has not been to reduce state dependency but to increase the strains on claimants. On the whole, they do not need encouragement to work. The study of long-term claimants by Dean and Taylor Gooby, which was cited in the last chapter, gives evidence of people's anxiety to find work for reasons mainly unrelated to, and independent of, any pressures from the social security system. On the other hand, the poverty trap had a disincentive effect, particularly on lone parents who felt directly constrained by the benefit system and the deficiencies of the labour market. 'As one such respondent put it, "It's quite a luxury to go to work really": a luxury she was no longer permitted and could not afford.'[31] But they do not want material assistance from their families because the burden of financial obligation was seen as standing in the way of the personal and emotional support which was what was valued within families.

The increasingly coercive and punitive nature of state intervention is also of questionable effectiveness as it may encourage claimants to view the state as adversary, reduce their inclination to co-operate with the state and undermine any inhibition they may feel about 'working the system'. Unease, anger and impotence may be endemic to the receipt of benefits, but Dean and Taylor-Gooby felt these feelings had been aggravated by recent changes. Claimants felt under constant suspicion of cheating and more than ever stripped of their privacy. 'If nothing else, it cannot be said that such widespread and often deep-seated feelings of resentment and mistrust are conducive to "good citizenship".'[32]

Private provision

In some of the areas covered by the social security system, there are also forms of private provision. About half of all employees (57 per cent men, 37 per cent women[33]) are covered by occupational pension schemes. Additionally some employers give enhanced maternity (and sometimes paternity) or sick leave and offer free private medical insurance. An increasing number of people now are contributing to personal pensions. Private insurance also allows those who can afford it to make additional provision against contingencies such as sickness or invalidity. Clearly in all these instances there is an issue of access and affordability. The long-term unemployed have no opportunity to safeguard their old age through occupational or private schemes. Even for many in work, the opportunity may not be there or their income will be too low to make it feasible. Similarly private health insurance will be totally outside some people's range.

The Government has been encouraging people to make private arrangements. For example, it has given tax relief and National Insurance rebates on personal pension schemes. How much it matters that a large section of the population will be precluded from making such personal arrangements depends upon the quality of state provision. If, as seems to be the case, the government is looking to private provision as an alternative to, rather than just an optional top-up to state provision, this is a worrying trend.

At worst, private insurance schemes can be mishandled through incompetence or fraud and, therefore, fail their subscribers. At best, they are concerned with their own viability and the well-being of their members. As such, they are constrained first of all in respect of the risks they can underwrite. For example, unemployment would not be an attractive proposition for them. They cannot encompass the social security system's overall requirement to give personal security and community stability with effective and fair provision for all.[34] Individuals putting their reliance on private provision and seeing themselves as getting no personal benefit from the state scheme, are unlikely to want to go on paying for it. The Government's capacity to raise the necessary income would be impaired, leading to a further erosion in the value of benefits, leaving those dependent upon them further behind. 'It is vital that a level of common provision, reflecting a concern for all in society, remains at the heart of social security policy.'[35]

In 1990, the responsibility for administering social security passed to a new executive agency, the Social Security Benefits Agency. Formally, it has no control over policy other than to ensure that it is operationally practicable. However, when a Social Security Commissioner's decision led people with learning difficulties to claim arrears of benefit going back as far as 1948, the Agency lobbied successfully to get the law changed. 'Thus in a situation where the legitimate rights of claimants unduly pressurised benefits administration, the Benefits Agency sought to protect the latter.'[36]

Lone parents

The social security system was also founded on the premise that men were the breadwinners and would provide for women. Women's disadvantaged situation in the labour market, their reduced chances of building up full National Insurance contributions and the continued assumptions about their dependency on men all combine to consign them to secondary status.

As the number of lone-parent families increases, so society's anxiety would seem to be increasing, too: *Whose 'fault' are they and whose 'responsibility'? What should be done about them? Should the role of policy be to discourage or support? Could it do both?*[37]

All political parties try to portray themselves as 'the party of the family'. But what is their conception of the family? Recent policy has been framed largely on the assumption that the two-parent, male-breadwinner family is both 'natural' and desirable. This has led to policies which curb welfare for lone parents and restrict the access of young people to social benefits which might enable them to leave home. Such policies are at odds with the reality of changes in the labour market affecting family life. They connect with more general issues than those specific to lone mothers concerning parental roles and the sometimes contradictory needs of childcare on the one hand and the family's financial needs on the other. They also expose the tensions between adopting a position on some moral high ground and responding to evident need. The needs of children in poverty are no less whatever judgement is reached about the responsibility or irresponsibility of their parents. In any case, stigmatization is no answer. Instead, struggling families, whether one or two parent, require positive support to ensure that children and young people do not suffer the ill-effects of the social and financial strain their parents are under. Preventative and ameliorative strategies are needed.

Who has really benefited?

Social security is concerned with two sorts of income redistribution. First it is intended to smooth income over the individual's life-cycle and in this it is evidently successful. Secondly, it is to redistribute income between individuals to reduce poverty and inequality. In this, it has been fighting more of a losing battle over recent years. Nevertheless, it has proved an important buffer against the impact of economic crises which could otherwise have precipitated much more social unrest. For example, it is surprising that mass unemployment, for all its side effects, has not created greater political backlash. Howard Glennerster argues that 'much of the credit for this is due to the welfare system, which not only permitted the economy to weather the storms without too much social distress, but also permitted it to make the subsequent economic adjustments. If the economic gains of the Thatcher government are real, then they were possible because there was a welfare safety net.'[38]

Nevertheless, the direction of social security changes in the 1980s was increasingly to isolate claimants by lowering their relative living standards and fuelling the fears and prejudices of others. The latter also influences the mood in the country about 'reasonable' levels of taxation. So, what have been the trends in taxation and what effects have they had on the distribution of income?

TAXES UP AND TAXES DOWN

In 1994, the Institute for Fiscal Studies published a study of personal taxation over a ten-year period.[39] It took 1985 as the baseline year, and the analysis follows changes up to 1995 when the measures announced in the 1993 budgets will have come fully into effect. The authors, Christopher Giles and Paul Johnson, look at changes to taxes on personal income, on personal property and on expenditure.

The growth in the UK economy around the mid-1980s yielded increased tax revenues which were used by the Government to cut the Public Sector Borrowing Rate (PSBR) and to increase spending, but also to fund tax cuts, in particular to reduce income tax. However, by 1993 the growing PSBR led to a package of tax increases in the two budgets which, in terms of the revenue raised, will reverse most of the reductions of the late 1980s. But these increases are very different from the earlier reductions. They therefore bring about a substantial reform of the UK tax system. Some of the major changes during the decade are shown below.

The major tax changes over the decade:

Income tax

- 1986 to 1988: a step-by-step reduction in basic rate of income tax from 30 per cent to 25 per cent;
- 1988: the top band of tax taken down from 60 per cent to 40 per cent;
- personal allowances increased in real terms in this period;
- 1992: a 20 per cent tax band introduced on the first £2,000 of taxable income;
- 1993: income tax allowances frozen;
- 1993: 20 per cent tax band widened to £2,500 and to £3,000 in 1994;
- Married Couple's allowance to fall to 20 per cent in April 1994 and to 15 per cent in April 1995.

National Insurance Contribution (NIC)

- 1989: reforms which cut NICs for most people;
- 1993: main rate of employee NICs to rise from 9 per cent to 10 per cent in 1994.

Mortgage Interest Relief at Source (MIRAS)

- 1991: MIRAS restricted to the 25 per cent basic rate of tax;
- 1993 Budget: value of MIRAS to fall from 25 per cent to 20 per cent in April 1994 and to 15 per cent in April 1995.

Domestic rates

- In 1989 in Scotland and 1990 for the rest of the UK, the Community Charge (Poll Tax) replaced domestic rates. This marked a change from a tax on the estimated value of a home to a *per capita* charge not related to either income or property value;
- 1992 Poll Tax replaced by Council Tax, which returned to a basis of property value (with a reduction for single-person households), payable according to the value band rather than constantly varying with rental values as under the old domestic rating system.

VAT

- 1991: VAT increase from 15 per cent to 17.5 per cent (to fund a Poll Tax subsidy of £140 per adult);
- 1993: VAT imposed on domestic fuel at 8 per cent in 1994 and 17.5 per cent in 1995. Its revenue partially offset by a compensation package of increases to means-tested benefits and to state pensions.

Excise duty

- the overall effect of changes 1985–95 has been a substantial increase in duty on leaded petrol and cigarettes in real terms and a fall in real duties on alcohol, especially spirits.

A number of policy moves reflect the unpopularity of specific measures, most obviously the Community Charge and VAT on domestic fuel. It was estimated that 83 per cent of the poorest tenth of the population paid more under the Community Charge whilst 71 per cent of the richest tenth paid less.[40] In general, those households whose property had a lower rateable value paid more. So did those with more registered Charge payers. The Community Charge was so widely believed to be unfair – as well as expensive – that, first it was subsidised by the Exchequer, funded by an increase in the level of VAT, and then replaced altogether.

The imposition of VAT on domestic fuel drew an instantly hostile reaction from across the political spectrum because, as it is 'a tax on a necessity, the consumption of which is relatively invariant with income, it would have hit the poor particularly hard'.[41] Conservative supporters' concern focused especially on its effects on the elderly. A survey conducted by Church Action on

Poverty showed that there was no predictable relationship between household composition, incomes and the size of fuel bills.[42] There was enormous disparity and the reasons for the variations were complex, including the size and age of the residential home, the age and state of health of the residents, the amount of time spent at home, the variable standards of heating systems and insulation in addition to personal habits and choice. And it was clear that those factors leading to higher bills – such as poor housing conditions, inadequate heating systems, unemployment and old age – were difficult if not impossible to change.

As a result of the controversy that greeted the imposition of VAT on domestic fuel after its announcement in the March 1993 Budget, a compensation package was announced in the second budget in November that year. While for pensioners, the compensation would come near to offsetting their higher fuel charges, it fell short for families with children on means-tested benefits. This was partly because of the wide variations of fuel bills, largely outside of individual control, but also because Income Support levels already fell short of the minimum needed for even a low-cost standard of living. A report published by Joseph Rowntree Foundation in November 1992 estimated that a two adults/two children family needed an extra £36 per week and a lone parent with two children needed an extra £25 per week.[43] In any case, compensation, of course, would not bring any relief to those poorer families not in receipt of means-tested benefits. The House of Commons Social Security Committee estimated in January 1993 that 4.4 million people have income less than Income Support.[44] In addition, Alistair Burt, the Social Security Minister, in a written Parliamentary answer, estimated that between 2.2 and 3.6 million people have an income which is less than £10 above benefit level.[45] These total up to 8 million people, most of whom would receive no compensation whatsoever for higher fuel bills.

Measuring the effects

The likely impact of the Poll Tax and VAT on fuel were immediately evident. Hence they were clear-cut issues which people could grasp. The effects of other equally significant trends have been less visible. Yet, the nature of the tax cuts in the 1980s and the continuing trend from direct to indirect taxation has had a marked impact on the distribution of taxation.

Giles and Johnson found a way of modelling the 1985 tax system in order to compare its effects with those of the 1994 system across the whole population.[46] Overall the tax changes since 1984 have meant that households' disposable incomes have risen on average by £4 per week. But the gains and losses were distributed very unevenly – 47 per cent gained, 37 per cent lost.

The main determinant of how much a household gained, or indeed whether or not it gained at all, was its income. High income households gained substantially from the reductions in income tax rates. For most high income households these outweighed the negative impact of indirect tax rises. For poorer households, however, who gained little or nothing from the reductions in income tax rates, the overall effect of the changes was to reduce post-tax incomes.[47]

Analysing households in deciles, that is, in 10 per cent blocks ranging from the highest to the lowest incomes, the pattern was clear – 'the richer the decile the greater the gain, with the poorest four deciles actually losing on average as a result of the changes'.[48]

Gains and losses can also be looked at across types of household. Most of those in non-pensioner households where no one was in work lost over the period. Over three-quarters of unemployed couples with children lost out from the changes and nearly two-thirds of single parent families. In part this reflects the unduly hard impact on these families of VAT on fuel. Even amongst earning couples, those with children were more likely to be losers than those without. Where both partners were earning they had twice the opportunity to benefit by direct tax cuts. Only a comparatively small proportion of pensioners lost out, reflecting the VAT on fuel compensation package.

Progressive or regressive

In 1985 and 1995, direct taxation is clearly progressive, that is, it takes a higher proportion of income from the better off than from poorer. In 1995, the proportions taken range from 7 per cent from the lowest decile to 30 per cent from the highest. Most of those in the bottom deciles have incomes so low that they pay no income tax at all. However, the gap between what is taken from rich and poor has narrowed since 1985. In other words, the changes since then have been regressive – the reduction in the proportion taken from the richer deciles has been greater than the reduction in proportion taken from the poorer. The greatest difference has been made to the very rich, that is, the top decile, whose direct taxation fell from 34.25 per cent to 30.5 per cent and for those in the top 1 per cent income bracket, there has been a striking 10 per cent drop in their tax bill from 46.2 per cent to 36.2 per cent, because they benefited in full from the cutting of the highest income tax rate from 60 to 40 per cent.

Indirect taxes are inherently regressive. This is because the basics of living consume a higher proportion of the income of poorer groups. In 1995, the poorest decile will pay nearly one-fifth of their gross income on indirect taxes as against the top decile paying only 8 per cent. But again, while increasing indirect taxation for everyone, the 1985–95 changes have increased the regressivity of this tax. The burden has not fallen proportionately across all income bands, but hits the poor harder, with a rise of 4 per cent at the bottom end of income distribution but only 1.5 per cent at the top end.

I have tried to avoid using the word 'burden' – so often applied to taxation – because we need to get away from the negative connotations invariably attached to taxation. But burden does seem the only appropriate word for the disproportionate load which has been heaped upon those at the lower end of the income scale as a deliberate act of policy.

This chapter has examined social security and taxation. Other policies affect living standards. Where the state provides free or subsidized services or benefits in kind, this makes a difference to income. The next chapter looks at how policies in housing, education, health and social care impact directly or indirectly on individual income. This will lead on to consideration of the urban, economic and employment policies which play a part by affecting the market-related economic processes that generate inequalities.

NOTES

1. Maurice Bruce, *The Coming of the Welfare State* (Batsford, 1965), p. 294.
2. See John Hills (ed.), *The State of Welfare: The Welfare State in Britain since 1974* (Oxford: Clarendon Press, 1991).
3. *Ibid.*, p. 20.
4. The Labour Party's Commission on Social Justice, which attempted just such a thoroughgoing review, published its report, *Social Justice: Strategies for National Renewal*, in October 1994.
5. Vic George and Paul Wilding, *Welfare and Ideology* (Harvester Wheatsheaf, 1994).
6. *Ibid.*, p. 190.
7. *Ibid.*, p. 192.
8. Pete Alcock, *Understanding Poverty* (London: Macmillan 1993), p. 264.
9. Beveridge Report, *Social Insurance and Allied Services*, Cmd 6404 (London: HMSO, 1942), para. 8.
10. The Commission on Social Justice, *Social Justice in a Changing World* (Institute for Public Policy Research, 1993), p. 1.
11. Alcock, *op. cit.*, p. 267.
12. *Ibid.*
13. Julien le Grand, *The Strategy of Equality* (London: Allen and Unwin, 1982).
14. Richard Titmuss, 'The Social Division of Welfare', in *Essays on the Welfare State* (London: Allen and Unwin, 1958).
15. Peter Taylor-Gooby, *Social Change, Social Welfare and Social Science* (Harvester Wheatsheaf 1991).
16. Nicholas Barr and Fiona Coulter, 'Social Security: Solution or Problem?' in Hills (ed.), *op. cit.*, p. 274.
17. The Social Security Act 1980.
18. See discussion in Carol Walker, *Managing Poverty: the Limits of Social Assistance* (London: Routledge, 1993), pp. 122ff.
19. *Reform of Social Security*, Vol. 1, Cmnd 9517 (London: HMSO, June 1985), pp. 2–3, para. 1.12.
20. *Ibid.*, preface by Norman Fowler.
21. Walker, *op. cit.*, p. 14.
22. Participant in a discussion with the author at Merseyside Trade Union, Community and Unemployed Resource Centre, 18 August 1994.

23. Calculation by the Family Welfare Association, quoted in Jacqui Moore, 'The Social Fund', Occasional Paper 3, in Hilary Russell (ed.), *Community Matters* (Centre for Urban Studies, University of Liverpool, 1988).

24. Barr and Coulter, *op. cit.*, pp. 302ff.

25. From Nina Oldfield and Autumn C. S. Yu, *The Cost of a Child: Living Standards for the 1990s* (Child Poverty Action Group, 1993).

26. Barr and Coulter, *op. cit.*, p. 310.

27. Madeleine Bunting, 'The abandoned generation', *Guardian*, 1 June 1994.

28. John Hills, *Changing Tax: How the Tax System Works and How to Change It* (London: CPAG, 1988), p. 29.

29. Example taken from Church Action on Poverty's response to the Review of Expenditure on Social Security, October 1993, p. 18.

30. Hartley Dean and Peter Taylor-Gooby, *Dependency Culture: The Explosion of a Myth* (Harvester Wheatsheaf, 1992), p. 85.

31. *Ibid.*, p. 95.

32. *Ibid.*, p. 111.

33. Figures given in The Commission on Social Justice, *Making Sense of Benefits* (Institute for Public Policy Research (IPPR), 1993).

34. This section draws upon the CAP response to the Review of Expenditure on Social Security, October 1993.

35. *Ibid.*, p. 14.

36. C. Walker, *op. cit.*, p. 8.

37. Louie Burghes, *One-Parent Families: Policy Options for the 1990s* (Family Policy Studies Centre, Joseph Rowntree Foundation, February 1993), p. 41 (emphasis in the original).

38. Julian Le Grand in Hills (ed.), *op. cit.* (1991), referring to Howard Glennerster, 'What Commitment to Welfare?', The Richard Titmuss Memorial Lecture, 1988.

39. Christopher Giles and Paul Johnson, *Taxes Down, Taxes Up: The Effects of a Decade of Tax Changes*, Commentary No. 41 (The Institute for Fiscal Studies, 1994).

40. Carey Oppenheim and Peter Esam, *A Charge on the Community* (London: CPAG and LGUI, 1987).

41. *The Rich Get Richer, the Poor Get Colder: VAT on Fuel – Its Impact on Low Income Households* (Church Action on Poverty, September 1993), p. 3.

42. *Ibid.*

43. *Household Budgets and Living Standards* (Joseph Rowntree Foundation, November 1992).

44. House of Commons Social Security Committee, *Low Income Statistics: Low Income Families 1979–89* (London: HMSO, 1993).

45. Hansard, 1 April 1993, column 420, House of Commons.

46. Giles and Johnson, *op. cit.*, see p. 9 for the method used.

47. *Ibid.*, p. 10.

48. *Ibid.*, p. 11.

CHAPTER 10

The Building Blocks of the Good Society

As long as men are men, a poor society cannot be too poor to find a right order of life, nor a rich society too rich to have need to seek it. (R. H. Tawney, *The Acquisitive Society*, Fontana 1961, first published 1921, p. 13)

... politics ought to be a moral activity and we should never be inhibited in stressing the moral basis of our approach. Of course, we have to take matters further forward. We have to undertake the intellectual task of applying moral principle in a way which results in a practical policy of benefit to our fellow citizens. (John Smith, in *Reclaiming the Ground: Christianity and Socialism*, ed Christopher Bryant, Spire, 1993, p. 128)

This chapter looks first at developments in housing over the past few years and identifies ways in which public policy has not only not compensated for market failure but at times has reinforced it. Similarly, in the spheres of health and education, which are social goods not catered for by markets, policies have had additional detrimental implications for disadvantaged groups and communities.

HOUSING

The Welfare State has been sneered at and, like any human institution, it has bred its own distortions and difficulties, but it was and remains a noble human ideal. Society as a whole assumed the role of provision for the poor. Enormous social distinctions remained, of course, but there was an underlying conviction that we were part of the same family and it was monstrous for some members of the family to be homeless while the rest of us were comfortable.[1]

Even at the most expansive period of the welfare state, it was never envisaged that government should make universal provision for housing on a par with education or health. Yet it was recognized that having a decent home is a social right fundamental to human well-being, and that the country's housing needs could never be met through the private housing market alone. Market forces operate here as elsewhere to disadvantage the poor. There is a need for state intervention both to set some minimum standards for the quality of housing and to ensure a supply of affordable accommodation for people on low incomes. Given the great importance of housing for individuals and for the country as a whole, it is surprising that it has not been higher on the political agenda for any of the major political parties. Housing is only one part of a junior minister's brief.

A failing supply

There is a simple stark fact that the number of houses provided for those in housing need has been reducing at the very time that homelessness has increased.[2]

We clearly have a housing shortage in this country. Calculating this is not just a matter of comparing the number of available dwellings with the number of households requiring them. They may not be the right type or size, or in the right place, or at the right price. The housing supply needs to be able to cope with change whether it is demographic, such as changes in household composition, or regional shifts of population as when families uproot in search of employment. Yet, housing is a long-term, high-investment commodity for public or private sector providers and for consumers wishing to buy or rent. It is slow, therefore, to adjust to changes in need or demand. Provision requires planning. But it also requires subsidy either to the providers or the consumers, or both, to bridge the gap between the economic cost of housing and people's resources. 'In no country does the market system provide good low-cost housing. This is a matter of prime importance and must everywhere be a public responsibility. Few things are more visibly at odds with the good society than badly housed or homeless people.'[3]

... if one sought a living instance of the enduring Galbraithian truth about the coexistence of private affluence and public squalor, the example of British housing could not be improved on. It fits the picture precisely because it was no accident. What has happened to housing – the downgrading of the public, the upgrading of the private – is exactly what was meant to happen.[4]

However, over the last fifteen years, past policy criteria – housing need, shortage, and condition – have been largely set aside in favour of 'what the country can afford'.[5] Housing policy has been determined more by considerations of taxation and public expenditure than a concern to redress disadvantage. Exchequer subsidies to housing costs have fallen dramatically and general subsidies benefiting all council tenants via rent control have been replaced by means-tested ones through Housing Benefit. There has been an increase in rents to a real level higher than at any time in the post-war period. At the same time, steps have been taken to extend the role of the private sector and encourage owner occupation. This was in line with the wider ideological push towards a property-owning democracy 'which emphasised the merits of ownership of capital rather than seeing home ownership as a means of achieving housing policy objectives'.[6] These measures did not signify a withdrawal of government from the housing field, rather a change in the type of state intervention.

The Right to Buy scheme for council tenants was introduced in 1980. Although this gave many people an opportunity to embark on home ownership which they could not otherwise have afforded, the scheme had severe consequences for other, still poorer people. It depleted the social housing stock by the sale of the better properties without provision being made for the renewal of that stock. Then the Housing and Planning Act of 1986 not only introduced higher discounts to make the Right to Buy more attractive, but measures to extend privatization through sales to private developers. This legislation, together with the 1986 Building Societies Act, paved the way for the 1988 Housing Act which was heralded by the 1987 election slogan 'the right to rent'. The new emphasis on rented housing was prompted by the problems stemming from the escalation of house prices and the impact of high interest rates. However, the solutions offered by government did not denote any return to municipalization. The 'right to rent' involved a fuller deregulation of private renting and a greater role for housing associations, whilst local authorities were left on the sidelines both with regard to making present provision and determining policy for future provision.

Owner occupation has risen from 57 per cent to 68 per cent since 1979. Over 3.5 million more people have become owner-occupiers. The push to home ownership was seductive. It evidently appealed especially to a distinctively English cultural attitude. If 'an Englishman's home is his castle', it is one he owns not rents. The high proportion of rented accommodation in the social housing sector has contributed to the feeling that renting is something people do only if they cannot afford to buy. It is different in other countries even within the UK. Traditionally renting has been more favoured in Scotland, though that too probably changed during the 1980s. But Britain certainly differs from others in the rest of Europe where in general the wealthier economies have more rented accommodation. Germany, for example, has only 40 per cent home ownership. There is less stigma attached to renting. Young people are less pressured into buying. Most importantly there are more housing options available. Britain has the highest percentage of personal wealth tied up in housing, which distorts the economy and makes it particularly subject to the volatility of the housing market.

The trend to ownership was driven by both positive and negative factors. The Right to Buy and tax relief both subsidized home ownership. But owner-occupation also became more attractive as rents increased and the rental sector declined in size and quality. The apparently inexorable rise in house values made ownership seem a good, safe investment and encouraged people to borrow to the limit – and sometimes beyond – of what they could afford. This proved falsely optimistic when the downturn came. The result in 1992 was 1.5 million home owners left holding £3 billion of negative equity – that is, living in houses worth on average £2,800 less than their outstanding mortgages. Up to 352,000 mortgagees were over six months in arrears and 68,540 lost their homes through repossession orders as unemployment took its toll of household incomes. Castles turned to prisons, assets to millstones. Ownership is predicated on a secure, steady income, but this no longer fits with the reality of the labour market for many people whose working lives are likely to be interspersed with periods of uncertainty and unemployment.

The public sector makes direct provision of housing to rent and it provides subsidies to local authorities and housing associations as providers and to individuals through housing benefit and tax relief. But this period has seen a reduction in housing available to lower-income households who cannot compete in the housing market. Between 1979 and 1987, the number of rented homes in Britain fell by 1.3 million. From 1981 to 1991, there was an average reduction in local authority housing of 9 per cent. The Right to Buy led to the loss of 1 million council homes in the ten years after its introduction. The impact was especially striking in new towns and some older industrial towns in the north which previously had a lot of council housing. Local authority house building declined to its lowest peace-time level since 1921 and housing association provision does not fill the gap. The 31,000 public sector and housing association completions in 1992 amount to less than a third of the 100,000 estimate of new units needed per year. The private rented sector has also massively declined, although there are signs of a slight upturn again in the mid-1990s. This decline partly reflected a reduction in tied housing, but also exposed the non-profitability of private letting at affordable rents.

The evidence given to the Archbishops' Commission on Rural Areas put a lot of stress on housing need. The increasing disparity between the cost of housing and rural incomes was highlighted. People often face a choice between moving away or remaining in substandard or overcrowded accommodation. The reduction of affordable housing stock in the countryside compounded by the purchase of rural houses as second homes was mentioned in Chapter 6. In some areas, over 10 per cent of houses are not occupied by permanent residents. ACRE (Action with Communities in Rural England) estimated a need for 25,000 new units a year at a time when the Housing Corporation planned to fund 1,100.

Misdirected expenditure

The system of housing finance was both inequitable and ineffective long before the Conservatives came to power in 1979. But action taken in 1980 exacerbated the shortcomings instead of remedying them. In the early 1980s, housing cutbacks accounted for over three-quarters of the public expenditure reductions, until housing expenditure was down from over 5 per cent to under 3 per cent of all government spending. Although this low level continued, the fall disguised a more complex picture. What was really happening was a transfer of resources from conventional housing programmes to other categories of expenditure. Two major sources of public costs associated with housing do not feature in the housing budget. Housing benefit figures appear instead in the social security programme. This inevitably escalated as controls were removed from rents. But also there are those items, including mortgage interest relief, capital gains tax exemptions, and discounts to council house purchasers, which are not classified as public expenditure, but nevertheless represent income lost to the public purse.

In the mid-1980s, housing benefit payments already exceeded housing expenditure and continued to climb. At the same time, the combination of mortgage tax relief and capital gains tax exemption was over double the amount spent on housing benefit. By 1990, mortgage tax relief alone was three times as high as housing public expenditure, partly because of high interest rates. In August 1994, John Perry, Policy Director of the Institute of Housing, reported to the Social Security Advisory Committee in the light of government concern to cut housing benefit expenditure which had become the fastest growing element of public spending.[7] He pointed to spiralling rents rather than benefit levels as the root of the problem. The pursuit of market rents, he said, was a 'false goal'. It could lead to rents of £200 per week and, if full benefit cover was withdrawn, intense hardship for poor tenants unable to pay the bills. Government plans to cut housing association grants would mean 85 per cent of new tenants being eligible for benefit so that, by the end of the century, he foresaw a £12 billion housing benefit bill amounting to 10 per cent of all social security spending.

Controls on local authority capital expenditure had been developed through the 1970s. Local authorities made bids for a central government allocation for their housing improvement expenditure through Housing Investment Programmes (HIPs). This arrangement, introduced in 1977, was thought to reconcile the central government concern to control public expenditure with allowance for local variation in housing requirements and local discretion over the appropriate balance of investment between new build and renovation. However, increasing limits on HIP allocations, and changing conditions placed on their supplementation and the use of capital receipts meant that they had decreasing impact on local investment patterns.

By 1987, the level of investment bore no relation to either local or national estimates of need and the pattern of investment depended on political and professional judgements about the use of creative accounting and of capital receipts. Allocations of permissions to spend bore little relation to needs or policies and were more strongly related to where capital receipts fell. From central government's viewpoint, however, the mechanism did enable it to check the total level of housing capital spending in the public sector.[8]

In other words, the balance of power had swung to the centre away from local discretion. The possibility of a rational allocation according to relative need nationwide was removed and the very mechanism which had been intended to encourage longer-term planning had been disabled by the abandonment of a forward planning structure and increasing uncertainty over levels of spending.

Most government spending on social housing now goes to the Housing Corporation for dwellings produced by housing associations, but this provision in no way makes up the reduction in the public sector. Additionally, the condition that housing associations must mix public and private finance is driving rents up which has implications for tenants whether or not they are on housing benefit. There is no guarantee that housing benefit will meet the increase. The rate of withdrawal of housing benefit has created a new poverty trap for those people who find work, amounting to a marginal tax rate of 97 per cent. And, those on low earnings not eligible for housing benefit are being priced out of this sector. A study of new housing association estates concluded that some were becoming ghettos, confined to families on benefits, with a very high proportion of lone-parent families and a very high ratio of children to adults.[9]

In poor condition

Throughout the 1980s, the depth of housing problems emerged more clearly. Improvement and clearance did not keep up with the effects of age and decay in private sector stock and a backlog was building up of expenditure needed to tackle under-maintenance and building defects in local authority stock. The English Household Condition Survey for 1991 estimated that about 1.5 million homes – 1 in 12 – were unfit for human habitation. Other housing professionals, the National Housing and Town Planning Council, put the estimate much higher, claiming that 1 in 6 were either in poor condition or lacking basic amenities. Almost 20 per cent had no inside toilet. These were most likely to be pre-1919 private terraced houses, many of which will also be very dilapidated. However, nowadays, the problem is less likely to be a lack of basic amenities and more likely to be disrepair. In the survey, 40 per cent were in a state of 'serious disrepair'. Many system-built 1960s estates were exhibiting the generic problems of that type of building – condensation, lack of insulation, drafts around windows and other structural defects. Deteriorating physical condition often led to increasing tenant dissatisfaction and a downward spiral of neglect and abuse.

Poor conditions were also evident in some owner-occupied housing. For example, there is a growing number of poor elderly home-owners unable to afford maintenance for their homes. The extension of home ownership as a result of government policy to those who are low-income owners, struggling to keep up their payments, means that an increasing number are competing for the scarce public funds to carry out repairs and renovation. Yet the Chartered Institute of Housing reports that the number of grants being awarded now is only about one-third of those awarded seven or eight years ago.

Homelessness – visibly at odds with the good society

> We believe that a home is more than bricks and mortar, more than a roof over one's head. Decent housing certainly means a place that is warm and dry and in reasonable repair. It also means security, privacy, sufficient space; a place where people can grow, make choices, become more whole people.[10]

> There is something peculiarly horrifying about the spreading incidence of absolute homelessness in our sophisticated society at the end of the second millennium.[11]

'Homelessness' can be used in different senses. It has a statutory meaning under the 1977 Homeless Persons Act (later consolidated in the 1985 Housing Act) which established a duty for local authorities to make adequate provision for certain categories of homeless people. This followed years of concern and campaigning about the plight of homeless people exemplified in the television play *Cathy Come Home*. Local authorities' fear that they would be swamped with homeless people led to a restricted definition of homelessness. People have a legal right to be seen as homeless if it is not reasonable for them to be living where they are or the accommodation is unsuitable, for example, if they are:

• living with family or friends who have told them to leave;
• experiencing threats of violence;

- split up as a family;
- having to leave their home within 28 days.

Second, they must not be intentionally homeless, that is, having done or failed to do something which led to the loss of accommodation. Leaving secure accommodation to seek work elsewhere can be deemed intentional home-lessness. A government survey in 1988 showed that over half of councils refused to designate people with young families moving into the area to find work as homeless. Third, they have to be in priority need. This means mainly those with dependent children or those who are vulnerable through age or disability or people being threatened, or homeless through an emergency such as fire or flood. Most single people and childless couples do not count. They must also have some local connection through work or length of residence or longstanding family links with the area.

The Act has since been criticized for its restrictive definition. But it was notable for its statutory recognition of local authorities' responsibility for households in urgent need of accommodation, whatever the authority's general inclination or attitude to individual cases. It also therefore underlined the limits on local autonomy. Councils' freedom of action is circumscribed by the broad policy framework set by central government.

The number of people accepted as homeless by councils in Britain rose from 73,951 in 1980 to 168,271 in 1992 – over 450,000 individuals. The number of households in temporary accommodation multiplied fifteen times in the same period to 68,540. Shelter estimated in 1992 that there were about 1,200,000 hidden homeless people and, when added to those sleeping rough, squatting or in hostels, and those private tenants with no long-term security, the unofficial homeless tally amounted to nearly 2 million. The number of homeless families in temporary accommoda-tion rose from 4,170 in 1980 to 62,740 in 1992. In 1992 an estimated 8,600 people were sleeping rough on the streets in England, including large numbers of young people and people leaving community care, more than half of them outside London. The 1824 Vagrancy Act remains in operation which means that sleeping rough and begging are still crimes for which 1,400 people were prosecuted in 1990. The average age at death of homeless people is 47.

In 1990–91, the Scottish Federation of Housing Associations said the number of applications to local authorities in Scotland had risen to over 34,600 per year, a 133 per cent increase over ten years. Of these, 23,155 households were actually assessed as homeless. The number of people involved was much greater. Not all applicants would be technically homeless. On the other hand, many homeless individuals and childless couples do not apply because they know they do not qualify for housing under the Act. Nearly a quarter of all homeless applicants that year were under twenty-five. Nearly 3,000 were under eighteen.

The National Consumer Council found that about 2.6 million people live in 'houses of multiple occupation', flats, bedsits or rooms in a house or hostel. They are mainly young or elderly and poor. Of these buildings, 80 per cent present fire hazards and 150 people die in them in fires each year and 2,500 are injured. Local authorities only have a duty to inspect the largest properties.

In 1994, the Government published a consultation paper reviewing current homelessness legislation and making proposals for change.[12] It concluded that the legislation was not working and was enabling some to take a short cut to re-housing, so that homes were not going to those with the best claim to them. As a result, it wished to:

- make waiting lists the sole means by which homeless and badly housed people may be allocated a tenancy;
- limit the local authority responsibility towards them to one year;
- withdraw the automatic entitlement to assistance of a homeless family who can no longer be accommodated by friends or family;
- encourage greater use of the private rented sector.

In its response, the Churches' National Housing Coalition said,

As Christians, we are disturbed by a document which appears to ignore the realities of homelessness, and the difficulties faced by low income households in securing housing in either the public or private sectors. The Consultation Paper is either a deliberate distortion of homeless people's experience, or hopelessly out of touch with it.[13]

The paper echoed earlier allegations by government Ministers that young girls were deliberately becoming pregnant to jump the housing queue. Commissioner Dinsdale Pender, UK Territorial Commander of the Salvation Army, says, 'It appears to be based on sweeping and unfounded assumptions about the motivation of homeless people.'[14] In general, the paper exemplified the strategy of obscuring the real problem – in this case, the lack of affordable housing – by focusing attention and blame on the very people who suffer as a result of it. It was an exercise in scapegoating, setting poor against poor, and reasserting the 'deserving' and 'undeserving' divide.

It was also misleading about the current position on allocations. The DoE's own research indicated that:

- there is only six months' difference between housing homeless people and those on the waiting list;
- 74 per cent of households rehoused as homeless are already on waiting lists;
- over half of all vacancies nationally go to the general waiting list. Only in London and the South-east is more local authority housing allocated to homeless households than ones on the ordinary waiting list.

Concern in the Churches

> ... the links between bad housing circumstances and other forms of social exclusion make it imperative that housing is tackled as well as other social inequalities.[15]

The Churches' National Housing Coalition (CNHC) is a coalition of over 500 Churches and Church-related housing organizations. It was established in 1991 as an expression of Christian concern about the growth of homelessness amongst young people and the continuing shortage of decent affordable housing.

In December 1992, CNHC organized the first ever Churches' national lobby of Parliament on housing and homelessness. Attended by over 3,000 people from all over the country, the lobby called on the Government to give housing a higher priority and to make 100,000 additional affordable homes available each year until the end of the decade. The Presidents of the Council of Churches for Britain and Ireland issued a statement endorsing the lobby's objectives. Preaching at a special service in Westminster Abbey on the eve of the lobby, the Archbishop of Canterbury, Dr George Carey, called for a 'moral crusade to rid society of the evil of homelessness'.

As well as campaigning about housing policy, CNHC seeks to promote good practice within the churches in response to housing and homelessness problems. It has a Church, Land and Property Project, part funded by the Department of the Environment, to encourage the use of surplus church property for affordable housing. CNHC also organizes an annual 'Homelessness Sunday' and provides resources, training and support to an extensive network of regional and local church housing groups.

CNHC policy objectives:

1. A commitment to greater investment in the provision of affordable rented housing
with a commitment to 100,000 new affordable homes each year to meet rural and urban housing needs, by bringing into use empty property in the public and private sectors and by an increase in house building. This should be funded in a variety of ways including:

- re-investing in housing provision all available proceeds from the past and future sales of council houses;
- incentives for private institutions and landlords to invest in housing provision and improvement;
- investing resources made available as part of the reform and re-structure of the housing finance system.

2. *Improvements in choice and quality for all tenants*, including:

- a legally enforceable 'tenants' charter' specifying minimum standards of quality of accommodation, repair and maintenance, participation and consultation;
- linking incentives to private landlords with the minimum standards laid down in a 'tenants' charter'.

3. *Further measures to tackle the growing problem of homelessness (especially for young people)* including:

- an inter-departmental government committee to investigate the replacement of bed and breakfast accommodation with more cost-effective and suitable permanent homes;
- restoration of entitlement to Income Support for all 16/17-year-olds with no recourse to other income who are unable to find employment or a suitable training scheme;
- recognition of the housing and living costs incurred by 18/25-year-olds living independently by restoring full entitlement to the full rate of benefits;
- re-instatement of DSS payment of deposits, thereby making rent payments in advance more easily obtainable.

4. *A reform and re-structuring of housing subsidies (especially Mortgage Interest Tax Relief) in order to direct support to those most in need*, including in particular, those:

- presently homeless;
- in inadequate accommodation;
- unable to form an independent household;
- unable to maintain a home.

HEALTH

Health to me is about having decent housing, nice neighbours, good friends, not feeling isolated, having enough money to live on, having a clean environment, and some community facilities and resources.[16]

Health is more than the absence of disease. Physical, psychological, social and spiritual factors all combine to make up 'health'. We understand more about health nowadays and know that all these elements are inextricably woven together, but somehow this understanding has not carried through to a recognition that we require healthier public policy more generally in spheres affecting income, employment, housing, nutrition, and the environment. A whole range of social inequalities prevent poorer people from enjoying optimum health. This is the context in which health care takes place and this section turns to looking at the health service to see how recent changes are likely to affect disadvantaged groups.

NHS – founded on equity principles

> The National Health Service was founded on equity principles. It is therefore extraordinary that in the current mammoth upheavals so little official attention has been paid to monitoring and ensuring the protection of these principles.[17]

Although the meaning of equity may never have been fully spelt out, there was general agreement that the National Health Service would be a fairer system than its predecessor. Margaret Whitehead, author of *The Health Divide*,[18] lists eight components of the NHS objectives which are equitable ones:

- universal entitlement;
- the pooling of financial risks so that payment is linked with the ability to pay rather than health care need;
- free at the point of use;
- equality of access to a comprehensive range and geographical spread of primary, secondary, tertiary and emergency services;
- the same high standard for all;
- selection on the basis of clinical need;
- a non-exploitative ethos, with health professionals' work not based on the profit motive;
- Bevan's 'feel-good factor' that society is more comfortable knowing that 'not only themselves, but all their fellows have access, when ill, to the best that medical skill can provide'.[19]

These last two are more intangible, not quantifiable, but Whitehead suggests that it may be 'some of the factors least amenable to precise measurement that are ultimately the most important in maintaining an equitable system'.[20]

Although it is debatable how far these basic objectives were ever fully achieved, and some principles have been eroded over time, the NHS remains more equitable than systems in many other developed countries. There have been radical changes over recent years intended to increase efficiency, widen choice and improve quality, though the assumption that this was the way to achieve these goals was based more upon ideological preference than empirical evidence. The reforms have been widely criticized inside and outside the medical profession, but it is only the anxieties about the likely effects of the reforms on disadvantaged groups which concern us here.

> Instead of 'get ready, take aim, fire' the Government chose 'get ready, fire, take aim'.[21]

In January 1988, Mrs Thatcher announced the setting up of a Working Party to review the NHS. A year later the White Paper, *Working for Patients*, was published. The NHS and Community Care Act was passed in June 1990, coming into force in April 1991. It introduced an internal market into health care, in which responsibility for purchasing services was separated from responsibility for providing them. Hospitals and other providers now have to compete for contracts from purchasers. On the purchasing side were the district health authorities, and their equivalents in Scotland and Northern Ireland, and the larger general practices holding their own budgets. On the providing side were the self-governing hospitals now competing with one another, with private-sector hospitals and with ones directly managed for the custom of purchasers. Accompanying reforms modified the management structure and systems, the financial arrangements and consultants' contracts in order to tailor the service to meet its business as well as its medical needs. More positively, however, the use of medical audit was promoted as a means of improving quality of care.

Working for Patients 'sparked off a propaganda battle of truly spectacular proportions that threatened at one time to deal a mortal blow to the Government's plans for the NHS, if not to the Government itself.'[22] 'Between its publication and the 1991 Act, changing vocabulary reflected a softening of the Department of Health stance.'[23] The canon of acceptable terminology gradually lost its more blatantly commercial flavour. The accent on change gave way to emphasis on continuity and stability. William Waldegrave, the incoming Secretary of State, when speaking to the Royal College of Surgeons in December 1990, admitted that the use of business jargon had alarmed people into thinking that 'we do not know the difference between a hospital and a supermarket'.[24]

Even before the White Paper was published, fears were being expressed that excessive dependence on the market would threaten the NHS's equity goals. As a result, instruments were brought in or reinforced to regulate the market under the umbrella term of 'managed competition'. It is still early days to judge the effects of the changes. 'The very fact that equity issues have been neglected means that there is little systematic evidence in terms of which the reforms can be evaluated.'[25] But, as Whitehead says, 'in a health care market, not just the weakest services, but also the chronically sick and economically weaker members of society could be the main losers'.[26] How will the services for the chronically sick rate alongside the potentially more profitable ones for acute conditions? Will the geographical spread and access be maintained? Some patients may be less attractive than others. Those from disadvantaged groups or neighbourhoods may be more expensive to treat because they have a higher prevalence of illness or take longer to recover as a result of poorer nutrition and living conditions and lack of social support.

A two-tier system?

In primary care, there has been concern about the effects of the GP contract. With the fundholding scheme, it is those larger, higher-income practices that are able to be more innovative and respond to the incentives on offer, and they are mainly in more affluent suburban areas. The scheme risks channelling resources to those areas least in need and being a two-tier scheme. Margaret Whitehead has drawn on a range of sources to examine the outcome of fundholding. She found that a two-tier system is developing in some places, though it was difficult to know how widespread this was and if it was more a product of the transition from one system to another than a lasting feature. The optimistic scenario is that fundholders are leading the way to improvements across the board, which will eventually reduce the two-tier effect. However, this relies on an expansion of public spending. If, as seems more likely, resources do not increase, fundholders' gains would be at the expense of others.

According to Glennerster *et al.*,

> Three years of interviewing in GP practices, that vary from dingy cramped premises with harassed receptionists in a poor inner city area, to quiet and efficient modern premises with rose gardens, branch clinics and computers linking the surgeries in a rural area, would disabuse anyone that there ever was a single tier system in Britain.[27]

However, the difference now is that 'a two or multi-tier system is openly condoned or even encouraged'[28] and therefore the principles of equality of access and selection on the basis of clinical need officially abandoned.

Assessing need

> I would like to improve my health by having a bigger income, a nice view outside my house, a community centre for people, play areas for the kids, and a cheap local food shop.[29]

On the plus side, the emphasis on effectiveness and on the assessment of need in the reforms had the potential to address existing inequalities if assessments covered the socio-economic distribution of ill health and its determinants, and if subsequent resource allocation took account of these findings. The health strategies of the four UK countries have varied. It is only in Wales, following the WHO *Health for All* principles, that tackling social inequalities is a stated objective and targets have been set for actions to improve the health of the most disadvantaged sections of the population. The other three have not gone along this road nationally even if local initiatives have tried to accommodate social and economic considerations in the priorities set in the national strategy.

Apart from the neglect of socio-economic factors in assessing health needs, some people are concerned that there are trade-offs between efficiency, effectiveness and equity. For example, pursuing the currently fashionable idea of 'health gain' can mean going for the quickest or easiest benefit at the lowest cost, with groups for whom improvements would take longer or bring smaller gains in life expectancy being sidelined.

Rather than taking steps to raise incomes or improve environments, the Government's approach to health promotion has been to emphasize the need for individuals to change their lifestyles. *The Health of the Nation* told people to avoid 'risk behaviour', adopt healthier diets and give up smoking, as though it is either ignorance or irresponsibility which prevents them.[30] Yet studies such as that conducted by NCH amongst families using its centres have found no evidence to suggest that parents are ignorant about what constitutes a good diet.[31] They knew all too well what they would like to buy if they had enough money. 'In terms of diet, well we all know what's healthy, but it's much harder to get to town, find out where is cheapest.'[32] If the levels of Income Support and Family Credit are insufficient to meet nutritional needs, as they are,[33] no amount of health education will solve the problem.

Similarly with smoking, there is a failure to understand why people smoke. Again studies find that people are aware of the dangers, but giving up constitutes a greater hazard. For someone living in cramped surroundings, who cannot allow the children out to play because of the traffic, smoking is a way of coping with stress and shielding the rest of the family from that stress. It is felt to be less damaging than rows or smacking the children. It may be the one perceived pleasure or a way of handling depression. Smoking has halved among better off families in Britain since the 1970s, but those on low incomes have continued to smoke at the same high rates. Half of those in the lowest income quarter smoked then and half still smoke now; six out of ten lone parents smoked then, six out of ten smoke now. The Government's policy of increasing tobacco tax above the rate of inflation has helped to reduce smoking overall but not amongst poor smokers. For them it has only increased their hardship.[34]

But it is in any case a false promise that health will improve if only people change their habits. Socio-economic circumstances are far more important. A study of civil servants on all grades showed that occupational or socio-economic status had a greater bearing on health than either smoking or drinking habits. Being on a higher grade counteracted the effects of smoking, so that a non-smoker on a lower grade still died earlier than a more senior smoker. Poverty, bad housing and unemployment are all health hazards. Doctors have found the extent and pattern of illness changing with the growth of poverty and unemployment.[35] Often non-medical interventions, such as employing an advice worker to help people handle debt or claim benefits, can be more effective than medical ones in enabling people to cope better, improve their health and therefore use the doctor less.

Inequality, as well as poverty, is significant. Peter Townsend and Richard Wilkinson both found that as inequality grew during the 1980s, improvement in health slowed down and wider gaps appeared in mortality and disability rates. Increasing national prosperity no longer ensures rising health standards. The health problems of developed societies show that eliminating absolute poverty does not break the connection between income and health. There comes a point when the increase in absolute standards makes little difference to health and what health differences reflect.

> Overall health standards in developed countries are highly dependent on how equal or unequal people's incomes are. The most effective way of improving health is to make incomes more equal. This is more important than providing better public services or making everyone better off while ignoring the inequalities between them.[36]

A caring society?

The numbers of people requiring care are increasing, whereas because of changes in family life and working patterns there are fewer people to provide it. Most people would support the idea of care in the community but, as yet, there are too few resources devoted to community care and there is insufficient co-ordination across the services involved. The number of psychiatric beds has fallen markedly. People are sometimes being discharged inappropriately without adequate support. Poor physical access, inadequate public transport and a lack of adapted housing combine to isolate people who are frail or disabled, and often also their carers. These together with restricted educational and employment opportunities create unnecessary dependency.

The Government still takes for granted that families, particularly middle-aged women, are there as a pool of care. In 1989 a Carers' Charter, *A New Deal for Carers,*[37] was drawn up to promote the need to acknowledge carers' physical, emotional and material needs through support services such as counselling, arrangements for respite care, home and transport adaptations and income to cover the additional costs of caring without precluding the carer from being employed or sharing the responsibility of care. Similarly in 1990, the House of Commons Social Services Committee, on the basis of evidence from the Carers' National Association, produced a report advocating three long-term objectives for any government in relation to carers:[38]

- improved income maintenance;
- improved opportunities to combine work with caring;
- improved availability of domestic and nursing services.

The principle of care in the community as an alternative to institutional care wherever possible is a welcome one. The issue is whether enough resources are being made available to enable it to work. The 1990 Community Care Act made local authorities responsible for assessing need, designing care arrangements and ensuring their delivery within available resources. They were told to make maximum use of the independent sector. Rather than themselves being the main providers, they were to spend 85 per cent of their grant on contracts to private and voluntary agencies. There was a delay in introducing the changes until April 1993, but one year after the reforms were brought in, a survey of 68 local authorities showed that unmet need was hampering the implementation of key areas of community care.[39] Their ranking of groups most in need were the elderly suffering mental infirmity or dementia cited by the majority, followed by young physically disabled people, people with learning difficulties and physically disabled people of all ages. For these groups respite care, day care and domiciliary care were in shortest supply.

However, despite this, the transition was smoother than many had feared. The pacing of the development of community care services varied in different parts of the country. The market of care is a complex one and it has yet to be seen how well it will work in terms of planning and balancing supply and demand, and ensuring quality of care.

Amongst the voluntary agencies that have now become part of this contract culture are many Christian ones. For them as for others, the move holds some threats as well as opportunities. The statutory agency will have identified the need and defined the service required. Being the provider in these circumstances could jeopardize or distort the original vision of the organization concerned. It could interfere with one of the traditional strengths of the voluntary sector which was to break new ground, to be at the forefront of responding to new or different needs. Being tied into a contract which also has to be regularly renewed might curb their role as advocates for the people with whom they work. The growth of organizations, their increasing bureaucracy and organizational complexity runs the risk of replicating the worst features of local government and squeezing out the voice of the poor and powerless.

> Voluntary organisations have learnt a lot over the past few years about working alongside local people, listening to their views and learning from their experience. Unless there is a determined effort to take these people and their views into the negotiations we shall be back to the worst sort of welfare paternalism.[40]

EDUCATION

> Every year a new race of 400,000 souls slip quietly into the United Kingdom – the purpose of the educationalist is to aid their growth. It should be easy to regard them, not as employers or workmen or masters and servants or rich and poor, but merely as human beings. Here, if anywhere, the spirit of equality might be expected to establish its Kingdom.[41]

Not surprisingly, the past fifteen years have seen considerable controversy over education policy. There is no necessary consensus about the goals of education, even during a period of stability. A time of painful economic change with attendant social problems was bound to produce reverberations for education. It has exposed disagreement over these goals and the way their balance is shifting. Much of the public debate may focus on means but usually at its heart there are different conceptions of what the education ought to be seeking to achieve.

Conforming or transforming?

Education can produce both individual and social benefits. For the individual, it offers general personal development as well as the acquisition of necessary skills which may be the route to social advancement. Society requires a workforce trained to meet the needs of an advanced technological economy, but also a population with the values and behavioural traits conducive to citizenship in a 'good society', however this is defined. In practice, education policy has to combine these diverse and expansive goals, which means that often incompatible aims are simultaneously and uneasily pursued. Individual interests may be at odds with social ones. Some people look to education as an agent of social change and challenge. Others want it to be an instrument of social control and integration, reinforcing existing values and culture.

The education service is faced by greater and more complex problems than ever before in trying to meet these conflicting demands. Urban Priority Area contexts frequently present enormous additional pressures. Although they are not peculiar to Inner London, it is here that problems are probably seen most acutely. Building stock is often in a very poor state. Teacher recruitment and retention can be a problem. At the end of the 1980s, the teacher vacancy rate in London was 3 to 4 times greater than other parts of the country and in boroughs such as Tower Hamlets had reached crisis proportions. Falling rolls in some areas have meant surplus places and often a slow run-down to closure, causing great demoralization in the process. Sixth forms, where they exist, are often not viable. In any case, 'the problems within 11–16 school provision are large and unsolved: frequent low achievement and poor academic results, high truancy rates and discipline problems, to much lack of motivation, and continuing low staying-on eats into any form of post-16 education and training'.[42] There are enormous differences in staying-on rates between inner-city and suburban schools. Multi-ethnic areas present exciting opportunities but also require extra resources. There are over 180 home languages spoken in inner London. One school in Pimlico has nearly fifty languages amongst its children for whom English is a second language. Being bilingual can be a tremendous asset, but for the one in six children in these schools whose English is not fluent, it is a major handicap.[43]

> There are great pressures on teachers who are often torn between going for exam success and trying to give an enriching educational experience to all; between raising ambitions which would never be satisfied and socialising children to accept an unsatisfactory situation.[44]

Tawney's dream of a spirit of equality reigning in education sounds innocent, but would actually be revolutionary. The history of education since 1940 can be reviewed as a succession of strategies for achieving social reform, tools of social policy used for different ends by governments of different complexions. The 1944 Education Act riding on the wave of social solidarity induced by the war extended opportunity for poor children and young people and introduced measures to enable them take better advantage of these opportunities, through grants, free milk and school meals. Later, the development of comprehensive schools, the expansion of higher education and increasing emphasis on community education were also all attempts to promote greater social equality. They were attempts that often got caught in the undertow of more powerful forces.

The rising tide of national educational change is not lifting these boats. Beyond the school gate are underlying issues such as poverty, unemployment, poor housing, inadequate health care and the frequent break-up of families. Education itself can only do so much to enable individuals to reach beyond the limiting contour of their personal and social circumstances and succeed.[45]

The failure of these strategies to achieve the progress envisaged in the early post-war decades demonstrates that, unless supported by broader economic and social policies, education is very limited in its capacity to effect change. Restructuring secondary education did not have the major impact on the inequalities of society that was desired. The vision of opening up opportunities for all has had to be incorporated into new diagnoses of the obstacles in the way of social justice and new prescriptions for their removal. Yet these are similarly likely to be thwarted if enacted in isolation from wider political and social action.

It was a lecture at Ruskin College in 1976 by the Labour Prime Minister, Jim Callaghan, that began the 'Great Debate' which culminated in the 1988 Education Reform Act. He criticized the education service for its failure to achieve basic standards of attainment and meet employers' needs. He was looking for a shift in emphasis towards education as a preparation for work, for further training and for improving the country's economic performance. This was an agenda quickly picked up by the Conservative Government when it came to power. Various pieces of significant legislation preceded the 1988 Act. In 1979, the Act requiring local authorities to establish non-selective secondary schools was repealed. In 1980, free school milk was finally abolished and the local authority obligation to supply school meals removed except for those entitled to free meals. The duty to provide nursery education was also removed. Numerous studies in this country and elsewhere have demonstrated the enormous value of pre-school education for three- and four-year-olds. Not only does it boost children's progress in primary schools, but it has been found to have effects lasting into adulthood amongst children who had been in poverty and were at risk of failing. 'The advantages of pre-school education are not confined to better school performance at six: they crucially include higher self-esteem and aspirations at 16 and therefore the potential for take-up of further education and training.'[46] One study of African-Americans showed that by the age 27, those who had received high-quality pre-school education were far less likely to have been in repeated trouble with the law, far more likely to have continued their high school or further education and to earn a good income and own their own homes. Every dollar's worth of public funds invested was reckoned to have produced over 7 dollars' worth of benefit.[47] Such studies demonstrate that 'pre-school education is part of the "reasonable start" that both social justice and pragmatic economics demand for every child'.[48]

Private choice or public interest?

> If all could choose between equally good if different alternatives with equal confidence and mobility – remember choice can mean how far you can push a pram or how long it takes the au pair in the Volvo – it would be real and its outcomes fair. It would also be so boring that nobody would discuss or vote for it any more. It is only the existence of inequality which makes it a subject, and while there is inequality 'choice' becomes a nice name for rationing or social segregation.[49]

The 1980 Act also began the process of widening parental choice of school, although the accompanying pressure to close schools in the face of declining school rolls effectively reduced choice. Extension of choice was taken further in the 1988 and 1993 Acts. Provision was made for schools to opt out of local authority control. This opened the way for covert forms of selection to return on social or cultural grounds as well as academic.

Amongst a host of other provisions in a very weighty piece of legislation, the 1988 Act also introduced the National Curriculum and assessment tests at 7, 11, 14 and 16, the results of which were to be publicized. Parents were being encouraged to 'shop around'. These tests have, of course, met with strong teacher union, and some parental, resistance. They accept their validity, if properly resourced, for diagnostic purposes but not as the basis of school league tables. Pressures on the curriculum and the weight of attention being paid to basic skills also jeopardize its breadth. 'Children whose homes can offer little stimulation suffer most from narrowing the curriculum: some won't go on a voyage of discovery unless they go to school.'[50]

> The proposed Curriculum lacks clear definitions of aims and purpose, save to say that it is designed to 'develop the potential of all pupils and equip them for the responsibilities of citizenship and for the challenges of employment in tomorrow's world'. An educational philosophy must go beyond such general principles and begin to be specific. Perhaps the difficulty is that such a philosophy depends in the end on a coherent philosophy of life. As it is, the only discernible approach is a somewhat mechanistic pragmatism. This may quite often produce the goods; but without a shared understanding of aims, and a shared educational vision, it will lack that coherence and harmony that makes for purposeful confidence among all those concerned in the enterprise – pupil, parent, teacher, and society at large.[51]

Merseyside Churches Unemployment Committee Education Group – response to the National Curriculum Consultation Document
Our main concern is the apparent narrowing of the purpose of schooling which permeates these proposals, shown in the emphasis on the content of the curriculum at the expense of the process of education. Using the education system to service the economy is one necessary function, but it should not override all others. The entire document appears founded on a deeply impoverished conception of the individual and community life. It endorses preparation for work, but fails to affirm the importance of the quality of social, personal, cultural and moral education. In a region where high unemployment levels are likely to persist, irrespective of the qualifications of the workforce, we believe it is essential to show young people that economic success is not the sole criterion either of personal value or social well-being.

Publishing academic results and encouraging schools to compete on performance also jeopardizes some schools and pupils. Some schools may be loathe to admit children who need special attention and who fare badly in examinations, while those schools that do take them in may be penalized for their efforts if it affects their place in the league tables.

Two other acts having considerable implications for education and, especially, its relationship to poverty, were the Local Government Acts in 1980 and 1981, which changed the way that local authority spending needs were assessed. When local authorities themselves decided on local needs and weighed up the readiness of local ratepayers to pay to meet them, areas with greater social problems were more likely to have good nursery provision and pupil–teacher ratios and take account of disadvantage in resourcing schools. This flexibility disappeared when the government established spending norms according to complex formulae and introduced rate-capping for 'overspending' authorities. In education, as in other policy sectors, this spelt the weakening of local autonomy as council decisions became constrained by national policy initiatives and tight control on resources.

The formula funding of schools is very largely numbers-based, with only about 15 per cent available to respond to the ways in which schools and their pupils differ in their needs or compensate for the additional pressures felt by schools in very poor neighbourhoods. Funding cuts have meant the introduction of payments for some activities previously part of mainstream provision, such as music lessons, extra books, school trips. These can be compensated indirectly by fund-raising activities or directly by charging parents. 'In poor schools where few parents can afford these things they just don't happen. Is this what the law means by "diversity"? Even in more favoured schools where some parents can pay, poor ones and their children will feel pressure if they are in effect "piggy-backing" on other families.'[52] Access for poor children after 16 has also been limited by cuts in maintenance allowances. It is paradoxical that there should be funding for vocational training but not for sixth-form studies.

A common thread running through the changes is increasing centralization. It was estimated that the Education Reform Act contained nearly 200 new powers for the Secretary of State. So many policy areas are now subject to direct ministerial control that the tradition of decentralized education in Britain has been put into reverse. The previous checks and balances in the relationships between central government, local government and the voluntary bodies (notably the churches) involved in education have been swept away. Local authorities have further been weakened by the provision for schools to opt for grant-maintained status. This, together with the switch to local management of schools, reinforced the trend towards encouraging people to see education as a consumer commodity and the education service as a market-place based upon self-interest.

There is no longer a single authority with an overview of the education situation within a given area and the scope to develop an effective and co-ordinated strategy. 'Placing more power in the hands of parents', as the Government put it, veiled increasing fragmentation as well as a real shift of power to central government. Decisions can be made by default or without reference to broader principles or consideration of the wider and longer term implications, particularly for those most likely to be victims of market forces. A 1993 report by the Office for Standards in Education (OFSTED) found the residents of disadvantaged urban areas poorly served by the education system, with weaknesses within individual institutions exacerbated by poor links between them.[53] It advocated a much better overall analysis of needs and more co-ordination between the sectors of the education service.

Having looked at aspects of income in the last chapter, this one has examined some of the main planks of public policy which determine whether or not we have a 'good society'. The next chapter broadens the focus further to consider how firm a foundation is being laid by economic and urban policy.

NOTES

1. Richard Holloway, Bishop of Edinburgh, 'The Scottish housing crisis: the churches' response', in the report of the Scottish Churches Housing Consultation, 14 November 1992 (Partick, Glasgow: Churches National Housing Coalition (CNHC) for the Scottish Churches Housing Coalition).
2. Alun Michael, 'Housing in Wales', in the proceedings of a Church in Wales Division for Social Responsibility and CNHC Consultation on Housing in Wales, 8 May 1992 (Gregynog, Newtown, Powys: Church in Wales Publications).

3. J. K. Galbraith, 'The good society considered: the economic dimension', Journal of Law and Society Annual Lecture, Cardiff Law School (26 January 1994).
4. Hugo Young, 'Thatcherism: did society survive?', Maisie Ward Sheed Memorial Lecture 1992, Catholic Housing Aid Society.
5. Statement by the Secretary of State for the Environment in *First Report from the Environment Committee*, Session 1979–80, in *Enquiry into the Implications of the Government's Expenditure Plans 1980–81 to 1983–84 for the Housing Policies of the DoE* (London: HMSO, 1980).
6. Peter Malpass and Alan Murie, *Housing Policy and Practice* (London: Macmillan, 3rd edn, 1990), p. 89.
7. Reported in the *Guardian*, 3 August 1994.
8. Malpass and Murie, *op. cit.*, p. 108.
9. Page Report, *Building for Communities*, Joseph Rowntree Trust, 1994.
10. *Faith in the City: A Call for Action by Church and Nation*, Report of the Archbishop of Canterbury's Commission on Urban Priority Areas (London: Church House Publishing, 1985), paragraph 10.8.
11. Richard Holloway, *op. cit.*
12. Department of the Environment, *Access to Local Authority and Housing Association Tenancies* (London: HMSO, 1994).
13. *Families Need Homes: The Churches' Response to the Government's Homelessness Review* (Churches National Housing Coalition, June 1994).
14. Quoted in CNHC 1994, *op. cit.*, p. 5.
15. Robina Goodlad and Kenneth Gibb (eds), *Housing and Social Justice* (The Commission on Social Justice, Institute for Public Policy Research, 1994), p. 3.
16. A 50-year-old lone mother, a resident of Ancoats for 25 years, speaking in Mary Catherine Dunne, *Stitched Up! Action for Health in Ancoats, Voices for Struggle, Hope and Vision* (CAP, 1993), p. 92.
17. Margaret Whitehead, 'Is it fair? Evaluating the equity implications of the NHS reforms', in Ray Robinson and Julian Le Grand (eds), *Evaluating the NHS Reforms* (King's Fund Institute, 1994), p. 208.
18. Margaret Whitehead, 'The Health Divide', in *Inequalities in Health*, which also contains 'The Black Report', first published as a single volume by Penguin Books in 1988.
19. Aneurin Bevan, quoted in Michael Foot, *Aneurin Bevan 1945–1960* (London: Davis-Poynter, 1973).
20. Whitehead in Robinson and Le Grand (eds), *op. cit.*, p. 210.
21. Sir Raymond Hoffenberg (President of the Royal College of Physicians 1983–89), letter to *The Times*, 4 August 1994, about the setting up of the Health 2000 initiative.
22. John Butler in Robinson and Le Grand (eds), *op. cit.*, p. 18.
23. *Ibid.*, pp. 22–3.
24. D. Brindle, 'Waldegrave shuns business jargon', *Guardian*, 13 December 1990.
25. Ray Robinson, 'Introduction' in Robinson and Le Grand (eds), *op. cit.*, p. 11.
26. Whitehead in Robinson and Le Grand, *op. cit.*, p. 211.
27. Howard Glennerster, Manos Matsaganis, Pat Owens and Stephanie Hancock, 'GP fundholding: wild card or winning hand?', in Robinson and Le Grand (eds), 1994, p. 102.
28. Whitehead in Robinson and Le Grand (eds), p. 225.
29. Jean Grey speaking in Dunne, *op. cit.*, p. 87.
30. Department of Health, *The Health of the Nation: A Strategy for the 1990s* (London: HMSO, 1992).
31. *Poverty and Nutrition* (NCH, 1991).
32. Dunne, *op. cit.*, p. 92.
33. Sean Stitt, Liverpool John Moores University, has done work which indicates that subsistence poverty in this country – that is, the inability to afford necessities for physical efficiency – has increased.
34. Alan Marsh and Stephen McKay, *Poor Smokers* (Policy Studies Institute, 1994).
35. See Stephen Fineman, *Supporting the Jobless: Doctors, Clergy, Police, Probation Officers* (London: Tavistock/ Routledge, 1990).
36. Allison Quick and Richard Wilkinson, *Income and Health* (Socialist Health Association, 1991), p. 5.
37. A. Richardson, J. Unell and B. Ashton, *A New Deal for Carers* (King's Fund Centre, 1989).
38. *Community Care: Carers*, fifth report of the Social Services Committee, May 1990 (London: HMSO).
39. Reported in *Third Sector*, 8 April 1994.
40. Ian Sparks, 'Markets in welfare', in *Poverty Network*, Autumn 1990.
41. R. H. Tawney, *Equality* (London: Allen and Unwin, 1931), p. 141.
42. Gerald Greenwood, 'The future of education in London', in 'A Vision for London', *Christian Action Journal* (Autumn 1990), p. 29.
43. David Mallen, 'Challenges for education', in Suzanne MacGregor and Ben Pimlott (eds), *Tackling the Inner Cities: The 1980s Reviewed, Prospects for the 1990s* (Oxford: Clarendon Paperbacks, 1990).

44. Hilary Russell (ed.), *Faith in Our City: the Message of the Archbishop of Canterbury's Commission on Urban Priority Areas for Faith and Public Policy in Merseyside and Region* (Liverpool Diocesan Publishing, 1986), p. 26.
45. *Access and Achievement in Urban Education*, A Report from the Office of Her Majesty's Chief Inspector of Schools, Office for Standards in Education (OFSTED) (London: HMSO, 1993).
46. Penelope Leach, *Guardian*, 18 April 1994.
47. L. Schweinhart and D. Weikart, *Significant Benefits: The High/Scope Perry Preschool Study Through Age 27* (High/Scope Press, Michigan), quoted in Patricia Hewitt and Penelope Leach, *Social Justice, Children and Families* (IPPR, 1993), p. 27.
48. *Ibid.*
49. Joan Sallis, 'Poor marks for education', *Poverty*, 87 (Spring 1994), p. 9.
50. *Ibid.*
51. Rt Revd David Konstant, Bishop of Leeds, Address to the School Curriculum Development Committee National Conference, 24 September 1987.
52. Sallis, *op. cit.*
53. OFSTED, 1993, *op. cit.*

CHAPTER 11

A House Built on Rock or Sand?

If you take away from the midst of you the yoke, the pointing of the finger, and speaking wickedness, if you pour yourselves out for the hungry and satisfy the desire of the afflicted, then shall your light rise in the darkness and your gloom be as the noonday. And the Lord will guide you continually, and satisfy your desire with good things, and make your bones strong; and you shall be like a watered garden, like a spring of water, whose waters fail not. And your ancient ruins shall be rebuilt; you shall raise up the foundations of many generations; you shall be called the repairer of the breach, the restorer of streets to dwell in. (Isa 58.9–12)

The fundamental economic failure to relate private or corporate wealth to the wealth of the nation as a whole is the root cause of the ever-growing poverty in Britain's underbelly. We desperately need some new vision, not of a Welfare Britain, but of a whole society, in which new commonality and cohesion is rooted in economic common interest and community inter-dependence. That is the political agenda hardly yet addressed. (Revd Dr John Vincent, letter to *The Guardian*, 5 September 1994)

THE ECONOMY AND EMPLOYMENT

The monetarist pilgrimage

The main monetarist goals of the 1980s were to limit public spending and control the money supply. Some of the costs of the first have already been noted. The outcomes of the second were slower price rises – a brake on inflation – and an explosion in unemployment. During this period, Britain had a long steep rise in unemployment contrasting with developments elsewhere. 'Before Britain started on its monetarist pilgrimage towards a free market, there were only four other countries among all the leading Western nations with a lower unemployment rate. By the mid-1980s only three of the same group had higher levels.'[1]

Some unemployment is structural and some cyclical. The structural component is that part which is not reversed by an economic upturn. But, in practice, there is a close interrelationship between the two sorts, with one exacerbating the other. Policies to reduce structural unemployment are those which will help the economy to adapt to pressures, such as new technology, globalization and increasingly intense competition. An OECD report suggests that none of these pressures *per se* necessarily leads to high unemployment, certainly not until all existing and potential demand is saturated.[2] Similarly, despite all evidence to the contrary, it sees fears of jobless growth as unfounded. But an economy's ability to retain or create viable jobs depends upon a supportive macro-economic climate, with adequate levels of investment and saving.

There are a number of ways in which national policies as well as international economic trends have shaped employment patterns over recent years. The loss of jobs was made far worse by 'the Thatcher Government's antipathy to manufacturing industry. The Government's conviction that the future lay in service industries became a self-fulfilling prophecy as it neglected alternative engines of growth.'[3] Major industries such as shipbuilding have been allowed to wither and their skills be dissipated. There has been a failure to invest in the physical infrastructure which would have generated employment and an overvalued pound exacerbated the recessions in the early 1980s and 1990s, killing off companies which might otherwise have survived.

Seeking a flexible labour market

Monetarists were also fixated about so-called 'rigidities in the labour market' which they perceived as interfering with the free operation of the market by making it difficult to achieve wage cuts, thus boosting unemployment. In their antipathy to the influence of trade unions, they put forward a 'nightmare vision of an employer trapped in a cage with a hungry lion'.[4] 'The unions', said Hayek, 'have become in Britain the chief cause of unemployment,'[5] so during the 1980s there was legislation limiting their activities. Pre-strike ballots were made compulsory; sympathetic action was banned; strikers were no longer entitled to social security benefit whether or not they were receiving strike pay. Pre-entry closed shops, where unions had some say in who was recruited, were outlawed; barriers erected in the way of post-entry ones. Yet, said Robbie Gilbert, special advisor to the Department of Employment in the early 1980s, the vision of employers powerless against excessive pay claims and disruptive action is far from credible. 'Most employers, if they stop to think about it, would not see in the monetarist account a picture of themselves or their firms.'[6] The lion, in other words, was a straw one set up in order to be knocked down.

The mechanisms for setting pay influence wage differentials. Disparity is lower when pay is set at an industry or national level and/or between unions and firms. Thus, another factor depressing pay rates at the lower end of the scale was the drop in union membership from 13.3 million in 1979 to 9.6 million in 1991 (58 per cent to 42 per cent of the workforce),[7] and in their presence with the number of workplaces with recognized unions falling from 64 per cent to 53 per cent.[8] So too was the decline in collective bargaining during the second half of the 1980s when the number of full-time employees affected by multi-employer, national agreements fell from 47 per cent to 34 per cent.[9]

Specific arrangements for protecting low-paid workers have been removed or weakened over the past fifteen years. The 1980 Employment Act abolished the requirement for any organization contracted to local or central government to pay 'fair wages'. Wages Councils, which had been in operation for over sixty years in trades where unionized collective bargaining had never developed, were abolished in 1993. The Councils recognized that individuals unprotected by a union were more at risk of exploitation by the employer. For the Government, setting such a floor below which wages should not fall was another 'rigidity'. The full effectiveness of Wages Councils is open to doubt because enforcement was modest – very few firms would ever have an inspector call – and penalties low for those who contravened, although they did have to pay back wages. Nevertheless, they served as a significant deterrent to sweated labour and put down an important marker about realistic wage rates. As was noted in Chapter 7, their demise has triggered a reduction in pay in many jobs formerly subject to their protection. 'Once labour becomes cheap, and especially if Government condones that development, the danger is that people will be treated cheaply.'[10]

Another perceived barrier to the 'downward adjustment' of wages is the level of state benefits and their disincentive effect. People, it is argued, will not work unless it pays them to do so. It is a dubious assumption. As Gilbert says, 'when asked, money is only one reason people give for working and often they do not rank it as the most important'.[11] In practice, there are many other relevant influences as is demonstrated by the number of people working for less than they could claim on the dole.

There is little evidence that if employers had a better chance of imposing lower pay rates, they would create thousands of full-time jobs at lower pay rates. Nevertheless, it was this belief that led the Government to introduce the Young Workers' Scheme in 1981, which gave a subsidy to employers taking on young people at less than £50 per week. 'Yet it was later admitted that this substantial carrot produced little additional movement from the donkey'[12] and the scheme was withdrawn as a failure four years later. Even so, schemes on the same principle followed, only to meet with equally little success. They also carry the danger that so-called new jobs are actually cheaper substitutes for old ones. Certainly, the abundance of jobs has not appeared and, for many of the unemployed, the labour market has become more stagnant not more flexible,[13] as is demonstrated by the sluggishness of movement off the unemployment register and the increasing proportion of long-term unemployed. This situation contrasts with that in the US where, though there might be a higher risk of becoming unemployed in the first place, there is nevertheless a greater chance of being re-hired quickly.[14]

Despite the often-repeated assertion that a national minimum wage would add to unemployment, studies in America and this country suggest the contrary. A study commissioned by the Ministry of Agriculture, Fisheries and Food, found no evidence that minimum wages set by the Agricultural Wages Boards, the only remaining system of minimum wages in the UK, had destroyed jobs. Britain is the only EU member state without legal pay protection for the poorest, yet its job creation record is unimpressive compared with, for example, France, Germany or Italy.

> The reason is simple: a minimum wage boosts spending power and therefore, generates employment elsewhere in the economy. It discourages employers from competing solely on the basis of cheap labour, and encourages investment in training and better techniques of production. A minimum wage reduces absenteeism and staff turnover.[15]

Research has shown that employers at the bottom end of the labour market underpay their employees by about 15 per cent of their productive value. 'This generates a double inefficiency: fewer workers are willing to work and incentives for increased productivity are reduced because workers receive so little of the proceeds.'[16]

Firms, too, are restructuring to increase their flexibility. Single status companies with everyone on broadly similar contracts are disappearing. Charles Handy talks about 'shamrock organisations',[17] in which the first leaf of the shamrock represents the professional core workers, qualified technicians and managers. These are the staff essential to the company. Much is demanded of them in hard work and long hours in return for high rewards. But cores are shrinking, companies are being 'downsized'. Non-essential work, that is jobs for which substitutes can easily be found, are increasingly contracted out so that, according to Handy, for some organizations as much as 80 per cent of the value of their operation is carried by people not inside the organization. The shamrock's third leaf is the flexible labour force, the part-time and temporary workers who are the fastest growing part of the employment scene, 'too easily seen as the hired help division, people of whom little is expected and to whom little is given. In crude terms, these people are ... a market into which employers dip as they like and when they need, for as little money as they have to pay.'[18]

The unreason of economic rationality

The payback of a minimum wage for the employer is its effect on worker morale. Labour markets are not like other sorts of market. Wages are not commodities. The labour market is a social as much as an economic institution, which is why wages are not as responsive to changes in unemployment and the removal of restrictions as the government and major financial institutions would like them to be. It also explains why performance-related pay works best where a basis of trust, a sense of fairness and high motivation already exist; that is, in precisely those circumstances which render it unnecessary. 'People, exasperatingly, refuse to obey the laws applying to the fish market.'[19]

Supply and demand in the labour market do not work in the way free-market text books would predict. There is 'some form of human agreement that raises the value of work above the market clearing level and so decommoditises the wage bargain'.[20] In the end, elements such as morale and motivation intrude in the human bargain and, if this is the case, achieving efficiency in the labour market entails building an industrial relations system which recognizes people's wish for fairness.

It is argued that we are creating a situation which combines American levels of inequality with high European levels of unemployment, but with real wages still rising for core workers.[21] As the flexible sector grew,

> those in full-time, permanent employment were largely insulated against external pressures, while those in other forms of employment suffered from job insecurity and falling relative earnings; and a growing rump of marginalised, jobless households had only marginal contact with the world of work.[22]

The shift to part-time jobs has been pushed along by *laissez-faire* employment legislation which makes part-time labour easy to hire and fire and exempts employers from having to pay National Insurance contributions. Many employers are taking advantage of this exemption by limiting both the hours of workers and their pay. The Low Pay Network reported an example of a new supermarket opening in Stirling, advertising 91 jobs in the local JobCentre.[23] Only seven paid more than the £56 a week over which employers and employees have to pay National Insurance contributions. About 60 jobs offered less than 16 hours' work a week for a wage of £45 or less, so that all workers would still be entitled to Income Support. Another 20 jobs offered less than 16 hours, but over £45 a week, in which case entitlement would depend on family circumstances.

On the one hand, this situation represents a massive disincentive to people because of the poverty trap it places them in. If people working less than 16 hours a week earn so little that they are entitled to Income Support, any additional hour worked to earn more is wholly offset by a cut in their benefit. It is, in effect, a marginal tax rate of 100 per cent. DSS figures show that the number of people facing this poverty trap rose during 1993 by about 25,000 to 200,000. On the other hand, the Exchequer is effectively subsidizing employers. More money has to be paid out in state benefits. But also, employing 91 part-timers instead of 28 full-timers, working the same number of hours, denies the Exchequer £40,000 a year in lost revenue.

'Flexibility' has come to mean stripping away employment rights, reducing collective bargaining to a minimum and welcoming the widening gap between the highest and the lowest paid. The employer's flexibility is the employee's insecurity. However, flexibility in the labour force need not mean this. An alternative approach would be to foster a more highly skilled workforce and tackle inequality. As it is, the economic growth rate is slowed by the waste of people and their incomes, spending and potential skills. To increase the supply of skilled labour would not only allow firms to respond to new opportunities, but would also gradually reduce earnings differentials.

Linking Up

Linking Up was set up in 1989, sponsored by the Church of England Industrial and Economic Affairs Committee, Church Action with the Unemployed (CAWTU),[24] and Manchester Diocesan Board for Social Responsibility, as a practical response to *Faith in the City*. Based in Manchester with an England-wide remit, its aim was to help the churches play a more effective role in regenerating the local economic life of Urban Priority Areas. Originally its full title was Linking Up – the Churches' Involvement in Local Economies. However, as early as 1990 it had started work with Hindu communities and after three years the interfaith emphasis was reflecting in its new title, Linking Up Interfaith – Faith in Action for Local Economic Development.

> One of the early discussions we had within Linking Up was – what is our 'product', what is it we're actually about? We came to distinguish ourselves by the fact . . . we were trying to promote a process or processes by which people could arrive at the conclusions about what is right for them, given their needs, resources and agendas. Linking Up is as much about the processes that go on inside communities, neighbourhoods and faith communities as it is about very specific projects, credit unions, community enterprises, etc.[25]

Linking Up works with local churches, temples, mosques, gurdwaras and religious groups to:

- identify individuals, groups and locations that have the potential to make a significant contribution to the economic regeneration of urban areas;

- support and enable the development of local economic initiatives; community businesses, credit unions, customized training, development trusts, fund raising;
- assist the sharing and transfer of ideas and experience in the field of economic regeneration between individuals and groups;
- encourage partnerships between religious and other organizations to benefit local people.

From the beginning, half the funding came from Government, first from the Inner Cities Unit of DTI, later from the Action for Cities Unit of DoE, with the rest of the finance coming from corporate sponsors and other Government departments.

> It strikes me that many of us are going on the same journey but some people actually feel quite invisible and quite ignored. Even though we are going in the same direction and are fellow travellers, we are not sure whether or not the people we are travelling with have recognised that we exist or that what we have might be worth hearing and listening to or receiving. The role of the churches with regard to community enterprise and economic initiatives is absolutely crucial in respect to this listening and hearing.[26]

Linking Up recognizes that economic and social needs have to be solved together. Many community groups are constantly in danger of falling over the edge of financial viability. The funding climate for them has become even colder over the past few years. Linking Up is helping to establish income generating initiatives and spread good practice about ways in which local projects can contribute to the economic well-being of their neighbourhoods. It stresses the need for partnership between local churches, different faiths, local authorities, central government, companies, voluntary organizations and local communities.

Training

Preparing young people for their future lives without either limiting their potential or inviting later disillusion requires a realistic appraisal of what sort of society we want and is likely to exist over the next few decades. Technological and economic changes are altering the traditional shape, extent and role of paid employment. We do not seem to be confronting the implications of this either in terms of meeting individual needs or addressing the country's requirements. Similarly, enabling adults to survive in employment in an economy in which most skills are always becoming obsolete requires both vision and a training strategy. Britain's record in this is abysmal.

Basically, there is just too little vocational education and training. Compared with other advanced industrial nations, the problem is not at degree or higher technician level, but in middle and lower technician and craft qualifications. France and Germany produce roughly twice as many qualified people. Two-thirds of our workers have no vocational or professional qualification, compared with only a quarter in Germany. 'This is bad for the nation as a whole. But it is particularly bad for the least skilled individuals. In task after task the IT revolution is replacing brawn with brain. Those without skill will soon have little future and become an increasing burden on society.'[27]

One main reason for our training deficiencies is the under-resourced and piecemeal approach to training by government, exacerbated by confusion about the role of the state. Ministers have wanted the private sector to take a more prominent role in funding and providing training. Employers, however, are reluctant to pay for general training which also raises the worker's value to other employers because it is an uncertain investment. The person may leave after obtaining the qualification. Their investment is more likely to be channelled into tailoring employees to the firm's specific needs. In large firms, at best, investment in training may rise and fall according to the state of the economy, and small firms may never feel able to afford it.

Since the establishment of the Manpower Services Commission in 1974, there has been a bewildering array of schemes and programmes and a succession of bodies responsible for them, with each new initiative introduced with an accompanying fanfare. Repeated changes were prompted by a desire to get away from the training's poor image. It was perceived by trainees and employers alike as of low quality and there was deep-rooted, and evidently justified, suspicion about the real purpose of the schemes. Will Hutton has said, 'Schemes are designed by the included for the excluded and their purpose is less creative training built around a shared vision of the future than simply to massage the unemployment numbers.'[28] This might be thought to be cynicism born out of a more fundamental distaste for government policies, but even the then Minister at the Department of Employment, Alan Clark, referred in his *Diaries* in June 1983 to 'a mass of "schemes" whose purpose, plainly, is not so much to bring relief to those out of work as to devise excuses for removing them from the Register'.[29]

There have been improvements in quality over time, but even in 1990, less than a quarter of people leaving Youth Training Schemes had achieved even National Vocational Qualification (NVQ) level 2,[30] although the target is for 85 per cent of young people to reach this level by the year 2000 and 60 to 70 per cent to reach level 3 and the same proportion of the workforce as a whole to be qualified to this level. The management of youth and adult training has now been passed to Training and Enterprise Councils, though the main part of vocational education and training (VET) continues to be provided in further education. Despite all the rhetoric about new initiatives, real expenditure on off-the-job vocational training has been falling. There are also disincentives for people to participate because, for non-degree level education and training for people over 18, the normal practice is to charge tuition fees.

> We praise VET, yet we charge for it. We lament that people prefer academic routes to vocational. Yet we provide every incentive for them to do so. This hypocrisy arises for class reasons: the children of professionals and managers are mostly not into VET. But the effect of it is disastrous.[31]

In education, our system selects people early and is thereafter geared to the needs of the minority. It is content with low achievement and because it is not meritocratic, it disregards a huge amount of talent, which is tragic for the people concerned and wasteful economically. The qualifications that are obtained do not compare well internationally. This leads to lower – and therefore more expensive – productivity plus the supreme irony of skill shortages while millions are unemployed.

Training and Enterprise Councils

> You can take it that if the government has passed the job to TECs then it is very difficult or impossible to achieve, or there is little governmental priority to allocate it resources.[32]

The White Paper *Employment in the 1990s* published in 1988 introduced the idea of Training and Enterprise Councils (TECs). These are called Local Enterprise Companies (LECs) in Scotland. They are independent companies that have contracts with the Secretary of State for Employment and are run by boards of directors led by private-sector business leaders. Department of Employment guidance for TECs set six major national priorities which included encouraging the growth of enterprise and business investment in skills, persuading individuals of the value of training and providing the opportunities for them, and helping unemployed people back into the workforce.

There are a number of tensions in respect of the philosophy and functioning of TECs. They are private companies, yet their funding largely comes from central government and they are publicly accountable for its use. They have been encouraged to move towards a private-sector culture, but governmental monitoring locks them into more bureaucratic practices. Early enthusiasm in the private sector seems to have given way to disillusion because although they were promised discretion to assess and address the specific needs of their local economy, they are subject to the government's priorities. Fears in other sectors have focused on the lack of proper local democratic accountability and expenditure control. The reality is that the government remains firmly in the driving seat. Scope for innovation, customized or even quality provision is severely curtailed by having to concentrate on quantity and deliver bulk training for the unemployed. Budget constraints limit the quality of training and those most in need of specialist attention are likely to be least well served. The basis of public funding has shifted from needs to performance-related criteria. An increasing proportion of the budget is output-related which encourages a conveyor-belt approach and risks pushing down standards.

This section has looked at the economy and employment policies in general. However, the greater than average fall in employment suffered by larger urban areas and the segregation of different types of housing and residential areas both affect the operation of their labour markets in a way not found in small towns that are more integrated and compact. Certain groups are clearly disadvantaged in employment, access to jobs and their duration, level of income and the development of skills. The next section goes on to look at how such spatial disadvantage is addressed through urban policy.

TACKLING 'THOSE INNER CITIES'

We've got a big job to do in some of those inner cities . . . and politically, we've got to get back in there – we want to win those too.[33]

We are disturbed that the situation to be found in many UPAs today is in reality a tale of two (inner) cities. On the one hand are to be seen shining new workshop units sprouting on sites which until recently were derelict eye-sores constituting the remains of once thriving industrial plant. On the other still exist decaying terraces or council estates where a large proportion of the residents are unemployed, lacking decent health care, education facilities and other amenities which most of us take for granted.[34]

The urban face of Britain has been transformed over the past quarter of a century. In the past, urbanization was linked with industrialization. Jobs and opportunities compensated for the grimmer aspects of urban life. That link has now been broken. This period has seen the decline of many traditional industries. Many cities have lost both people and jobs. Migration into cities was selectively reversed. The better-off and the employed have moved to the suburbs and beyond. The economic and fiscal base of cities has declined. Their physical environments have deteriorated. They have experienced a concentration of socially and economically vulnerable groups. But at the same time as economic and social problems have increased, so the autonomy and capacity of cities to address them have declined.

The language of enterprise

It is clear, then, that the inner cities – or parts of them – have not shared the benefits of rapid economic growth. Why is this so? Why, if there are available resources in terms of labour and land, has the 'invisible hand' not reached further into these pockets of urban deprivation?[35]

The 'inner city problem' was redefined in the 1980s. There was a move away from the idea of inner cities as concentrations of deprived people for which a welfarist solution was appropriate. Instead, economic regeneration was seen as the key to the revival of inner cities with the stress put on economic and infrastructural issues carried through into a switch of spending from revenue to capital. The logic of this did not necessarily point towards dependence upon private-sector funding, but this was the route which corresponded with the ideological preferences of the Government. From Michael Heseltine's announcement of a review of inner-city policies in 1979 onwards, 'the language of the enterprise culture has flavoured all the government's pronouncements on policies for inner urban areas. And their packaging has become glossier (some would say in inverse relation to substance)'.[36]

An Audit Commission report published ten years after the Conservatives returned to power noted the different ideological views about public sector intervention in the economic environment.[37] At one end of the spectrum were those who blamed distortions in the economy on intervention of one sort or another and, therefore, wanted a further withdrawal from any attempted manipulation in favour of leaving market mechanisms to correct the imbalance. At the other extreme were those who saw an overwhelming social case for correcting economic differences, even if this meant jeopardizing the economy's overall ability to generate wealth. In practice, there was a legislative and regulatory framework which allowed for some intervention in the market process, 'justified in some circumstances by the need to correct certain inefficiencies in the market and to compensate for certain externalities'.[38]

However, with the dissolution of a bipartisan approach nationally came a clash of agendas between central government and the Labour administrations in many cities who were still convinced that only the public sector was capable of 'staunching the haemorrhaging caused by private sector disinvestment'.[39] This period also saw, therefore, a growth in local government intervention in economic development, covering such activities as physical redevelopment, enterprise development, co-operative and community development, promotional policies and municipal interventions in the labour market. The impact of this activity was limited because the resources available to local authorities to put into it were severely restricted. The scope for economic development programmes was further reduced by the removal of the Metropolitan County Councils. They were often the lead players and, in part, it was precisely to stem this type of activity that they were abolished in 1986.

Quasi-democracy

The word quango, short for quasi-autonomous non-governmental organisation, was coined as a joke in the late 1960s by Professor Anthony Barker to describe bodies outside the civil service, but publicly funded, appointed by ministers and, in theory, arm's-length from government. Despite the Conservative Party coming to power in 1979 pledged to cut quangos, their number has vastly grown since then, they wield greater powers than before and spend more public money. A study by the Democratic Audit and Charter 88 Trust found that there are over five thousand quangos now spending nearly one-third of all public expenditure in spheres as diverse as health, education, training, public housing, employment and urban regeneration.[40]

They have taken over the powers and responsibilities previously subject to democratic control. 'Virtually all the safeguards of a mature democracy are missing.'[41] The Government looks not for democratic accountability but, in William Waldegrave's term, 'consumer responsiveness'. However, this represents a greatly impoverished view. 'The consumer is a poor and passive shadow of the self-confident citizen of a mature democracy, who is entitled to choose who runs his or her services, to participate and be consulted in the way they are run and to know what decisions are taken in her or his name.'[42] Although this may portray an ideal that has never been fully realized, it is no longer even potentially realizable. Power has been taken away from Parliament and local elected members and concentrated in the hands of government ministers who can dispense it through patronage to bodies which are free to be secretive, unregulated and unaccountable. New unelected elites are emerging as key players in national and regional life. Examining quangos in the West Midlands, the Institute of Local Government Studies at Birmingham University predictably found the same names cropping up as board members. The Institute concluded that although clearly, within their own terms, there are many examples of good practice, 'Boards can follow policies to which local people object, they can fail to provide adequate services, they can abuse their position and there is no way that local people can replace them.'[43]

More icing less cake

The Government's move to enlist the private sector as the key driver of regeneration was part of a bigger strategy to redistribute political power. It was determined to reduce the power of local authorities and break their control as monopoly suppliers of public services. In urban finance, increasingly complex grant mechanisms were created intended to restrict cities' revenue and capital spending. Government substantially reduced the level of resources provided to cities and restricted their ability to raise their own resources or spend those they have. There was an increasing imbalance between the 'icing' in the form of Urban Programme funds and a disappearing 'cake' in terms of main programmes. Many urban services were privatized or deregulated either by the enforced sale of city assets or by opening the way for private companies to supply local services. Attempts were made to enable citizens to become more discerning consumers in the hope that they would then want to curtail spending. This was one of the objectives of the Community Charge. The overall effect has been to reduce the coherence of the financial system and make it increasingly difficult for cities to plan or control their environment and deliver high quality services.

In trying to minimize the role of local government, the Government not only looked to the private sector to play a bigger part in regeneration. It also enlarged its own role. First, financial incentives were offered to local authorities to collaborate with the private sector in development programmes. Later, the Urban Regeneration Grant and City Grant cut out the local authorities altogether and offered central government funds direct to the private sector. The Government created Urban Development Corporations (UDCs) to lead regeneration in inner-city areas. These are the most complete illustration of the thrust of government policy because they are bodies established, empowered and funded by central government to whom UDCs are directly accountable. They have extensive powers in land acquisition, finance and planning. In this sense, they control a fiefdom carved out of the local authority area. UDCs are run by boards whose members are appointed by government, usually heavily weighted by local business representatives. Government increased their substantial budgets through the 1980s at a time when expenditure on other parts of the Urban Programme and for the mainstream local authority services of housing, education, welfare and transport was being cut back.

The track record of UDCs has been chequered. They have often achieved considerable physical improvement in their areas. However, they have not proved able to turn the tide of a locality's economic fortunes. Rather they themselves are affected by an area's market potential as the relative performances of the Merseyside Development Corporation and the London Docklands Development Corporation showed in the 1980s. Their achievements have also been confined geographically and socially. Thus the jobs created were in the skilled service sector and often required importing labour. The houses built were at the top end of the private market. Environmental improvements did not extend to neighbouring run down areas. There was very little positive impact on adjacent communities. Their actions were not designed to meet the training, employment or housing needs of the residents on their doorstep. In this way, they symbolized the failure of the government's private-sector and property-led approach to regeneration to 'trickle down'.

Apart from being a source of political tension, the contrasting trends and levels of investment between UDC areas and inner cities generally raised wider issues about the nature of regeneration. They pointed up the danger of creating 'islands of private excellence amidst seas of public squalor'.[44] UDCs and other initiatives such as Enterprise Zones have been seen as tinkering at the edges of the problems facing millions of residents in urban areas and having little real significance in relation to the range of essential services needed by many for whom the ability to choose in a free market is non-existent.

Inner Cities Religious Council

Faith communities have the potential to offer sustainability to local regeneration initiatives based upon the permanence of their presence in, as well as their commitment to, difficult areas.[45]

Religious faith, that great power house, has been passive too long in the face of inner city problems.[46]

It was following the disturbances on estates around the country, such as Meadowell and Elswick in the North-east and Blackbird Leys in Oxford, that Robert Key, a Minister in the Department of the Environment proposed to the Archbishop of Canterbury the setting up of an Inner Cities Religious Council, chaired by a Minister, with representatives from the main faith communities living in deprived urban areas of England. In January 1992, the Revd Chris Beales was seconded by the Church of England to the DoE to service the Council.[47] The Council's work has three main strands:

- enabling Government and faith communities to consider policy issues together, such as youth unemployment, housing and homelessness, crime, religious discrimination;
- sharing information and listening to people in local communities through running conferences and seminars around the country;
- facilitating the development of practical local initiatives such as a Hindu Action Research Project in the Black Country, and a Multi-Faith Youth Challenge across five cities in the summer of 1994.

The ICRC exemplifies the more general problem of how Ministers of State and their civil servants can actually meet as equals people from these diverse groups and communities, some of which they know 'only as a persistent problem governments have been grappling with for most of this century'.[48] Conversely, members of the Council have to struggle with how to represent people's interests convincingly and authentically and find the scope for effective participation.

> This is a new experience for all of us. Some of us are more used to inter-faith dialogue with its long and painful growth in trust and friendship followed by specific social action in local communities. Here we are beginning rather than ending with the consequences, and picking up each other's various ways of thinking through and implementing faith as we go along. Our ways of looking at things are as diverse as our beliefs. Some think of the whole nation and its needs, others stress the morality of their particular tradition, some have particular regard for the equality and well-being of the minority group they represent and some of us have more direct experience of the inner city than others. We are growing in understanding and all the time learning from each other.[49]

David Horn, who succeeded Chris Beales in September 1994, would also say that as members grow together, they are also gaining confidence about what the Council can do as a group

Who wins, who loses?

> The dreadful lesson of those outbreaks seemed to be that, from the Prime Minister downwards, the plea for social justice only gets a hearing when it takes the form of outright disorder. It was a desolating thought that after so many years of commitment to the service of the Granby ward, violence appeared to be the only means of securing the remedying of just grievances. The outbreak of unrest on such a scale and of such intensity surely stood for a condemnation of me and my kind which was hard to bear. Had we been wrong to plead for patience? Had they been wrong to heed us and not take to the streets long years ago?[50]

The DoE report, *Assessing the Impact of Urban Policy*,[51] identified the social and environmental problems of British cities since the 1960s. It found cities suffering from significant population and job losses, a withdrawal of investment, extensive physical dereliction and growing social problems associated with poverty, disillusionment and lawlessness. The study reviewed the whole package of Action for Cities policy instruments. It tried to measure changes in the conditions of different cities and decide what had been the impact of government policy. The evidence it found was mixed. On the measures used, government policy had improved the position of the fifty-seven cities in greatest need, that is, those designated as Priority Areas. Resources spent seemed to have reduced unemployment, attracted younger residents and increased the demand for private housing compared with other towns not receiving that expenditure. Also the gaps between those fifty-seven areas and the rest had narrowed.

However, the largest cities in the country did not share in this relative improvement. The seven largest cities experienced both relative and absolute decline. There was an intensification of economic distress at their hearts, irrespective of the resources put in, and their problems seeped out more generally across these bigger cities. Thus polarization grew between these city residents, especially those in central areas, and those living in smaller or less deprived cities.

The following is an extract from an account of how an inner-city church in the part of Liverpool containing the greatest concentration of social problems, found itself forced by sheer weight of circumstance in the 1960s to move from a 'gathered church' pattern of ministry, focusing largely on its own membership, to one which acknowledged the importance of accountability for and to the community it was there to serve. The paper combined the recollections of Don May, a Methodist Minister, and Margaret Simey, a City Councillor. This is Margaret Simey, not herself a church member, talking about the way the church for her represented an enduring, faithful presence, a 'stability zone' so that the flux and uncertainty all around could be more bravely confronted. Hopelessness waited round every corner because of the scale of human need. The Church shared the anguish but also embodied a future hope.

In effect, the churches stood for an alternative way of life to that of the individualism and materialism which threatened our survival as a human society. Their efforts were often as futile as our own but I am convinced that merely to exist amongst us on those terms was a positive contribution. I know that I personally found that my own sense of commitment to what I call socialism and they call Christianity was refreshed by even the most casual contact at some committee meeting or youth club. Those whose values are put to the test of extreme and continuing stress learn by harsh experience that no man can live wholly unto himself, but the struggle to keep alive any sense of social duty is often a desperate one. The mere existence in our midst of a handful of people who were there for no other reason than to keep that flag flying I believe to have been a greater importance than we, or perhaps they, realised. There was unspoken comfort to be derived from the fact that someone still had faith in the ideal of the caring community even though bitter disillusion had eroded our own conviction.[52]

Other research conducted by the Policy Studies Institute similarly concluded that major conurbations particularly suffered from a rise in unemployment during much of the 1980s and that deprived areas saw a deterioration in housing conditions.[53] They also benefited less from the boom in 1988/9, although the subsequent recession affected relative conditions across the country. The North was less badly hit precisely because it had not made the same gains as the South, where new service sector jobs were especially vulnerable to the economic down-turn. So, there was a higher *increase* in unemployment in, say, Southend than in Liverpool during the recession of the early 1990s. But this was from a much lower base and did not alter the fact that Liverpool's *rate* of unemployment stubbornly remained much higher. There was a country-wide increase in homelessness. In many deprived areas, there were below average increases, but much higher ones in London and parts of other large cities.

Across the board of policy areas, it was found that the general state of the economy and government policy were the most important influences on employment, the numbers on Income Support and housing issues. For example, housing problems were compounded by the depletion of council stock and low levels of new build resulting directly from government policy. In some respects, people in deprived areas shared in nation-wide improvements such as in perinatal and infant mortality rates but the gap in standards was not closing.

The allocation of resources was also problematic. First, although a growing proportion of designated urban funding was targeted at the 57 cities in most need, the major sources of funding remained the Rate Support Grant and the Housing Investment Programmes. These were considerably reduced during the 1980s. In addition, the amount of *per capita* resource going into cities through the 1980s did not necessarily fit with the classification of local authorities as UPAs. The top 57 cities in terms of size of financial resource included 12 non-UPAs, displacing 12 UPAs, one of which fell as far down the list as eighty-seventh. Even during the late 1980s when the 57 UPAs were officially designated target areas, the pattern of expenditure remained similarly ill-matched. Specific resources were not necessarily well targeted. For example, Estate Action and other special programmes – for which funds were in any case modest and not new – 'have not in general resulted in improvement and renovation being given higher priority in deprived areas than in other areas'.[54]

A further problem is insufficient co-ordination between the policies and activities of different government departments. Government does not speak with one voice and different departments believe very different things about UPA problems and their solutions. They may focus on different-sized areas – regions as against cities. Or they may not work spatially at all and hence have no manifest commitment to cities. There are inadequate links between different policy sectors such as training and employment or job creation and building the capacity of local communities.

In addition to these administrative and institutional problems in central government, there has been what has been called a 'culture of disdain' from the centre towards local government, so that mutual goodwill cannot be taken for granted. Although the stated intention of Task Forces and City Action Teams was to foster co-operation, their creation was indicative of this antagonism. Resources to democratically elected bodies have been steadily cut back and, where there have been additional resources, they have gone to quangos and other Non-Governmental Public Bodies.

Church Urban Fund

Faith in the City was a call for *action*. One direct outcome was that many churches tried to relate more closely to their neighbourhoods through opening up their church buildings to greater community use and/or through specific social and community action projects, often based upon a preliminary audit of local needs. The Church Urban Fund was established in 1987 as 'a practical demonstration that the Church as a whole is concerned for and stands with the deprived',[55] to grant aid locally based initiatives as a means of helping 'people of deprived urban communities find ways of meeting the spiritual and material needs of their own communities'.[56] By the end of its first five years, the Fund had made grants totalling nearly £17 million. (The Methodist scheme, Mission Alongside the Poor, was a similarly motivated fund, and more recently a Baptist one, Against the Stream, has been set up to give small pump-priming grants to local projects.)

CUF projects have brought many benefits to UPAs, as have other similar ones. An evaluation report notes that 'at the level of "service delivery" a significant proportion of local schemes supported by the Fund offer opportunities that either would not be available to their users at all or provide them in a particular way'.[57] In general the report finds that most users spoke very positively about the projects and especially valued the commitment of project workers and the flexibility and informality of the work.

However, questions are raised about project management in some cases, and about project sustainability once CUF funding ceases. Also, the report expresses some reservations about the lack of strategy to steer the use of the Fund. The major issues raised in *Faith in the City* –

structural change, political marginalization and racial injustice – are not central to most CUF activity. Although the Fund has overall aims, it might now be timely and possible, in the light of early experience and listening to grassroots voices, to develop some 'middle principles' which could guide a more focused programme. They might also provide criteria for the harder decisions required to avoid spreading the Fund too thinly and to put more emphasis on better resourced and mutually reinforcing initiatives. ' "Thin jam" would be replaced by a more limited number of projects, building upon current good practice, which could really fulfil the Fund's aspiration to provide "city lights" which others might follow.'[58]

CUF has undoubtedly served to prompt new thinking, focus people's thoughts on local needs and galvanize energies in local areas and in the wider Church. But schemes of this sort are not without risk. By channelling specially raised monies to UPAs, they may allow the Church to duck the challenge of re-ordering mainstream budget priorities or relinquishing power to people in UPAs. They can erect a convenient smokescreen behind which to carry on business as usual and thus compound the confusion between 'charity' and justice.

Looking for coherence and consensus

Urban policy has been modified again in the early 1990s. On the one hand, quantitatively, resources being directed at urban regeneration continue to shrink. On the other, the Government's approach has changed partly to take into account the reduced resource base and partly to incorporate lessons of the 1980s. *Assessing the Impact of Urban Policy* drew five main lessons for future policy:

- the importance of creating effective coalitions of local players to attempt urban regeneration;
- the need to give greater opportunities to local authorities to play a significant part in such coalitions in their new roles as enablers and facilitators;
- the equal need for local communities to have opportunities to play a part especially because evidence of increasing polarization suggests the need for specific resources to address the scope for community capacity building;
- the need to improve the coherence of programmes across and within government departments, requiring strategic objectives to be identified to guide departmental priorities. Where separate programmes had been successfully linked, area targeting had played an important part;
- part of such coherence must derive from better targeting of resources and this could be best done at regional level to reflect the varying constraints

and opportunities across different regions and achieve more effective co-ordination across programmes and departments.

Two Government initiatives of the early 1990s clearly take account of these policy messages. First, City Challenge incorporated these principles. Despite reservations about authorities having to compete for funds and the fact that the money was top-sliced from existing programmes, many features of the design of City Challenge made it more promising than previous initiatives. It:

- recognized that urban problems cannot be tackled singly: an effective strategy must be comprehensive and integrated;
- returned a key role in spearheading and co-ordinating such an approach to local government;
- appreciated that to be effective in meeting local needs and having lasting effects, any such strategy must be owned by local people. So the community, as well as the private sector, is brought in as a partner.

In 1994, similar principles informed the introduction of Government Offices for the Regions, the Single Regeneration Budget (SRB) and stream-lined arrangements in Whitehall for promoting regeneration through a new Ministerial Committee. The SRB brought together 20 separate programmes from the Departments of Environment, Trade and Industry, Education, Employment and the Home Office, with the intention of enabling a more flexible response to urban problems. Most of the money (£1.4 billion in 1994–95), however, is committed to existing programmes. Initial bids were made in the autumn of 1994 for a share of the 1995–96 budget, which amounted to about £100 million uncommitted money spread across the ten English regions. They were to be projects which would either contribute to a city- or town-wide strategy or promote small area regeneration and, like City Challenge, they were to be comprehensive, targeted and supported by a cross-sectoral partnership.

In the end, judgements about City Challenge and SRB projects must rest not only on their practical achievements but on whether they have also been able to deliver some of their wider ambitions. Have they achieved quality, innovation and local flexibility in their programmes? Have they resulted in sustainable development? Have they produced organizational arrangements which enable local authorities and communities to play more substantial strategic roles? Have other partner agencies become more responsive to local circumstances?

The churches as partners

The Bidding Guidance for the SRB says 'Bids should also aim to harness the talents and resources of the voluntary sector and volunteers and involve local communities.'[59] Clearly there are going to be increased opportunities for churches to join in regeneration initiatives. What can local churches bring to the partnership table?

- The churches should bring their clear value base, their understanding of both human worth and fallenness, and the moral credibility which comes from their longstanding presence in neighbourhoods under stress;
- The churches' ministry should reflect the Christian gospel's concern for all people and for the whole person including the social and economic dimensions of life in their enabling and capacity building role;
- Churches have a role as advocate with other voluntary and community sector partners;
- Churches may themselves provide a variety of social and environmental projects, with or without outside funding.

Potentially local churches have a lot to offer. However, how far this potential is fulfilled will depend upon the extent to which they are already equipped to contribute, not so much in terms of their material resources as their motivation, outlook, existing local involvement and way of working. Some questions may serve to illustrate:

- Does the church itself allow for full participation? Churches and their leaders are just as prone as other agencies to impose solutions on others, to think they know best, to undertake meaningless so-called consultation exercises, to act *for* instead of *with* people.
- Is this type of local involvement and action fully integrated with the worshipping life of the church or is it a matter of running two sorts of organizations – and possibly different participants – alongside each other with little interchange?
- Are the implications of this local way of working being taken on board by the wider Church and influencing its priorities, deployment of resources, organization, and mission? Two-way communication is required. Very often local churches or branches of sector ministry complain that they are overlooked or misunderstood. But, in addition to having a responsive parent body, they must articulate what they are doing and show its relation to the Church's wider ministry if they are to effect more deep seated change in the Church itself.

Partnership has become the buzz word of the 1990s. But it is necessary, too, to extend the idea of social partnerships beyond specific programmes and projects to the country as a whole. If the market system is here to stay, all interested parties should have a stake – and rights and obligations – in its management. As already noted, the balance of power has swung heavily towards employers, with trade unions playing a diminishing role. It is notable as well that trade unions are very often absent from the table in more local partnerships. Yet they, or some reformed version of them, have a key part to play if gains are to be spread equitably. As the cracks in 'the Great Market Experiment'[60] have appeared, it is vital to re-create social stability and cohesion. This takes us into the next chapter.

NOTES

1. Robbie Gilbert, *Employment in the 1990s* (London: Macmillan, 1989), p. 119.
2. *The OECD Jobs Study: Facts, Analysis, Strategies* (Organisation for Economic Cooperation and Development, 1994).
3. Victor Keegan in 'Girls on top in jobs market', *Guardian*, 9 April 1994.
4. Gilbert, *op. cit.*, p. 109.
5. F. A. Hayek, *1980s Unemployment and the Unions*, IEA Hobart Paper, No. 87, p. 62.
6. Gilbert, *op. cit.*, p. 110.
7. See *Employment Gazette*, May 1993.
8. See Amanda Gosling, Stephen Machin and Costas Meghir, *What Has Happened to Wages?* (Institute for Fiscal Studies, June 1994).
9. See *Employment Gazette*, September 1993.
10. Gilbert, *op. cit.*, p. 117.
11. *Ibid.*, p. 114.
12. *Ibid.*, p. 116.
13. See Paul Gregg and Jonathan Wadsworth, researchers at the National Institute of Economic and Social Research, 'How to liberate British workers from the country's economic apartheid', *Guardian*, 23 May 1994.
14. *OECD Jobs Study*.
15. Chris Pond, Director of the Low Pay Unit, in a letter to the *Guardian*, 10 June 1994.
16. Andrew Glyn and David Miliband, 'Why an unequal Britain is paying the price for "efficiency" fallacy', *Guardian*, 25 April 1994.
17. Charles Handy, *The Age of Unreason* (Business Books Ltd., 1989), pp. 70ff.
18. *Ibid.*, p. 79.
19. Will Hutton, 'An end to the rule of fish market economics', *Guardian*, 25 July 1994.
20. *Ibid.*
21. David Blanchflower and Richard Freeman, 'Did the Thatcher reforms change British labour market performance?' in Ray Barrel (ed.), *The UK Labour Market* (Cambridge), quoted in Gregg and Wadsworth, *op. cit.*
22. Gregg and Wadsworth, *op. cit.*
23. *Independent*, 22 March 1994.
24. CAWTU ceased to operate in September 1994 when it handed its remaining assets to Church Action on Poverty, which then took over responsibility for organizing Unemployment Sunday and other activities to continue informing the churches about the issue of unemployment.
25. Tony Addy in his summing up of the 1990 Linking Up Conference, in William Temple Foundation Occasional Paper 21, p. 44.
26. Chris Beales, 'Why ought the churches to be involved in community enterprise and economic initiatives?' Address to the 1990 Linking Up Conference, *ibid.*, p. 28.
27. Professor Richard Layard, Economic and Social Research Council Annual Lecture, December 1992.

28. Will Hutton, 'Conservatism's basic flaw amounts to more than ill-chosen slogan', *Guardian*, 14 February 1994.
29. Alan Clark, *Diaries* (London: Phoenix, 1994), p. 10.
30. National Vocational Qualifications are ranked at five different levels of competence.
31. Richard Layard, *op. cit.*
32. A TEC Chief Executive quoted in Robert J. Bennett, Peter Wicks and Andrew McCoshan, *Local Empowerment and Business Services: Britain's Experiment with Training and Enterprise Councils* (UCL Press, 1994), p. 286.
33. Mrs Thatcher, the night after winning the 1987 General Election.
34. *Living Faith in the City*, a progress report of the Archbishop of Canterbury's Group on Urban Priority Areas, General Synod of the Church of England, 1990, p. x, paragraph 17.
35. Audit Commission, *Urban Regeneration and Economic Development: The Local Government Dimension* (London: HMSO, 1989), p. 12.
36. Nicholas Deakin and John Edwards, *The Enterprise Culture and the Inner City* (London: Routledge, 1993), p. 26.
37. Audit Commission 1989, *op. cit.*
38. *Ibid.*, p. 13.
39. Michael Parkinson, 'British urban strategy', in Parkinson and Le Gales, *National Policies for Cities in France and Britain: A Comparative Assessment*, Report to the Franco-British Council, April 1994, p. 39.
40. Stuart Weir and Wendy Hall (eds), *Ego Trip: Extra-governmental Organisations in the UK and Their Accountability* (Democratic Audit and Charter 88 Trust, 1994).
41. Nick Cohen and Stuart Weir, 'Welcome to Quangoland', *Independent on Sunday*, 22 May 1994.
42. *Ibid.*
43. Quoted in Nick Cohen, 'One-party Britain', *Independent on Sunday*, 3 April 1994.
44. Parkinson and Le Gales, *op. cit.*, p. 42.
45. Tony Baldry, MP, Parliamentary Under-Secretary of State, DoE, in a speech to the East Midlands Inter-Faith Conference on Inner Cities, 11 May 1994.
46. Revd Alan Greenbat, Consultant to the Chief Rabbi and member of the ICRC, 'Getting involved – faith and the inner cities', Address to the West Yorkshire Multi-Faith Conference on Inner Cities, 27 October 1992.
47. Chris Beales was also central to setting up Linking Up.
48. Bryan Rippin, Chairman of Sheffield District of the Methodist Church and Free Church representative on the Inner Cities Religious Council, 'Inner Cities Religious Council' in *Poverty Network* No. 20 (September 1993), pp. 22–23.
49. *Ibid.*, pp. 23–24.
50. Margaret Simey, *Government by Consent: The Principles and Practice of Accountability in Local Government* (Bedford Square Press, 1985), p. 43.
51. Department of the Environment Inner Cities Research Programme, *Assessing the Impact of Urban Policy*, Brian Robson, Michael Parkinson *et al.* (London: HMSO, 1994).
52. Don May and Margaret Simey, in Hilary Russell (ed.), *The Servant Church in Granby*, Cross Connections Occasional Papers on Church and Society (Centre for Urban Studies, University of Liverpool, 1989), p. 21.
53. Peter Willmott and Robert Hutchison (eds), *Urban Trends 1: A Report on Britain's Deprived Urban Areas* (Policy Studies Institute, 1992).
54. *Ibid.*, p. 65.
55. Church Urban Fund document, *Our Policies* (no date).
56. *Ibid.*
57. Richard Farnell, Sue Land, Robert Furbey, Paul Lawless, Benita Wishard and Peter Else, *Hope in the City? The Local Impact of the Church Urban Fund* (Centre for Regional Economic and Social Research, Sheffield Hallam University, 1994), p. 161. (See also the separate evaluation report by the same group of the Broad-Based Organising funded by CUF.)
58. *Ibid.*, p. 162.
59. Government Offices for the Regions, *Bidding Guidance: A Guide to Funding from the Single Regeneration Budget*.
60. Will Hutton, 'Brother, can you spare a deal?', *Guardian*, 8 July 1994.

CHAPTER 12

Relationships of Justice

Jesus . . . was warning them that fidelity to the Kingdom of God and the relationships of justice amongst themselves would be the crucial issue in which people would find salvation or collapse. (Thomas Cullinan, 'The Passion of Political Love', in *The Passion of Political Love*, Sheed and Ward, 1987, p. 5)

. . . what is important is to make the connections, the connections between spirituality and social involvement, prayer and protest, contemplation and action. (Patrick Woodhouse, *In Search of the Kingdom: Private Faith Public Discipleship*, Marshall Pickering, 1989, p. 125)

WEAVING THE THREADS TOGETHER

In this final chapter, I want to draw together some of the themes running through the book and summarize the questions it has explicitly or implicitly raised for the future. The proposition throughout has been that poverty raises crucial personal, political and theological questions for us as Christians and as members of British society. I hope the book goes beyond polemic. It is not part of my intention to harangue the reader. No easy answers are offered, but I also hope that, by clarifying some of the issues, peeling away some of the layers of prejudice, misunderstanding and deliberate obfuscation which frequently envelop the issue, the book goes a little further than just saying 'it's all very difficult'.

The subject has been approached from various angles. Poverty is structural. It arises from the organization and operation of the main economic and social institutions. Over recent decades, poverty in Britain has deepened as a result of the potent mix of global economic trends with their wider repercussions, and deliberate acts of public policy and their intended or unintended consequences. Poverty is the flip side of free-market economics. It accompanies growth as well as recession. This presents a fundamental challenge to the conventional wisdom. Economic growth as the undisputed goal is proving socially divisive as well as ecologically short-sighted.[1] Poverty is also a cultural and political problem because our attitudes and political will express and affect the level of poverty we are prepared to tolerate. Historically Britain has swung between a compassionate and a punitive response. Not only does poverty touch the lives of those immediately affected in myriad ways, its existence diminishes everyone, the comfortable as well as the poor. It eats into the social and moral fabric of the nation as a whole. So, it requires a corporate and radical response, not just running repairs to a few patches here and there where the tears are most apparent. The material is worn too thin and would only rip again. This chapter looks at the scale of the task ahead. It sets out the need to develop a vision and a strategy for restoring full citizenship to all members of our society.

At the beginning, I quoted words of Thomas Cullinan. Christian hope, he says, 'always takes the mess seriously'. I have been trying to take the mess seriously by examining poverty, analytically and descriptively, and also reflecting upon the interrelationship between the Christian message and our public and personal attitudes and actions. I have deliberately avoided breaking the book up into sections separately labelled 'church' and 'society' because, although the end result might have been tidier, it would not have been true to life. We straddle two spheres, the religious and the secular, God's and Caesar's, the church and the world, the desert and the city, the kingdom of God now and not yet. They cannot be disentangled. Christian discipleship would be far simpler if we could discern a clear, signposted road through the world's messiness. It is not to be. 'From its biblical beginnings onwards . . . Christian thought reflects a qualified dualism between God and creation, whereby an irreducible difference is related through an indissoluble bond.'[2] God forged that bond – crossed the divide – and made himself known to humanity through his incarnation in Jesus Christ. We have to hold these two spheres in tension. The 'world' is not just the backcloth to our lives, it is the substance of them. All our experience of God is experience of things and people. Many of the issues that we face, therefore, we have to tackle in 'secular' territory, using 'secular' tools, and working alongside people with a wide range of beliefs and starting points.

But as Christians we should be able to bring something more to this task. 'Experiences of God are experiences of the ordinary seen in the context of an otherness which enfolds them all and lives within them all.'[3] Anthony Dyson talks of a Christian task

> of searching for, holding to, living and struggling, and dying in, the *creative centre of culture* . . . not an artistic conception, nor is it a geographical location. It is found at those critical points in society where God's creativity and redemptive acts are contending with forces of meaninglessness, dispersion, disorder and despair . . . To be and to persist, to bear portions of the world's sufferings, to fall and to be picked

up, to seek to be 'salt' and 'light' at these points, in the day-to-day fabric of our human lives, *is* the common Christian calling.[4]

Philip Wogaman looks at the two extremes of response on the 'right' and 'left'. He sees some naivety and imbalance amongst those on the left who would 'designate the actual world as the locus of God's whole intention' and identify the kingdom of God simply with the establishment of just economic and social relationships, 'forgetting that loving relationships and ultimate meanings can never be derived simply from concrete historical accomplishments'.[5] On the other hand, those on the right seeking to establish an absolute discontinuity between the physical world and the real world of the spirit, have been complacent about the physical distress and injustices which activated the social gospellers. 'If anything, their solution has been less relevant and less faithful to the gospel than that of unsophisticated social activists. The latter are at least prompted by an instinctive belief that physical needs and social justice are important in the light of the Christian faith. Moreover, the latter have the weight of Christian scripture on their side.'[6]

Wogaman refers to Dietrich Bonhoeffer's concept of the penultimate helping to put the relationship of the two worlds into perspective. Whereas the 'ultimate' is not identified with the structures of our this-worldly existence but 'the reconciliation of man with God through Christ and the final consummation of God's purposes beyond history',[7] the penultimate both derives its meaning from the ultimate and prepares the way for it. The material, social, economic and political structures of this world represent the conditions upon which the ultimate depends.

Part of our equipment as Christians should be the capacity to glimpse the transcendent through the here and now. It should be to know that we are not wholly bound by the historical moment; to realise that there *is* such a thing as structural wrong and institutionalized evil, *yet* redemption requires change on a profounder level than simply institutional change. We should be involved in the political realm but not imprisoned by it. 'God is always the transcendent source of judgement holding all human life in tension. No human agent can be absolutised as divine; God transcends them all.'[8] Just as no human agent can be absolute, nor can any government, ideology or political party. We must be open and self-critical; hold to a vision but attend to the 'small particulars'; balance the ideal with the practical. Institutions and systems require to acknowledge human failings through having checks and balances on the exercise of power, but also recognize human potentialities by leaving space to create new and better alternative futures. In addition, as Wogaman says, faith in the transcendent sovereignty of God absolutely precludes using people merely for economic or political ends or subjecting them completely to the power of others.

A SYSTEMIC PROBLEM

Put in these terms, the sovereignty of God becomes a highly political statement and connects closely with the issue of poverty. Poverty fetters people socially and psychologically as well as materially. It goes beyond the lack of physical resources. It can also mean being trapped; lacking opportunity, fulfilment and security; having no recognized contribution to make. It can mean living in appalling housing in a blighted neighbourhood, suffering from constant chest infections as a result of damp conditions or asthma aggravated by a polluted environment. It can mean being in bed and breakfast accommodation, isolated but also lacking privacy; living, cooking and sleeping in one room, without anywhere safe for the children to play or quiet for them to do homework. It can mean always running short at the end of the week, having a restricted diet, never being able to afford to have a holiday or treat the children. It can mean feeling on the scrap-heap and humiliated by having to depend upon state benefits or handouts from charities, family or friends.

Poverty arises not because poor people are inherently lazy or incompetent. No doubt individuals are, but so are those who are not poor. It stems from the economic and social character of society. There is now a division between those who are manual or non-manual workers in primary labour market jobs and those who are not. On the whole, the former will have access to decent housing, schooling and health care. However, the long-term unemployed and those in insecure, low-paid employment are increasingly excluded not only from a sufficient income but from these other essential components of an adequate lifestyle in the Britain of the 1990s. There are young people who do not know what it is like to have a job; women struggling to bring children up alone; ethnic minorities for whom exclusion is reinforced by discrimination; and those whose poverty and insecurity are carried into old age. These are the groups most dependent upon welfare and consequently most vulnerable to welfare cuts and sanctions.

Given this analysis of poverty, it has to be treated as a systemic problem, not as something marginal. It requires preventive change not just amelioration. The reason for the failure of so many attempted remedies is that they have tried to contain the problem (and the poor) and patch matters up rather than attack the root causes. To realize that poverty and growing inequality are symptoms of a malfunctioning society opens the way to recognizing that arguments for eliminating poverty do not rest on compassion or social justice alone. There are also sound pragmatic reasons based on the self-interest of the non-poor majority.[9] These are concerned with the social and economic waste and the social fragmentation that result from a divided society.

Poverty and exclusion are extremely expensive, both directly in terms of transfer payments – social security benefits – and indirectly in the opportunity costs of failing to develop human potential to the full. There is a common interest in cutting these costs and, therefore, in providing social frameworks which will maximize the opportunities for individuals to develop their talents. In economic terms, this is expressed as human capital which is recognized as a vital component of national competitiveness. When Howard Davies, Director-General of the Confederation of British Industries (CBI), called for a concerted attack on poverty and investment in better education and training to bring the long-term unemployed closer to the labour market, he did so because it makes economic sense. He wanted to close Britain's skills gap with the rest of the world.[10]

This argument goes against the thesis of the political right for whom efficiency necessarily leads to inequalities, so that society faces a trade off between equality and efficiency. They argue that redistribution policies have disincentive effects and lead to loss of efficiency. However, even in solely economic terms, this is disputable. In several policy areas, redistributing the resources of society can result in positive gains for all because

> the impact of the redistribution on the productive contributions of the poor leads to greater economic efficiency. This benefits not only those who can now find work, or work more productively: there are external effects in this case too as tax revenues rise and benefit expenditures fall, allowing lower tax rates (or better public services) for all.[11]

Redistribution here applies beyond income. Although transfer payments lessen inequality, they only alleviate the problem, not solve it. Insofar as they also stigmatize and subordinate people, welfare measures can exacerbate inequality and reinforce feelings of a lack of self-worth even while they relieve some of the material pressure. On the other hand, redistributing the means for people to participate fully in the economy and society would remove the need for perpetual income redistribution. It would also release society from the burden of costs accruing from the results of material deprivation – the costs of exclusion – such as mental and physical ill health and anti-social behaviour.

This leads onto the other line of pragmatic argument in favour of minimizing poverty, which focuses on the social disorder that follows in the wake of growing levels of poverty and inequality. Perhaps in a rigidly hierarchical society, inequalities could be accepted as legitimate, with the poor man quite content to be at the rich man's castle gate, so that social cohesion was not threatened. However, in a society which apparently offers mobility and opportunity, those at the wrong end of a widening divide are more likely to express some form of resentment. Such discontent is scarcely politicized in this country but is expressed in crime and conflict. Thus it is in the majority interest to curb socially divisive inequalities.

So far the response has been largely one of trying metaphorically and literally to pull up the drawbridge and shelter behind it, which can only be effective in the short term, if at all. At one extreme, there are 'no-go' areas; at the other, private enclaves of high-tech security. Stores and shopping precincts are monitored by cameras. Homes are fitted with alarms, window locks and security lights. Chain-link fences encircle factories and industrial estates. Security guards patrol them. It is all too easy for these physical security measures to be seen as the 'keep out' signs of a wider exclusion for those on the wrong side of the fence, shut out from the economic activity inside and the material security or social recognition that goes with it.

Not only are the financial costs of exclusion escalating, but other sorts of damage are taking place. Shops close down because of repeated break-ins. Potential investors are deterred from bringing their businesses to areas which have, or are reputed to have, a high crime rate. People are afraid to go out at night, or leave their homes unattended, or live alone. Mistrust grows and fear of the stranger. Although very often it is those living in the poorest neighbourhoods who are also the chief victims of this phenomenon, the consequences of the boredom and resentment of those people cut off from economic success diminish life for everyone.

REDEFINING CITIZENSHIP

> If we listened to the poorest, not only those living on minimum income but those who never take part in anything, those who feel inadequate and excluded from mainstream society, they would reveal everything in our society that crushes or tramples people down. They would ensure that all change, all progress and all political trends are used for everyone's benefit. Their experience could teach us the demands of a true democracy, where all citizens have rights, where all citizens are heard, because they are human beings.[12]

If poverty is rooted in economic and social structures and processes, action against poverty must address it on a number of levels – access to education, training and job opportunities; housing and nutrition; enhancing self-esteem and the confidence to participate in community life. In sum, this means reasserting the full citizenship of those in poverty. The material base for citizenship assumes an interrelationship between three major institutions: the labour market for employment, the family for practical and emotional care, and the welfare state as a source of cash and services.[13] A large section of this book has been concerned with the major changes that have taken place within these institutions as we have moved from an industrial to a post-industrial society, and their profound implications for the intensification of poverty:

- The labour market has polarized; patterns of male and female involvement in the labour market altered; insecure employment and unemployment have grown. At present all the signs are that with a continuation of current policies, unemployment will remain around at least 2 to 3 million.
- Accompanying these labour market developments and the increasing pre-occupation with material consumption in advanced industrial societies has been disruption in former patterns of family life. Families are more likely to be physically distanced, with grandparents, aunts and uncles less likely to be on hand to share in child care and adult children less available to give support to ageing parents. More marriages break down. More people remarry and start second families. More children are apparently at risk of neglect and abuse.
- The welfare state is overstretched as a result of higher demands on it and reduced public funding. Some of its functions have been hived off to other agencies or put within the realms of private provision. As a result, although it has been a significant buffer against further erosion in social cohesion, people are increasingly being asked to find alternative routes to meeting basic material, health, education and social care needs. The poor lose out again.

All these changes have altered the patterns of dependence and independence. Citizenship for all, therefore, needs to be rethought and poverty addressed via these institutions.

Materially, there are two key challenges: to give people labour market security and to tackle their right to a decent income. Both depend to some extent upon reconnecting the wealth creation in the hands of private companies and large, often multi-national corporations, with the rest of society. It is not a matter of disparaging this sort of wealth creation – a criticism sometimes (justly or unjustly) levelled at church leaders. Rather it is a question of recognizing that it has a social as well as a private role. It arises out of, and is made possible by, society as a whole and must feed back into society's overall well-being. In the past, a large part of the connection was in the mass employment industry provided. However, while advanced technology has increased productivity, it has also cut the traditional link between investment and jobs. Higher investment is now more likely to be labour saving than labour generating. We saw this first in manufacturing, but it applies increasingly in any information processing situation. In other words, wealth creation (in the narrow sense) requires a smaller employment base. It therefore provides a living for fewer people, with a consequent loss of taxation and spending power. This results in a smaller revenue stream to the public purse to fund other activities, necessary for the public good and which would themselves generate more employment and promote greater money circulation. We cannot just write off the public sector as 'unproductive'. It *is* productive of many essential and desirable social goods. Rather it is a question of rebalancing the way that the whole economy works for social as well as private ends.

Within the labour market, most attempts to get people into work rely upon supply-side policies, such as improving infrastructure, developing human resources through training programmes, promoting regional policies. Nevertheless, the question of whether full employment is achievable still has to be asked. And, what would full employment mean in today's type of labour market? Would it still rely considerably on part-time and insecure jobs which on their own could not provide a sufficient level or security of income? The report of the Commission on Social Justice summarizes proposals for the reduction and eventual elimination of long-term (over 12 months) unemployment. It gives seven conditions:[14]

- a high and sustainable growth rate in demand;
- low inflation entailing pegging average money earnings in line with productivity;
- a large and competitive tradable sector to ensure a full employment level of demand;
- greater intensity of employment through expanding non-tradable, labour intensive sectors, such as personal services, and greater flexibility in hours of employment;
- re-integrating the long-term unemployed into one labour market using measures such as high quality help with education and training, wage subsidies, childcare, sponsoring small-scale entrepreneurs, regenerating the most disadvantaged areas;
- developing tax and benefit systems providing incentives instead of disincentives through greater flexibility, less reliance on means-tested benefits and a gradual reduction in taxes on employment, especially less skilled and lower paid jobs;
- a new balance between employment and family across life cycles through arrangements such as employment breaks for men and women for family needs or additional training and flexible retirement packages.

Clearly such an agenda needs translating into firm policy proposals, but at least its principles are sufficiently broad to address this basic need to re-align employment, the family and the welfare state.

The second challenge is to ensure that everyone has a decent income. There are a number of proposals for basic income schemes to give each individual a tax-free state payment, irrespective of employment or family status, age or gender.[15] Such basic income would be 'a citizenship-based share of national income'.[16] The idea is attractive not just as an anti-poverty strategy but also because of its underlying principle of ethical collectivism, 'the idea that we are all equal inheritors of society's productive capacity and contributors to society's current production whether through full-time or part-time employment, through personal, familial or other unpaid carework, or in other ways'.[17] But proposed schemes tend to suffer from problems of complexity and practicality as well as affordability. In any case, a single policy instrument cannot solve all the interwoven problems associated with poverty. Such arguments for distributional justice in income cannot be detached from issues to do with the labour market, the family and other aspects of the welfare state.

Alongside these economic and social trends, there has been a change in the nature of politics.[18] Geoff Mulgan argues that politics have suffered a demise for a number of reasons. One is the passing of the Cold War. The rubble of the Berlin Wall also buried the old competing ideologies. While it had communism to oppose, the anachronism of the New Right was obscured. Although at first apparently vindicated by the Soviet collapse, New Right economics have since been found to have few answers to post-industrial forms of economic organization and political expectation. Also, the nation state is now a less obvious vehicle for dealing with many political issues. For example, basic income schemes tend to take national sovereignty for granted whereas nowadays such proposals should consider the future of income policies and rights within the European Union. Some issues, too, have extended into hitherto non-political arenas. Global economic and ecological questions transcend national boundaries; at the other extreme, personal lifestyle, gender and identity, domestic and neighbourhood issues slip through the national net. Politics has become either everything or nothing. All issues are political yet formal politics and political institutions have weakened. In other words, the context of politics has changed and with that change comes the need to redefine – re-imagine – democracy and democratic structures.

This is closely related to the issue of citizenship because those with less economic stake in society are also those with least say and those for whom democratic participation risks being an empty ideal. In any case the national picture has changed over the past fifteen years. Much Government policy in the 1980s, though it purported to minimize the role of the state, in fact centralized power by curbing the autonomy and spending power of local authorities and constraining other intermediary institutions such as trade unions. On the other hand, many local authorities are moving towards greater decentralization in their management of local services, taking planning and implementation nearer to residents. There have also been some urban policy moves by Government towards bringing in 'the community' as a full and active partner, though such talk of 'the community' should not distract from the more fundamental issues of citizenship. There is a long way to go to make such participative democracy a reality for most people and to bridge the credibility gap which often exists at both parliamentary and local council level between elected members and their constituents.

THE ROLE OF THE PUBLIC SECTOR

Questions arise from all these changes – economic, social and political – about the relationship between the state and the market and between public and private domains. The public sector has gradually been made more subject to market forces, but without any debate about what people now view as public goods and what role they want the public sector to play. When specific policy moves are in the offing, people and parties line up for and against them but the conception of the public sector which informs their thinking is not necessarily explicit. There are competing views about its function. It can be seen as offering broad income protection based upon insurance-type contributions combined with uniform benefits. This may or may not be linked with a more thoroughgoing goal of using it as a system of redistribution and social engineering. On the other hand, some would reduce welfare to a minimal safety-net and redefine some of its present provision, such as health, pensions, education, as private goods which should be supplied by the market.

Consumer goods have become the model of values for social goods. Yet their character is very different. Roads and clean air, for example, cannot be made into individualized commodities. Other goods and services, ranging from energy and water to health and education, combine the characteristics of public and private goods. Choices in the sphere of social goods are never totally private ones but have implications for society as a whole. Similarly, the benefits of public provision are not simply enjoyed by the immediate 'consumer' but more widely, because there are common benefits in minimizing contagious diseases, for example, or caring for the mentally sick or raising standards of education.

Reorganization within the public sector has been driven by the desire to contain public spending. Privatization and user charges have been introduced and financial controls have been tightened. The move towards contractual relationships within internal markets has gone along with separating the determination of ends from the means of implementation, as with the purchaser–provider split in health care and the use of quasi-independent public bodies working on contract from central government. Another shift has been to take funding away from providers and give it to consumers, for example, in rent subsidies or training vouchers. This rests partly on the questionable assumption that consumer choice can act as a cost discipline on providers. Uniting all policy moves has been the theme of competition as a means of pinning down costs and promoting greater entrepreneurialism. The private sector has been the model. Value for money (vfm) and outputs – the priorities of managers and accountants – are more centre stage, as against the discretion of the professionals such as teachers and doctors providing the services. In fact, competition can drive costs up. The 'contract culture' brings with it increased spending on marketing, accounting and consultancy. It risks greater commercialism. Proceeding on the assumption that economic motivation rules over all can become a self-fulfilling prophecy. If life is seen as nothing more than a series of transactions, it jeopardizes the sense of service and altruism which has traditionally motivated individuals and imbued the ethos of particular professions and public services.

The other side of the picture is the citizen turned consumer. Here is 'a model of society drawn from neo-classical economics. It is a world of perfect information and sovereign individual consumers, a world in which the only incentives are monetary and the only discipline that of competition.'[19] It assumes that individuals can exercise choice in the various markets. Such moves as the introduction of school league tables are meant to inform that choice. The plethora of 'charters' for citizens, passengers, patients and so on, carry the idea a stage further by clarifying the terms of the contract between provider and user. Only of course the world is not like this. Shifting power towards users, strengthening the direct accountability of providers, making organizations more transparent, are all welcome. However, often they only underline the lack of real choice open to people, the fragmentation of services and policy making, and the extent to which the balance of power remains with the provider, especially when providers feel governed by cost constraints. A doctor may drop an 'expensive' patient from his or her list or a school may tailor its intake to avoid children with learning difficulties. For some people in some spheres, choice will be non-existent and the barriers to meaningful choice will always be greatest for those most weakly positioned in the market place.

Although Christian teaching can give no policy prescriptions, it can provide values and principles to guide us as well as giving the motive force for change. The concept of the common good is closely linked with that of social justice. It has been especially prominent in Roman Catholic teaching. It expresses a mistrust for individualism and is, therefore, very far from being equated with the sum of individual self-interest. Such a guiding concept is clearly open to differing interpretations and its application must inevitably be modified in relation to historical and cultural circumstances. However, in acknowledging the importance of the role of the state in setting the institutional and legal framework for the common good and promoting the conditions in which *all* individuals can best flourish, it articulates a challenge which must always be faced.

RIGHTS AND DUTIES

The citizenship debate also revolves around balancing, in principle and in practice, individuals' rights and entitlement on the one hand, and obligations and responsibilities on the other. Governments since the end of the 1970s have acted on the premise that the pendulum had swung too far towards rights, and that this contributed to the dependency culture. The view that the enforcement of obligations is, in words quoted by Ruth Lister, 'as much a badge of citizenship as rights'[20] has strongly influenced recent British social policy. This links back to the two challenges of material citizenship. 'Workfare', entailing work or training as a condition of receiving benefit, is an example of enforcing an obligation to work. For Ruth Lister, the development of the rights of social citizenship partially neutralize the excessive inequalities generated by capitalism, whereas social obligations as conceived by the New Right reinforce them. Workfare, for example, is more likely to carry the obligation to take usually low-paid, often dirty, unpleasant jobs, than offer the sort of work opportunities enjoyed by more advantaged members of society.

Advocates of a state basic income for all differ over whether they would attach any kind of work condition to the scheme. To reject the New Right formulation certainly does not necessarily mean totally discounting any form of obligation. For most people the idea of rights is firmly linked with duties. Countering state paternalism by asserting the potency of individual responsibility has its attractions. But, as Ruth Lister's sentiments imply, it is important to look at the social and economic framework within which these rights and duties have to operate and which will determine how fair they are perceived to be. An obligation to work will be far more palatable in a society committed to full employment and the protection of workers against very low pay or poor conditions.

Over the past fifteen years or so, the government has passed responsibility from the state to families and individuals by such means as introducing workfare type training schemes, social security loans instead of grants and allowing schools to opt out of local authority control. It has been a period characterized by selfishness and greed. This is not surprising when the very concept of responsibility is a social one. It presupposes the mutual answerability of people bound together in a community, recognizing their common interests and interdependence. Inevitably it sits ill with monetarism, the market and an individualistic ideology.

For this reason, too, attempts to promote 'active citizenship' have failed. At the end of the 1980s, some Conservatives became concerned that the government appeared too uncaring. They feared that Mrs Thatcher's comment, 'there is no such thing as society',[21] gave the impression of disparaging the idea of mutual responsibility. Ministers such as Douglas Hurd portrayed active citizenship as the natural counterpart to the enterprise culture for those with money and time to spare for charitable giving and voluntary activity. However, despite their concern for social cohesion, their message was addressed to the beneficiaries of 1980s' prosperity and was, therefore, essentially inegalitarian.

> Thus lurking behind the active citizen is the successful, self-reliant, enterprising citizen, alias the consuming, property owning citizen. The unsuccessful and unenterprising are thereby excluded from the ranks of citizen (even though unskilled manual workers give a higher proportion of their income to charity than do those in the administrative and managerial classes).[22]

Where does the voluntary activity qualifying as active citizenship begin and end? The number of people engaged in community groups, tenants' associations, credit unions, welfare rights groups and play schemes testifies to this form of activity flourishing in poorer neighbourhoods. It cuts across the argument that the welfare state has undermined self-reliance. But it all depends on how active citizenship is defined. ' . . . it seems clear that the government regards the poor as the objects, not the subjects, of active citizenship. There is a tacit understanding that while the philanthropy of the middle classes is the hallmark of active citizenship, the campaigning of welfare rights groups and the like constitutes the undesirable face of political activism.'[23]

Both left and right focus on decentralizing power. For the right, consumerism brings the 'democracy of the marketplace', but this uncouples power and responsibility and detracts from communal concerns. The left look more to constitutionally guaranteed rights and empowering people through local democratic institutions. The Commission on Social Justice stresses 'the need for accountability and democracy within institutions . . . '.[24] Here the danger is that the idea of responsibility becomes too one way, that in asking the powerful to be answerable to the powerless, mutual answerability is over-looked. A social contract, like any other, must be two way. Nevertheless, the priority is to start with measures to counter 'the accretion of invisible and irresponsible power by national governments and transnational companies and organisations'.[25] Mulgan claims that 'Any serious programme for spreading responsibility would have to start not with those at the bottom of society, those out of work and on welfare, but rather with the most powerful.'[26] This is also a sound gospel principle.

GOD IS HERE, BUT WHERE IS THE CHURCH?

If there are pragmatic reasons for eliminating poverty, there are also compelling moral and Christian ones. The Christian gospel *is* good news to the poor. God has acted in history to liberate the poor. But more than that, he has identified himself with the weak and the poor. In taking human form, he was successively a refugee in Egypt, an immigrant in Galilee, a carpenter and an itinerant teacher with no settled home and dependent on others' hospitality. His ministry was defined by his relationship with the poor. When John the Baptist asked from his prison cell if Jesus was the awaited Messiah (Matt 11.2–6), the reply Jesus sent to convince him was that 'the blind receive their sight and the lame walk, lepers are cleansed and the deaf hear, and the poor have good news preached to them'. His parables spoke of God's love and the inclusiveness of his kingdom. He taught that it is in the hungry, the thirsty, the stranger, the naked, the sick and the imprisoned that we find him (Matt 25.31–46). The parable of the sheep and the goats is not an ethical lesson. It tells us about experiencing God. 'What does it mean to feed and clothe the Creator of all things? We cannot know. We can only look on the poor and oppressed with new eyes and resolve to heal their hurts and help end their oppression.'[27]

This is the road of discipleship. But we come back to the point that ending the oppression of the poor entails political as well as personal action, a social as well as an individual response. So often it has been found easier to touch someone's instinct to pity than any impulse towards social justice. For Ruth Lister, 'part of the challenge that has always faced groups like CPAG has been how the generous, charitable impulse that is tapped by individual stories of hardship can be translated into support for redistributive tax-benefit poli-cies'.[28] *Faith in the City* similarly records that 'while many members of the Church of England have generally found it more congenial to express their discipleship by helping individual victims of misfortune or oppression, fewer are willing to rectify injustices in the structures of society'.[29]

Responding to the report of the Commission on Social Justice, Melanie Phillips said,

> The Welfare State is above all a moral issue. Are we prepared as citizens
> to form a moral community of reciprocity, duty and altruism? ... The
> last election posed the urgent and disturbing question of whether
> better-off people were prepared any longer, after years of shameless
> individualism, to dig into their pockets so that *everyone* could fare well.
> This report has crucially failed to tell us whether in a decent society
> they should.[30]

There is no ducking the question and the Church – Christians – above all
should have a clear affirmative answer. To disturb the *status quo* may threaten
our comfortable position, yet this vulnerability and form of renunciation is
demanded of us. This takes us directly into the social, economic and political
territory already discussed and, in entering it, the Church must accept its
reality without being confined by it. It must retain a vision – even an
unattainable one – to give direction to the hard day-by-day struggle to work
with that reality, to let the kingdom that is 'not yet' inspire the 'now', but to
grapple with the 'now' *en route* to the 'not yet'.

There are many parallels between theology and politics. Both should be
rooted in the whole of people's lives, their relationships, their hopes and fears.
To look at church life this is not always evident. David Cockerell criticizes the
Anglican Church for the way its culture and organization have led to a dualism
between 'the community of believers' and those outside the Church as
'religious language and practice is no longer the language of common human
experience but rather that of a group having its own distinctive interests,
concerns and ideas'.[31] Many local churches strive to avoid such a tendency but
this is a dualism which members of other denominations will surely also
recognize. According to Wogaman, 'Religious practice increasingly focuses
upon mutual support and fulfilment within the religious group. But the group
is distant from the public sphere, and the practice of the religious group is
neither preparation for nor encouragement of participation in that sphere.'[32]
Morality is thereby redefined as exclusively personal, not social; private, not
public. Theology becomes individualistic and religion experience is privatized.

Churches like other institutions need to be scrutinized in terms of their
organization, power systems and deployment of resources. What the Church
says must be consistent with the way that it *is*. Dyson distinguishes between
the 'visible' and the 'invisible' Church, the sociological and institutional
reality compared with the theological, spiritual reality. He points out that to
talk of the former in the theological and devotional language of the latter, as
often happens, invites confusion. It shrouds the 'visible' Church in an aura of
irreproachability and inhibits self-criticism. 'In fact, the "visible" Church is a

tangled mixture of asceticism and affluence, courage and compromise, devotion and destructiveness, faith and frailty, prayer and perfidy, sanctity and sin.'[33] This blurring between the 'visible' and the 'invisible' has also tended to cut the Church off from the public realm. While the laity have been 'exposed to rapid social change, cultural dislocation, the loss of shared moral languages and to economic insecurity',[34] the 'visible' Church has tended more towards offering them a refuge from this experience than equipping them for it or supporting them in their task of being salt and light at the 'critical points in society'.

SIMPLY NO CHOICE IN THE MATTER

Don't ask what the Church can do for the Inner City; ask what the Inner City can do for the Church.[35]

Within the Church's 'tangled mixture', there are signs of hope. Scattered throughout the book are examples of Christian and Church responses to people in poverty. It would be possible to draw up a typology of possible responses: prophetic voices, protest, campaigning, empowering, pastoral care, social action, prayer and the worshipping life of the Church. Few of these examples could be neatly slotted under a single heading; they would be far poorer if they could. Varied as they are, what they have in common is that they are all at those critical points in society.

They are not just *for* the poor, they are trying to be *with* the poor. They are longing to be part of a Church *of* the poor. Pat Logan asks why local churches have shifted the pastoral care of the homeless onto specialist church agencies while themselves focusing on the care of the 'settled community'.[36] The question might be broadened to ask why all concern for the excluded has been marginalized. When members of Church Action on Poverty talked about their vision for the organization, the recurrent theme was that we looked towards a time when CAP and other such groups would not be needed; not just redundant because there is no more poverty, but because the Church no longer needs such 'fringe' organizations. Poverty will be integral to the life of the Church, not just seen as a specialist concern or a hobby for a few people who happen to be interested.

Father Austin Smith speaks out of his experience as a religious and a priest based for many years in inner-city Liverpool,

It is quite scandalous that such a term as 'fundamental option for the poor' should be a theologically debated topic: in terms of the hopefulness of the kingdom of God, there is no option of any kind, let alone a fundamental one. For the Christian faith there is simply no choice in the matter, a confrontation with evil and the identification and purging of it are at the heart of the human and Christian journey. But the purgation does not apply only to my personal journey: it is an obligation to be honoured with regard to the ideologies and structures of this world and especially so, when such ideologies and structures oppress, alienate and stigmatise the powerless.[37]

The Church's place must be at the margins, not at the centre talking about the margins. For the Church only to be *for* the poor means keeping hold of the reins, staying with the powers, still accommodating to them, remaining a church of the powerful – surely a contradiction in terms. To be *with* and *of* the poor means being prepared to be sidelined and scorned as they are. Realizing this produces unbearable tensions for those of us who are members of comfortable Britain. Living with these tensions, allowing the agony of the world to encroach upon our consciousness,[38]acknowledging our helplessness, is perhaps our cross. It is also our way to new life.

I asked earlier in the book, 'who owns the story?' A better question might be: 'whose story are we living?' ' . . . the real story of a people is not written by the manipulations and coercions of those in power, ready to sacrifice people to economic theory and national security. It is written by the emerging hope and involvement of the poor.'[39] Which is our story? There is an option, but for Christians there is simply no choice.

NOTES

1. I am indebted to Tim Beaumont for emphasizing the importance of sustainable economics to me. See such publications as H. Daly and J. Cobb, *For the Common Good* (Green Print, 1990); Tony Beamish, *No Free Lunch: The Urgent Need for Sustainable Economics* (T. Beamish, 1993).
2. Leroy S. Rouner, 'Dualism', in Alan Richardson and John Bowden (eds), *A New Dictionary of Christian Theology* (London: SCM Press, 1983).
3. John V. Taylor, *The Christlike God* (London: SCM Press, 1992), p. 25.
4. Anthony Dyson, 'Clericalism, church and laity', in *All Are Called: Towards a Theology of the Laity*, Essays from a Working Party of the General Synod Board of Education under the Chairmanship of the Bishop of Oxford (CIO Publishing, 1985), p. 16.
5. J. Philip Wogaman, *A Christian Method of Moral Judgement* (London: SCM Press, 1976), p. 66.
6. *Ibid.*, p. 66.
7. *Ibid.*, p. 67.
8. J. Philip Wogaman, *Christian Perspectives in Politics* (London: SCM Press, 1988), pp. 152–3.
9. See for example, Geoff Mulgan, *Politics in an Antipolitical Age* (Cambridge: Polity Press, 1994), pp. 48ff; Andrew Glyn and David Miliband (eds), *Paying for Inequality: The Economic Cost of Social Justice* (IPPR/ Rivers Oram Press, 1994); *Social Justice: Strategies for National Renewal*, The Report of the Commission on Social Justice (Vintage, 1994).
10. Howard Davies in an interview before the 1994 CBI Annual Conference, reported in Larry Elliott, 'CBI chief urges action on poverty', *Guardian*, 3 November 1994.
11. Glyn and Miliband, *op. cit.*, p. 14.
12. John Penet, *ATD Fourth World Journal*, Spring 1994, p. 3.
13. Maurice Roche, *Rethinking Citizenship: Welfare Ideology and Change in Modern Society* (Cambridge: Polity Press, 1992).

14. *Social Justice: Strategies for National Renewal*, pp. 155–7.
15. See for example, Hermione Parker, *Instead of the Dole* (London: Macmillan, 1989); T. Walker, *Basic Income* (London: Marian Boyars, 1989).
16. Bill Jordan, *The Common Good: Citizenship, Morality and Self-Interest* (Oxford: Basil Blackwell, 1989), p. 119.
17. Roche, *op. cit.*, p. 185.
18. See Mulgan, *op. cit.*, pp. 7ff.
19. Mulgan, *op. cit.*, p. 145.
20. Lawrence Mead, *Beyond Entitlement: the Social Obligations of Citizenship* (The Free Press, 1986), p. 229, quoted in Ruth Lister, *The Exclusive Society: Citizenship and the Poor* (London: CPAG, 1990), p. 8.
21. Margaret Thatcher in an interview in *Woman's Own* (31 October 1987).
22. Lister, *op. cit.*, pp. 15–16.
23. *Ibid.*, p. 19.
24. Commission on Social Justice 1994, *op. cit.*, p. 307.
25. Mulgan, *op. cit.*, p. 64.
26. *Ibid.*, p. 67.
27. Ronald L. Sider, *Rich Christians in an Age of Hunger* (London: Hodder and Stoughton, 1977), p. 62.
28. Lister, *op. cit.*, p. 18.
29. *Faith in the City: A Call for Action by Church and Nation*, Report of the Archbishop of Canterbury's Commission on Urban Priority Areas (London: Church House Publishing, 1985), p. 49, paragraph 3.7.
30. Melanie Phillips, 'Weasel words mask a moral vacuum', *Observer*, 30 October 1994.
31. David Cockerell, *Beginning Where We Are: A Theology of Parish Ministry* (London: SCM Press, 1989), p. 7.
32. J. Philip Wogaman, *Christian Perspectives on Politics* (London: SCM Press, 1988), p. 133.
33. Dyson, *op. cit.*, pp. 13–14.
34. *Ibid.*, p. 16.
35. Austin Smith, *Journeying with God: Paradigms of Power and Powerlessness* (London: Sheed and Ward, 1990), p. 126.
36. Patrick Logan, *A Life to Be Lived: Homelessness and Pastoral Care* (London: Darton, Longman and Todd with UNLEASH, 1989), p. 3.
37. Smith, *op. cit.*, p. 108.
38. See the end of Chapter 6.
39. Cullinan, *op. cit.*, p. 93.

Index

Action with Communities in Rural
       England   209
Against the Stream   248
Albert, Michel   18, 93, 94, 95
Alcock, Pete   42, 46, 189
Archbishop of Canterbury's Commission on
       Urban Priority Areas (ACUPA)
   Faith in the City   xiii, 44, 53, 135, 236, 248,
       267
Archbishops' Commission on Rural Areas
       (ACORA)   115, 209
   Faith in the Countryside   xiii
Arnold, Matthew   56
Assessing the Impact of Urban Policy   245, 249
ATD Fourth World   81
Atherton, John   70, 99, 100
Atkinson, A. B.   50
Attwood, Tony   154
Audit Commission   241

Barker, Anthony   242
Barnardos   162, 172
Barr, Nicholas   194
Beales, Chris   244, 245
Beatitudes   37, 129
Benn, Tony   60
Bevan, Aneurin   217
Beveridge, William   134, 189
   Beveridge Report   36, 190
Bevin, Ernest   50
Bialock, Carol   130
Blackbird Leys,   *see* Oxford
Boerma, Conraad   87
Bonhoeffer, Dietrich   256
Booth, Charles   80
Boyson, Rhodes   69, 80
Bracknell   117
Bradbury, Nicholas   175
Bradford   122, 162
Breadline Britain   31, 47, 48, 49, 50
Britain   20, 76, 77, 94, 103
Brueggemann, Walter   128–9
Brussels   175
Burgess, John   147

Burt, Alistair   202

Caborn, Richard   154
Calderdale   146
Callaghan, James   225
Calvin, John   16
Campbell, Beatrix   126, 168
Campbell Johnston, Michael   5
capitalism   15–16, 53–4, 67–9, 90, 93–5
   and Christianity   98–100
   neo–American model   94ff
   Rhine model   94ff
Carey, Archbishop George   215
Carlyle, Thomas   30
Cassidy, Sheila   130
Catholic social teaching   97–8, 264
   Pope John XXIII   98
   Pope John Paul II   98
Charter 88 Trust   242
Cheshire   143
Child Poverty Action Group   46, 50, 51, 267
   The Cost of a Child   46
   Hardship Britain   51
Child Support Agency   19, 167
Children's Society   51, 123, 172
Christian Aid   32, 65, 95, 151
Church, and churches   4, 7, 8, 9, 32, 103, 123,
       152, 153, 183, 184, 215, 236, 244, 246,
       248, 251–52, 267–70
Church Action on Poverty (CAP)   3, 4, 62, 89,
       124, 154, 163, 164, 201, 269
   Hearing the Cry of the Poor   3, 21
Church Action with the Unemployed
       (CAWTU)   236
Church Urban Fund (CUF)   124, 248–9
Churches' National Housing Coalition
       (CNHC)   176, 214, 215
   Church Land and Property Project   215
   Homelessness Sunday   215
   Reflections on Faith Statement   176
citizenship   259ff
   active citizenship   266
City Action Teams   248
City Challenge   250

City Grant   243
Clark, Alan   238
   Diaries 238
coalfields
   Coal Campaign   153–4
   Coalfields Chaplains' Network   154
   Coalfields Churches Conference   154
Cockerell, David   268
Commission on Social Justice   261, 266
common good   97–8, 264–5
Cone, James   102
Coulter, Fiona   194
crime   113, 118
   and unemployment   149–51
Cullinan, Thomas   255

Dahrendorf, Ralf   76
Davies, Howard   258
Davis, Kingsley   59, 114
Dean, Hartley   81, 82, 179
debt   161–3
de la Torre, Ed   9
Demant, V. A.   99
Democratic Audit   242
Department for Education   250
Department of Employment   136, 147, 232, 238,
   250
Department of the Environment   244, 250
   Action for Cities Unit   237
Department of Health   218
Department for Social Security   50, 216, 235
Department of Trade and Industry   250
   Inner Cities Unit   237
Dickens, Charles   29
Dickinson, David   149
disability   58, 147–8, 173
   Disabled Persons (Employment) Act 1944   147
   United Nations Declaration of the Rights of
        Disabled People   173
Disraeli, Benjamin   28, 29, 30
Duchrow, Ulrich   99
Dyson, Anthony   255, 268

East Anglia   143
Easterhouse,   *see* Glasgow
Economic Trends   50
education   67, 223–8
   1944 Education Act   224
   1988 Education Reform Act   226–8
   'Great Debate'   225
Eggar, Tim   154
elderly   172–3
Ellison, Ralph   35
Ellwood, David   81
El Salvador   5
Elswick   244
employment   58, 91, 133–56
   Agricultural Wages Boards   234
   Wages Councils   137, 138, 139, 233
Employment in the 1990s   239

Engels, Friedrich   30
England
   North   143
   North-east   244
   North-west   143
   South-east   215
   South-west   143
Enterprise Zones   244
equality and inequality   52ff
ethnic minorities   93, 112ff, 173ff
   and employment/unemployment   146–7
   racial tension   88
   racism   76, 92, 147
   and schools   224
   and the underclass   76
Europe
   Eastern Europe   93
   European Commission   51, 91
      Eurostat   51
      Poverty Programmes   51
   European Union   88, 90, 137, 234
   Towards a Europe of Solidarity   89

Field, Frank   75, 78, 167
   Losing Out   75
Fineman, Stephen   134, 151
France   234
   Lyon   93
   Marseilles   93
   Paris   93, 175
Friedman, Milton   68, 69

Galbraith, J. K.   10, 11, 43, 44
   The Affluent Society   43
   The Culture of Contentment   10
Gaskell, Elizabeth   30
   Mary Barton   30
George, Vic   188
Germany   94, 234
   East Germany   91
   Frankfurt   95
   Rhine model   94, 95
Gifford Enquiry   147
Gilbert, Robbie   232, 233
Giles, Christopher   200, 202
Glasgow   117
   Easterhouse   117
Glennester, Howard   199, 219
Gloucestershire   140
Government Offices for the Regions   250
Griffiths, Brian   100

Hall, M. Penelope   71
Halsey, A. H.   74
Handy, Charles   19, 90, 234
   The Empty Raincoat   90
Harrison, Paul   51, 111
   Inside the Inner City   51
Hayek, Friedrich   54, 68, 232
   The Mirage of Social Justice   54

health and social care   39, 216–23
   Carers' Charter: A New Deal for Carers   221–2
   Carers' National Association   222
   Community Care Act   218, 222
   The Health of the Nation   220
   N.H.S.   189, 217–21
   WHO *Health for All*   220
   Working for Patients   218
Heath Town   121
Heseltine, Michael   119, 122, 153, 241
Himmelfarb, Gertrude   24, 26
Hindu Action Research Project   244
Holman, Bob   72
Home Office   250
Horn, David   245
Households Below Average Income   50, 157
housing and homelessness   39, 175–9, 206–16,
   247
   Building Societies Act 1986   208
   English Household Condition Survey   211
   Homeless Persons Act 1977   212, 213
   homelessness   212–15
   Housing Act 1985   212
   Housing Act   1988   208
   Housing and Planning Act 1986   208
   housing associations   208, 210
   housing benefit   208, 210
   Housing Investment Programmes   210–11, 247
   negative equity   19, 209
   owner occupation   208–9
   Right to Buy   117, 208–9
   right to rent   208, 209
   rural housing   117, 209
   Vagrancy Act 1824   213
Housing Corporation   211
Hurd, Douglas   266
Hutton, Will   19

Index of Sustainable Welfare   20
Industrial Mission in South Yorkshire   124
inner cities   chapter 6, 240ff, 269
Inner Cities Religious Council   244–5
Institute for Fiscal Studies   58, 200
Institute of Housing   210, 212
Institute of Local Government Studies,
   Birmingham University   242
International Labour Office   142
Italy   234
   Naples 175

Jackson, Tim   20
Jenkins, Bishop David   5, 7, 9, 154
Jeremiah   127ff
Jesus   5, 6, 10, 11, 13, 23, 24, 34, 52, 53, 92, 97,
   129, 170, 176, 254, 255, 256, 267
Johnson, Paul   200, 202
Johnson, Samuel   24, 25
Joseph, Keith   44, 74, 77

Kairos Documents   8, 9, 89

Kairos Europa   89, 90, 93, 96, 99
Kee, Alistair   102
Key, Robert   244
Keynes, John Maynard   189
Kingdom of God   1, 6, 9, 65, 129, 176, 256
Kirklees   146
Knowsley   70, 118ff
   Cantril Farm   119–23
   Kirkby   123
   Stockbridge Village Trust   122

Landes, David   16
Lansley, Stewart   49, 51
Lash, Nicholas   34
Latin America   16, 102
Leech, Kenneth   76, 99, 112
Leeds Industrial Mission   141
Le Grand, Julian   190
Leicester   141
Lewis, Oscar   73
Linking Up Interfaith   236–7
Lister, Ruth   265, 267
Liverpool   4, 92, 114, 118, 122, 138, 247, 269
Local Enterprise Companies   239
Logan, Patrick   269
London   34, 122, 140, 177, 215, 224, 247
   Inner London   112, 224
   Kensington   162
   London Docklands Development
      Corporation   92, 243
   Notting Hill   126
   Pimlico   224
   Tower Hamlets   174, 224
London School of Economics   195
lone parents   164ff, 198–9
Low Pay Network   235
Lunn, David   153

MacGregor, Suzanne   113
Mack, Joanna   49, 51
Macmillan, Harold   12
Major, John   56, 60
Maltby Rainbow Projects   152–3
Malthus, Thomas   28
   Essay on Population   28
Manchester 34, 122
   Ancoats   89
   Diocesan Board for Social
      Responsibility   236
Manpower Services Commission   238
Marks, Nic   20
Marx, Karl   7, 134
May, Don   246
Mayhew, Henry   31, 51
Meadowell,   *see* North Shields
Merseyside   125, 143
   Ecumenical Department for Social
      Responsibility   125
   Merseyside Churches' Unemployment
      Committee   226

Merseyside Development Corporation   125,
        243
Merseyside Homeworking Group   141
Merseyside Trade Union, Community and
        Unemployed Resource Centre   138
    see also Liverpool and Knowsley
Merton, Robert   150
Metz, Johannes B.   101
Ministry of Agriculture, Fisheries and
        Food   234
Mission Alongside the Poor   248
Moltmann, Jurgen   101
money   14ff,   34, 60–1
Moore, John   44
Morris, William   134
Mulgan, Geoff   262, 267
Multi Faith Youth Challenge   244
multiple deprivation   117ff
Murray, Charles   76, 77, 168
Myrdal, Gunnar   75
    Challenge to Affluence   75

National Association of Citizens' Advice
        Bureaux   137, 138, 139
National Child Development Study   167
National Children's Home   51, 162, 170, 172,
        179
    Deep in Debt   162, 163
    Poverty and Nutrition   163
    Your Place or Mine?   178
National Consumer Council   214
National Housing and Town Planning
        Council   211
New Right   53, 55, 68, 187, 262, 265
Northern Ireland   126, 143
    Belfast   126
    Derry   126
North Shields
    Meadowell   4, 126, 164, 244
        Cedarwood Centre   164
North Tyneside   164
Novak, Michael   100

Office of Population Censuses and Surveys   148,
        173
Organisation for Economic Co-operation and
        Development   231
Orwell, George   51
    The Road to Wigan Pier   51
Oxford   244
    Blackbird Leys   244

Paxman, Jeremy   60
    Friends in High Places   60
Pender, Dinsdale   214
Perry, John   210
Phillips, Melanie   267
Piachaud, David   46
    The Cost of a Child   46
Plant, Raymond   53, 55

Policy Studies Institute   193, 247
poverty
    definitions   42ff
    explanations   65–105
        cultural   73ff
        individualist   66ff
        structural   85–105
        underclass   74ff
        welfare dependency   79ff
    poverty trap   196
powerlessness   4, 59ff
Preston, Ronald   99

Quangos   242

Rate Support Grant   247
Rawls, John   53, 55
Reagan, Ronald   10, 11, 35, 94
Reed, John   18
Retail Price Index   194
Rowntree, B. S.   42, 46, 51, 80
Rowntree Foundation, Joseph   202
Royal Commission on the Distribution of Income
        and Wealth   50
Rural Development Commission   116
rural poverty   114ff
    see also housing
Ryan, William   78
    Blaming the Victim   78

Said, Edward   101
Sampson, Anthony   14, 16
Schumacher, E. F.   134
Scotland   201
Scottish Federation of Housing
        Associations   213
Scruton, Roger   56
Seabrook, Jeremy   51
    Landscapes of Poverty   51
Sheffield   121
    Diocesan Social Responsibility
        Committee   154
Shelter   177, 213
    Homes Cost Less Than Homelessness   177
Shuttleworth, Lord   116
Simey, Margaret   246
Simmel, Georg   15
Single Regeneration Budget   250
Smith, Adam   27, 28, 44, 70
    The Wealth of Nations   27
Smith, Austin   269
social exclusion   88ff
social security   79, 82, 179, 190–200, 210
    Benefits Agency   198
    Fowler Review   192
    Social Fund   193, 195
    Social Security Act 1986   192, 194
    Social Security Advisory Committee   171,
        202, 210
    Social Security Commissioner   198

Social Security – *continued*
  Social Trends 50
  types of benefit 191
South Africa 8
South Wales 138, 139
South Yorkshire 153
Southend 247
Sweden 95

Task Forces 248
Tawney, R. II. 52, 53, 54, 55, 56, 57, 98, 99,
  224
  Equality 56
taxation 200–204
  Community Charge 201–2, 243
  direct and indirect 203–4
  excise duty 201
  mortgage interest relief 200, 209
  tax relief 200
  VAT on fuel 201–2
Taylor Gooby, Peter 81, 82, 179
Tebbit, Norman 69
Temple, William 99
Thatcher, Margaret 60, 69, 76, 94, 96, 100,
  218, 232, 266
  Thatcherism 11
theology xiii, 1, 6ff, 15, 32, 40, 100ff
  Black 102ff
  Critical 100ff
  Feminist 103
  Liberation 62, 102ff
Titmuss, Richard 71, 190
Torkington, Protasia 174
Townsend, Peter 44, 46, 50, 51, 221
training 237ff
  VET 238–9
  see also young people
Training and Enterprise Councils 70, 238,
  239–40

unemployment 58, 88ff, 133–56
  and crime 149–51
  and health 148–9
  male 145
  workfare 265

United States of America 10, 18, 20, 35, 59, 73,
  75, 76, 77, 78, 100, 102, 233, 235
  neo–American capitalism 94, 95
  New York 14
Urban Development Corporations 243, 244
  see also Merseyside and London
Urban Programme 243
Urban Regeneration Grant 243

Vallely, Paul 86
  Bad Samaritans 86

Waldegrave, William 218, 242
Walker, Alan 77
Weber, Max 15, 16
welfare dependency 81–2, 197
welfare state 185ff, 231, 206, 263ff
Wells, John 142
West Midlands 140
West Yorkshire Homeworking Group 141
Whitehead, Margaret 217, 219
  The Health Divide 217
Wilding, Paul 188
Wilkinson, Richard 221
Willmer, Hadden 126
Wilson, Andrew 123
Wilson, Robert 51
  The Dispossessed 51
Wilson, William Julius 75, 78
Wiltshire 140
Wogaman, J. P. 100, 256, 268
Wylie, Donovan 51
  The Dispossessed 51

York University Family Budget Unit 171
Yorkshire Low Pay Unit 139, 141
young people 170–2, 195–6
  and training 237ff
  and unemployment 88
  Young Workers' Scheme 233
  Youth Training Schemes 145, 238